Arendt, Natality and Biopolitics

D1610790

Incitements

Series editors
Peg Birmingham, DePaul University
and Dimitris Vardoulakis, Western Sydney University

Editorial Advisory Board
Étienne Balibar, Andrew Benjamin, Jay M. Bernstein, Rosi Braidotti, Wendy Brown, Judith Butler, Adriana Cavarero, Howard Caygill, Rebecca Comay, Joan Copjec, Simon Critchley, Costas Douzinas, Peter Fenves, Christopher Fynsk, Moira Gatens, Gregg Lambert, Leonard Lawlor, Genevieve Lloyd, Catherine Malabou, James Martel, Christoph Menke, Warren Montag, Michael Naas, Antonio Negri, Kelly Oliver, Paul Patton, Anson Rabinbach, Gerhard Richter, Martin Saar, Miguel Vatter, Gianni Vattimo, Santiago Zabala

Available
Return Statements: The Return of Religion in Contemporary Philosophy
Gregg Lambert

The Refusal of Politics
Laurent Dubreuil, translated by Cory Browning

Plastic Sovereignties: Agamben and the Politics of Aesthetics
Arne De Boever

From Violence to Speaking Out:
Apocalypse and Expression in Foucault, Derrida and Deleuze
Leonard Lawlor

Agonistic Mourning: Political Dissidence and the Women in Black
Athena Athanasiou

Interpassivity: The Aesthetics of Delegated Enjoyment
Robert Pfaller

Derrida's Secret: Perjury, Testimony, Oath
Charles Barbour

Resistance and Psychoanalysis: Impossible Divisions
Simon Morgan Wortham

Reclaiming Wonder: After the Sublime
Genevieve Lloyd

Arendt, Natality and Biopolitics: Toward Democratic Plurality and Reproductive Justice
Rosalyn Diprose and Ewa Plonowska Ziarek

Visit the series web page at: edinburghuniversitypress.com/series/incite

Arendt, Natality and Biopolitics

Toward Democratic Plurality and Reproductive Justice

*Rosalyn Diprose and
Ewa Plonowska Ziarek*

EDINBURGH
University Press

Edinburgh University Press is one of the leading university presses in the UK. We publish academic books and journals in our selected subject areas across the humanities and social sciences, combining cutting-edge scholarship with high editorial and production values to produce academic works of lasting importance. For more information visit our website: edinburghuniversitypress.com

Edinburgh University Press Ltd
The Tun – Holyrood Road, 12(2f) Jackson's Entry, Edinburgh EH8 8PJ

Typeset in Bembo
by R. J. Footring Ltd, Derby, UK, and
printed and bound in Great Britain.

A CIP record for this book is available from the British Library

ISBN 978 1 4744 4433 0 (hardback)
ISBN 978 1 4744 4436 1 (webready PDF)
ISBN 978 1 4744 4434 7 (paperback)
ISBN 978 1 4744 4435 4 (epub)

Contents

Acknowledgements

We thank the anonymous reviewers of Edinburgh University Press for their thoughtful engagement with our work, Carol Macdonald for her editorial expertise and support, and Peg Birmingham and Dimitris Vardoulakis, the editors of Incitements series, for their encouragement and interest in this project. Thanks also to James Dale, Rebecca Mackenzie and Kirsty Woods at EUP for their assistance in getting the book to press. We appreciate the cheerful and expert assistance of Emily Hughes in preparing the full manuscript for publication. Special thanks to Ralph Footring for his skilful and patient approach to the copy-editing and typesetting tasks.

We are grateful for the institutional support that allowed us to work together in the same place for short periods. Rosalyn Diprose visited the University at Buffalo (UB) in August–October 2014 as a guest of the UB Humanities Institute (and its then Director, Erik Seeman) and the Comparative Literature Department (and its Chair, Krzysztof Ziarek) with the generous support of the Eileen Silvers/WBFO Visiting Professorship in the Humanities. Thank you to Eileen Silvers for her unwavering support for the humanities, to faculty at UB who engaged with Rosalyn's research for their hospitality, to the administrative staff who helped with that visit and to the graduate students involved in the seminar 'The Human Condition' whom we co-taught – their insights did much to stimulate our thinking on Arendt's political ontology. We also had three opportunities to work together on the book in Sydney: initially for two weeks in 2013 with support from the University of New South Wales, and then, for a week in December 2015 and another in December 2016 to integrate different drafts into a single manuscript. These meetings occurred while Ewa Plonowska Ziarek held the positions of Visiting Senior Research Fellow at Western Sydney University (WSU) (December 2015) and Adjunct Professor in the College of Fellows, WSU (2016–19). We are grateful to those programmes and to colleagues at WSU for their support.

The book has benefited from our numerous stimulating joint discussions about Arendt's philosophy over the six years we were writing the book. However, the writing and the research were largely conducted with the two of us working independently. Hence, we have different colleagues and friends to thank for their support in that.

For stimulating her initial interest in Arendt's politics of action, Rosalyn Diprose is grateful to Sarah Sorial and Mark Kingston, graduate students at UNSW in the mid-2000s, and to Catherine Mills for introducing her to connections between Arendt and Agamben's biopolitics while co-teaching an honours seminar at that time. Ideas from those and other collegial events have no doubt leaked into this book via Rosalyn's research papers on Arendt and Foucault's biopolitics noted in this volume, which also benefited from the comments and/or institutional support of Bruce Braun, Danielle Celermajer, Nigel Clarke, Judith Still and Sarah Whatmore. Rosalyn's research on Arendt continues to be sustained by the wit, wisdom and friendship of members the UNSW Arendt Study Group of 2013–14: Robyn Ferrell, Joanne Faulkner, Melanie White and Simone Bignall. Thanks also to the following valued colleagues and friends for providing feedback on, or hosting presentations of, Rosalyn's research on biopolitics and phenomenology in this decade: Marsha Rosengarten, Martin Savransky, Leonard Lawlor, James Bono, Simone Drichel, Gay Hawkins, Ann Murphy, Niamh Stephenson and Alex Wilkie. Rosalyn's research would not have progressed far over the past decade without the love and support of Alison Ritter, to whom she gives her heartfelt thanks.

Ewa Ziarek is indebted to Vivian Liska, Idit Alphandary, Leszek Koczanowicz, Ryszard Nycz, Roma Sendyka, Alison Stone, Emilia Angelowa, Jana Schmidt, Roger Berkowitz, Karen Jacobs, Laura Winkiel and Krzysztof Ziarek, for their helpful comments and suggestions, and for providing opportunities to present her work in progress. Thanks also to Cheryl Emerson for her expert help in preparation of Ewa's written drafts. Ewa is especially grateful to Krzysztof Ziarek, as well as other family members, for their sense of humour, patience and support along the way.

Earlier versions of a few sections of this book have been published previously and we are grateful for permission to use these materials here in their substantially revised form:

- Earlier versions of sections II and III of Chapter 3 appeared in Rosalyn Diprose and Ewa Plonowska Ziarek (2013), 'Time for beginners: natality, biopolitics, and political theology', *PhiloSophia*, 3(2), 107–20.

- Sections I and III of Chapter 4 borrow revised text from two sources: Rosalyn Diprose (2009), 'Women's bodies between national hospitality and domestic biopolitics', *Paragraph: Journal of Modern Critical Theory*, 32(1), 69–86; and Rosalyn

Diprose (2010), 'Responsibility, sensibility and democratic pluralism', in Andrew Schaap, Danielle Celermajer and Vrasidas Karalis (eds), *Power, Judgment, and Political Evil: In Conversation with Hannah Arendt*, Farnham: Ashgate (reprinted by London: Routledge, 2013).

- Earlier versions of sections I and II of Chapter 5 were published in Ewa Plonowska Ziarek, 'Aesthetics and the politics of gender: on Arendt's theory of narrative and action', *Routledge Companion to Feminist Philosophy*, ed. Ann Garry, Serene Khader and Alison Stone (London: Routledge, 2017), 474–84, used and revised by the permission of the publisher of the Routledge imprint, Taylor and Francis, Ltd.

Abbreviations

Books by Hannah Arendt

BPF   *Between Past and Future: Eight Exercises in Political Thought*, New York: Penguin, 1977.

EJ   *Eichmann in Jerusalem: A Report on the Banality of Evil*, New York: Penguin, 2006.

EU   *Essays in Understanding 1930–1954: Formation, Exile, and Totalitarianism*, edited with an introduction by Jerome Kohn, New York: Schocken Books, 1994.

HC   *The Human Condition*, second edition with introduction by Margaret Canovan, Chicago: University of Chicago Press, 1998.

LKPP   *Lectures on Kant's Political Philosophy*, edited with an interpretive essay by Ronald Beiner, Chicago: University of Chicago Press, 1982.

LM I   *The Life of the Mind, Volume I: Thinking*, San Diego: Harcourt, 1978.

LM II   *The Life of the Mind, Volume II: Willing*, San Diego: Harcourt, 1978.

LSA   *Love and St Augustine*, edited with an interpretive essay by Joanna Vecchiarelli Scott and Judith Chelius Stark, Chicago: Chicago University Press, 1996.

MDT   *Men in Dark Times*, New York: Harcourt Brace & World, 1968.

OR   *On Revolution*, London: Faber and Faber, 1963; new edition with introduction by Jonathan Schell, New York: Penguin, 1977 (page numbers to both editions are cited in this order).

OT   *The Origins of Totalitarianism*, new edition with added prefaces, San Diego: Harcourt, 1968.

OV   *On Violence,* San Diego, New York: Harcourt Brace, 1970.

PP   *The Promise of Politics*, edited with an introduction by Jerome Kohn, New York: Schocken Books, 2005.

RJ   *Responsibility and Judgment*, edited with an introduction by Jerome Kohn, New York: Schocken Books, 2003.

RLC   *Reflections on Literature and Culture*, edited with an introduction by Susannah Young-ah Gottlieb, Stanford: Stanford University Press, 2007.

RV   *Rahel Varnhagen: The Life of a Jewess*, translated by Richard Winston and Clara Winston, New York: Harcourt, 1974.

Introduction

A key question that motivates this book is why, in liberal democracies, recurring restrictions of human plurality, manifest for instance in intensification of hostility toward immigrants and refugees, are usually accompanied by attempts to restrict women's reproductive self-determination. The concurrence of those two trends is not restricted to nations ruled by ultra-conservative democratic governments. Their coincidence is also apparent, and has been on and off over the past fifty years, in what are considered the most liberal of Western democracies, such as the US and Australia. As if to demonstrate our claim about this connection, Donald Trump began his term as US President in January 2017 with several Executive Orders and Presidential Memoranda that consolidated both trends. For example, four of his first twelve Executive Orders targeted either 'undocumented' immigrants, new arrivals from a list of eight Muslim countries (including banning Syrian refugees indefinitely), or the security of the border with Mexico.[1] In the midst of these, surrounded by a gaggle of suited men Trump publically signed a Presidential Memorandum reinstating President Reagan's 'global gag rule' that bans US AID money from going to non-government organisations that provide or counsel on abortion as a family planning

1

option.[2] This Memorandum is widely seen as merely the first of a potential avalanche of moves against women's reproductive self-determination that were on the Republican agenda during the presidential and general election campaigns of 2016.[3]

While this book does not attend to the details of the US situation regarding either trend, the analysis does reveal them as manifestations of forms of biopolitics that present a danger to what we will refer to as 'democratic plurality'. By refiguring Hannah Arendt's philosophy of natality in terms of biopolitical and feminist theory, we show how her work provides the means of diagnosing interconnections between these two forms of biopolitics. And we show how her revised understanding of the political and her notions of agency, freedom, responsibility and collective political action offer reasons for, and ways of, redressing both kinds of biopolitics.

'Natality' is the concept within Arendt's philosophy that facilitates the diagnosing and countering of the latent dangers in some forms of biopolitics. Arendt defines 'natality' *not* as the birth of new 'life', but variously as a 'new beginning' and the human 'capacity of beginning something anew' (HC: 9). While she does not always use the term 'natality', the concept of a beginner 'beginning something anew' persists throughout her oeuvre. She considers 'natality' to be both the central feature of human existence (as the basis for new notions of agency and 'humanness') and the 'central category of political [. . .] thought' (HC: 9). Defining human existence and politics in terms of the appearance of new beginnings emphasises novelty, unpredictability and frailty as central features of the human condition and human affairs. On this basis Arendt locates the 'degradation of politics', exemplified by the forms of biopolitics just mentioned, in attempts to eliminate natality from human affairs (for example,

HC: 230–3). This tends to happen when unpredictability is viewed and experienced negatively as uncertainty and insecurity.

In the opening pages of *The Human Condition* Arendt gives natality three inter-related meanings that help explain the concept further. *First*, natality refers to the '*new beginning inherent in birth*' (HC: 9, emphasis added), the fact that human existence begins with a birth that is not initiated by the being who is born, but that nevertheless makes a difference to the socio-historical world in which we first appear. While Arendt distinguishes between this 'fact of birth' and the 'second birth' into the political order of speech and action (HC: 176), she usually grants that the two orders are intertwined. This first-order birth, like death, is not a 'simple natural occurrence' – human birth and death presuppose a fabricated, meaningful and human world 'whose relative durability and permanence makes appearance and disappearance possible' (HC: 96–7). There are two connected ways of understanding the relation between the 'new beginning inherent in birth' and the socio-historical-political world (the 'common' or 'human world' in Arendt's terminology) in which the newborn first appears to others. From the (external) perspective of those already dwelling in the world, human birth signifies a new beginning (the birth of a unique and distinct human agent). Because a new beginning by definition has an unpredictable impact on the world, governments are inclined to control human birth as part of wider regulation of so-called 'biological' life. As we argue in Chapter 3, this is a form of biopolitics that can go too far in dampening natality by curtailing women's reproductive self-determination. The other way of understanding the relation between human birth and the socio-historical world is from the (internal) perspective of the political actor's relationship to her/his own birth and with regard to Arendt's unique notion of the political. As Peg Birmingham explains, in this formulation Arendt develops aspects of Augustine's concept of the self, giving it a phenomenological bent: since we 'cannot recall' our own birth, our own relation to this beginning is such that we are 'estranged' from ourselves in that our status as natal beings (beginners of the new) requires ongoing witness of others (Birmingham 2006: 76–83). As we will see, this aspect of our inter-relation with others is central to Arendt's definition of 'the political' and it means we also rely on others for a sense of 'who' we are (our 'life story').

The *second* related meaning of natality describes the *human agent as a perennial beginner*, who, by acting and speaking, can *begin something new in history*, or, to use Arendt's words, can 'set something in motion' (HC: 177). This second sense of natality is dependent on the first: we are 'prompted into action' and are 'beginners by virtue of birth' (HC: 177), the significance of which is disclosed by others. At its simplest level this means we are prompted to act and speak because we are distinct from others who surround us. But for these actions to begin something new in the world requires the witness of these others and the notion of a historical world into which these actions protrude and which they transform (a secular notion of time between birth and death that Arendt attributes to Augustine (OR: 17/19–20)).[4] As we will see in Chapter 1, the key point about natality and time is that the appearance of a beginner and a new beginning disrupts both linear and cyclic temporality characteristic of historical and/or biological determinism to open human existence and the world to an undetermined future. Moreover, the 'new beginning inherent in birth can make itself felt in the world only because the newcomer possesses the capacity of beginning something new' (HC: 9). What Arendt means by 'capacity' here is complicated and, as the discussion in Chapter 1 reveals, it is not simply that 'natality' is the result of an individual aptitude or specific human faculty (for example, of mind). A human being *is* a new beginning by virtue of their 'appearance' in the socio-historical world and, whatever the person is doing, their actions begin something new in the sense that they have a unique and unpredictable effect on others and on the course of events.

Third, and crucially, the notion of natality points to the centrality of *being-with a plurality of distinct others* to the event of natality and to both human existence and the realm of the political that it grounds. Arendt suggests that the 'capacity of beginning something new' through action and speech is inseparable from the condition of community (the 'presence of other human beings') and human plurality (HC: 22, 27). She rarely uses the term 'community' because of the philosophical baggage of sameness that comes with the concept after some interpretations of Hegel and the political baggage associated with the concept after communism, especially in Stalinist Russia. Hence, in Chapter 1 we dissociate her notion of the '"web" of human relationships' (HC: 183), and hence her notion of the political, from these other ideas of community. Meantime, it is clear that, from the outset, Arendt considers the public disclosure of natality through speech and 'action [to be] entirely dependent on the constant presence of others' (HC: 23). Moreover, the plurality of human existence is not just in terms of a multiplicity of distinct entities (it is not an individualistic notion characteristic of neo-liberal pluralism). Rather, natality is witnessed, 'welcomed' and 'disclosed' *to and by* others as a 'who' (a beginner whose 'personal identity' is undeterminable, or 'unique distinctness' per se) as opposed to a 'what' (a set of particular characteristics) (HC: 9, 180). This idea of the disclosure of natality to and by others forms the basis of Arendt's unique notion of the political, which is not the realm of representative government but the public 'space of appearance' consisting of the inter-relational disclosure of natality through speech and action. The disclosure of natality or uniqueness within the together-ness of human affairs is also the basis of Arendt's notion of what Kant calls human 'dignity' (OT: ix; RJ: 48) and the principle underlying human inter-relationality, democratic plurality, and ethical community.

Taken together, all these inter-related meanings of natality – the new beginning inherent in human birth, beginning the new through action, and the appearance of human uniqueness and plurality within the 'togetherness' of public affairs – indicate that all spheres of human activity, including labour and work but especially the political realm of speech and action, are 'rooted in natality in so far as they have the task to provide and preserve the world for […] the constant influx of newcomers who are born into the world as strangers' (HC: 9). From the perspective of political ontology, the event of 'natality' can be understood as the unique philosophical concept that Arendt adds to political theory to explain the play of the conditioned and unconditioned that underlies human existence and hence to explain the 'principle' underlying democracy. Her thesis, in summary, is this: through actions that begin something anew, activities that are 'disclosed' by others as such and as originating with a 'beginner' (that is, a human agent), we not only open ourselves to an undetermined future (that is, we retain our 'unique distinctness') but also we alter those conditions and thereby keep the 'common' world that we share open to 'potentiality' rather than governed by necessity.

Despite Arendt's own appraisal of the central role of natality in human existence and in political life, commentators vary on what exactly she means by the concept and its significance. Patricia Bowen-Moore (1989), in an especially thorough treatment, views Arendt's concept of natality as the core concept of her philosophy and the key 'theme' underlying three dimensions of human 'experience': 'primary natality' (the fact of our birth from which we derive the 'capacity' to begin something new); political natality, manifest in debate and action within public affairs; and 'theoretical natality', by which Bowen-Moore means the new beginnings characteristic of the life of the mind apparent in thinking, willing and judgement. Anne O'Byrne (2010: 78–106) also argues that the idea of natality pervades Arendt's philosophy, although in different terms to Bowen-Moore. For O'Byrne, as for the analyses in this book, 'natality' heralds a 'new understanding of our being in time', which O'Byrne (2010: 80–1) calls 'syncopated temporality' for the way natality disrupts any apparent linearity and necessity in history and in one's path between birth and death. Other commentators focus on the application of natality to politics and some are critical of the concept. Seyla Benhabib, while admiring aspects of Arendt's political philosophy, especially her championing of human rights and her diagnosis of totalitarianism, claims that the concept of natality not only fails to provide a normative foundation for politics (that is, 'it is not adequate to lead to an attitude of moral respect among equals'), but also actually 'involves' the reverse: it underlies 'inequality and hierarchies of dependence' (Benhabib 2000: 81).[5] Peg Birmingham (2006) takes a more positive approach to the concept of natality and its potential for rethinking the political, one that accords with the approach taken in this book. She argues, in her compelling analysis of Arendt's political philosophy, that the 'anarchic, unpredictable' and 'archaic event of natality' is the 'principle of common humanity' (it marks us as unique, human and of equal worth – Arendt, EU: 336) 'that grounds the right to have rights' (Birmingham 2006: 3, 9). While concurring with Birmingham's analysis of the status of the event of natality as the 'principle of common humanity', we take that insight in a different direction to examine how the event of natality provides the normative basis for a more general notion of the political, of human inter-relationality, and of political action that includes but extends beyond the 'right to have rights'.

Instead of the foci of these approaches, the analyses in this book explore the relationship between the event of natality and *biopolitics*. Biopolitics, broadly speaking, is the politicisation of biological 'life' apparent in modern democracies since at least the late nineteenth century. Or, to take Michel Foucault's definition, biopolitics is political 'power [. . .] situated and exercised at the level of life' (Foucault 1980a: 137). More specifically, biopolitics is the state-centred exercise of the *power to 'foster' or 'disallow'* human life (the power to 'make live' or 'let die') through regulation of the biological 'life' of a population (Foucault 1980a: 138; Foucault 2003: 241).[6] Despite the resurgence of interest in Arendt's political philosophy, until recently her philosophy of natality has been rarely discussed in the context of biopolitics, which is usually viewed as a critical approach to modern politics initiated by Foucault and refined by Georgio Agamben and Nikolas Rose (and, more recently, Roberto Esposito and Antonio Negri, among others).[7] This neglect is surprising given that, even though Foucault does not acknowledge any debt to Arendt (and, hence, nor does Rose), Agamben and Esposito do acknowledge in different ways Arendt as the first thinker of biopolitics: Agamben does in *Homo Sacer* (Agamben 1998: 1–14) and Esposito in *Bios* (Esposito 2008: 149–50) and other places.[8]

In exploring Arendt's philosophy of natality in the context of biopolitics we take seriously the suggestion that Arendt is the first thinker of biopolitics even though she does not use the term. We argue that Arendt's critiques of two forms of modern politics – what she calls the 'rise of the social' and 'totalitarianism' – are tantamount to analyses of how *biopolitics suppresses or, in the extreme, eliminates natality from human existence, human relationships and political community.*

While political philosophy has tended to embrace Arendt's philosophy for its approach to human rights, there are two related reasons why we sidestep the language of rights (and the 'right to have rights') in favour of biopolitics in using Arendt's philosophy of natality to diagnose threats to democratic plurality. First, in a liberal tradition such as ours, human rights are too closely tied to *individualism* and assumptions about the need to *defend oneself* against the state and other persons. Liberalism's rights discourse begins with the Hobbesian idea of a 'natural right' to preserve one's own life against the threat of others, as Birmingham has analysed (Birmingham 2006: 35–42), which has developed, via Locke and later liberal theorists, to include the notion of protecting the individual from the omnipotent state. Consequently, rights tend to be understood in the defensive and aspirational sense of the individual's right to particular kinds of treatment (for example, the right to respect) and 'goods' (for example, the right to free speech, to bear arms, to refuge) to which an individual is said to be entitled without discrimination.[9] This entitlement of the individual to rights is assumed to be inherent to being human, where 'human being' is understood in terms of the notion of the sovereign individual embedded in modern liberalism and in Christian thought (according to Marx).[10] The concept of natality (a beginner beginning something anew) is a less defensive, other-oriented notion of what is inherent to human being that points to the expansive and dynamic 'potentiality of being together' (HC: 201) that is also central to the human condition. The notion of natality thereby challenges usual understandings of the relation between a person, political community and government, and with that undercuts the model of the liberal individual as a defensive bearer of protective rights against others and against the state. For these reasons, the concept of natality is more suited to the task of diagnosing and countering the harmful effects of the kind of biopolitics with which we began. Hence, we go beyond the issue of rights to examine some of the wider consequences for politics of Arendt's notion of natality as the principle of human existence, of human coexistence, of collective action and of democracy.

The second reason for considering Arendt's philosophy of natality in the context of biopolitics rather than rights follows from the first: even in liberal democracies, the 'humanness' (our 'appearance' to others as beginners of the new) that gives us the 'right to have rights' is at best skewed, precisely because of the dominance of biopolitics in democratic nation states whereby state institutions assume control of what is considered to be the most fundamental of human rights, namely the right to (foster or disallow) life. As Werner Hamacher argues, following Arendt, while human rights supposedly protect the individual against the power of the state and 'are determined as natural and inalienable rights', they have been 'placed under the legal and executive sovereignty of exactly the same historical powers – the powers of national governments' (Hamacher 2004: 350). Consequently, even democratic liberal governments can, while attending to citizens' health, welfare and security, easily undermine the rights of individuals through discriminatory biopolitics or by rendering people stateless.

Rendering people stateless (and hence rights-less) is one kind of state-centred biopolitics that Arendt includes in her genealogy of totalitarianism. It is also the primary focus of Agamben's subsequent biopolitical theory, which is why, when commentators think of Arendt in the context of biopolitics, it is usually by associating her work with Agamben. For Agamben, in the modern democratic state people can be deprived of rights in the following way: through the exercise of a form of sovereign power and the biopolitical 'rule of exception', the state incorporates the citizen as both biological life and political subject in such a way that there is always the possibility of reducing some people to 'bare life', deprived of rights, held in 'camps', excluded from legal protection and exposed to violence and death (Agamben 1998: 9–11). Refugees, prisoners and the brain dead are contemporary examples that Agamben cites. As we show in Chapter 2, while Arendt's analysis of 'totalitarianism' had already covered much of the salient ground of Agamben's biopolitical theory, it differs in some important respects. For a start, Arendt's account is broader: she examines various ways that biopolitics can end in the suppression of natality and, hence, the obscuring of the foundation of the human condition that gives us the 'right to have rights'. Agamben's approach to biopolitics is more limited in that it focuses on the extreme end-point of biopolitical government – the production of 'bare life' and the concentration camp – and then in terms of the exercise of a form of sovereign power. While Arendt's account reveals how biopolitics can tip into the elimination of natality characteristic of totalitarian genocide, she does not explain this in terms of the operation of sovereign power (which matters for reasons that become clear in Chapter 2) and her analysis of the elements of totalitarianism contains insights that Agamben fails to develop. Nor does she share Agamben's view that the production of 'bare life' is a central (hidden) structural feature of the democratic state such that there is, according to Agamben, an 'inner solidarity between democracy and totalitarianism' (Agamben 1998: 10). Some critics of Arendt suggest that she shares Agamben's pessimism about the liberal democratic state essentially harbouring tendencies toward totalitarianism. Those criticisms are addressed explicitly in Chapters 2 and 3. For now we offer three points regarding Arendt's wider approach to the biopolitical suppression of natality aimed at moderating this sort of criticism. First, her exemplary account of how totalitarian biopolitics aims at eliminating natality in all senses outlined above throws light on how non-totalitarian biopolitics can suppress natality in ways that are unjust and a threat to democratic plurality but not necessarily lethal. Second, we argue in Chapter 1 that Arendt's concept of natality provides a normative principle underlying democratic plurality and political action, which rules out any suggestion that, for Arendt, robust democracy harbours an *inevitable* tendency toward totalitarianism. Nevertheless, and third, throughout this book we apply Arendt's analyses of some precursors of totalitarianism and what she calls the 'rise of the social' to diagnoses of totalitarian elements in some forms of normalising biopolitics apparent within contemporary democracies (the opening examples being cases in point), while concurring with Arendt on a disjunction between normalising and totalitarian biopolitics.

Arendt's critiques of the 'rise of the social' and the normalising precursors of totalitarianism indicate a more subtle operation of discrimination and normalisation within public life that is not obviously directed by a single (sovereign) agent of power or the result of instituting a state of exception. These analyses of how biopower suppresses natality have more affinity with Foucault's subsequent approach to biopolitics, which is why we rely initially on his definitions of biopolitics, rather than Agamben, to frame Arendt's approach. Commentators have been slow to link Foucault's biopolitics with Arendt's political philosophy, presumably because, on the surface, the foci of their political genealogies seem worlds apart. For instance, in *The History of Sexuality, Volume I*, the book where Foucault first defines biopower, his focus is on the history of the emergence of sexuality (within the discourses and practices of medicine and the social sciences) as one key category through which political power takes hold of the biological life of a population and does its normalising and 'corrective' work. On closer inspection, however, the reader will find that here (and in his recently published lecture courses) Foucault also accounts for a range of normalising categories embedded in biopolitics that are similar to those mentioned in Arendt's genealogies of the politics of modernity, including race, class, age, health and even fertility and women's reproductivity.[11] Like Arendt, Foucault is also clearly concerned with the potentially lethal consequences of the discriminatory aspects of the biopolitical focus on enhancing the life of a population.

Another possible reason why Arendt and Foucault are rarely discussed together is the influence of Nikolas Rose's work on biopolitics, particularly in the early days of Anglophone social science reception of Foucault studies regarding biopolitics and governmentality, especially in the UK and Australasia. Rose's work has arguably steered Foucault studies away from Arendt's and Foucault's concerns about the impact of various kinds of normalising biopolitics on public life and democratic plurality toward a focus on biopolitics at the 'molecular level' and with regard to the biotechnological somatic manipulation of human life (for example, Rose 2007: 3–4).[12] Without denying the importance of that work, we reject Rose's claim that the growth of both molecular and privatised medicine means that biopolitics is no longer focused on the health and biological 'quality of the *population*' with attention to 'eliminating pathology to protect the destiny of the nation' and concerns about the 'future of the race' (Rose 2007: 3–4, emphasis added). Our opening examples, and others presented in this study, suggest that biopolitics remains very much concerned with the 'quality' and 'preservation' of human 'biological life' across *the population* and hence the nation. Analyses in this book show how various macro-political issues and government policies to do with public health, immigration, labour and work, security, war and so on not only have a direct bearing on attitudes about the preservation and enhancement of 'life' at a molecular level, but also consolidate notions of 'biological citizenship' (tying a person's biological characteristics to their political identity) with attendant discrimination and injustice.[13] Hence, it is our conviction that Foucault's and Arendt's approaches to biopolitics not only enhance each other but also are entirely relevant to diagnosing threats to democratic plurality and (reproductive) justice apparent at the macro or 'public' level of contemporary liberal democracies.

We therefore agree with André Duarte, who argues that Arendt can be considered a pioneering and significant biopolitical theorist who stands out for the way she addresses *both* Agamben's concerns with the 'extraordinary violence of totalitarianism' and Foucault's concerns with the way 'life' has become a 'constitutive political element, managed, calculated, and normalized by means of biopolitics' in ways that can be harmful, dehumanising and discriminatory without being universally lethal (Duarte 2008: 193–5). Hence, our analyses also show how Arendt pre-empts Foucault's definition of biopolitics as political power 'exercised at the level of life, the species, the race, and the large-scale phenomena of population' (Foucault 1980a: 137). With regard to this non-totalitarian normalising biopolitics Arendt considers the ways that natality, including the 'capacity' to begin something new through action, is suppressed by the way the politics of modernity has been subsumed under concerns about managing and enhancing human 'life processes' of labouring, consuming and the reproduction of life to the point where the human agent is reduced to *animal laborans* driven by private interests and biological need (HC: 46–7). For now we can take *animal laborans* to mean a 'labouring body' that (in various ways discussed by Arendt and examined here in Chapter 1) has been 'conditioned' and rendered compliant to the point that it does not appear to begin the world anew (what Foucault calls a 'docile body' – for example, Foucault 1979: 136–8). As we will see, the effect of this kind of normalising biopolitics is not so much elimination of the basis of the 'right to have rights' in the first instance but, according to Arendt, the stifling of political action and contestation of the status quo by the dominance of predictable activity and 'thoughtless' or conformist attitudes (for example, HC: 321).

Mention of *animal laborans* raises a final preliminary point to be made about Arendt's approach to normalising biopolitics. The reduction of human existence to a compliant subject is actually the second of two ways that biopolitics can be normalising mentioned so far. Even though the two are related and sometimes appear together in Arendt's work, we note the difference now with regard to how the suppression of natality manifests in each as a guide and further background to some of the analyses in this book. The first kind of normalising biopolitics, mentioned earlier, is normalising in the sense that socio-political norms of 'viable life' and of (biological or social) identity guide assessments of what forms of life should be 'fostered' and what can be 'let die', what kinds of 'life' are to be considered a 'new beginning' to be included in public life and what should be excluded. As we discuss in Chapter 2, Arendt's work on the precursors of totalitarianism and totalitarianism itself indicates clearly how this type of normalisation operates in precluding recognition of some people as beginners of the new and, hence, as human agents. In Chapter 3, we also apply this idea of bio-political normalisation beyond Arendt's concerns to analyse how the biopolitics of reproduction works against women's repro-ductive self-determination. But the second kind of biopolitical normalisation that Arendt discusses in *The Human Condition*, the reduction of human life to 'the level of a conditioned and behaving animal' (HC: 54) (*animal laborans*), is less obviously discriminatory (insofar as she applies this across modernity per se); nor is it potentially lethal. It is also less clear how or whether natality is foreclosed through this kind of normalisation so that, as Arendt seems to suggest, so-called labouring bodies are driven and determined solely by 'life processes' (like biological need) and are unable to 'act to start new unprecedented processes' (HC: 230–5). Arguably the primary concern that drives Arendt's analyses of this kind of normalising biopolitics is not so much the injustice and violence attached to the kind of biopolitics displaying totalitarian elements, but the failure of her contem-poraries in 1930s Germany to speak out or act against these elements in the rise of National Socialism, a kind of inaction and general complicity with normalising biopolitical government that she claims characterises modernity in general – the conformity and abdication of political agency that Arendt characterises as 'degradation of politics' and an 'abstention from the whole realm of human affairs' (HC: 234). As this sort of erasure of natality is also apparent in contemporary democracies[14] – and we agree with Arendt that it does, therefore, present a threat to democratic plurality – we provide an account in the book of Arendt's later critique of this normalisation in terms of 'co-ordination' of the population, the suppression of 'conscience' or (moral) judgement and a failure of responsibility. But we also join a number of political, feminist and race theorists in questioning Arendt's characterisation in *The Human Condition* of *animal laborans* and related distinctions between biological life (*zoe*) and political life (*bios*) and private activities and public action because of how these tend to limit what Arendt counts as political 'action' that begins something anew, and because of her apparent assumption that keeping biology, bodies, particular feelings and private concerns out of politics will redress the bulk of the problems arising from biopolitical normalisation. We discuss these criticisms as the need arises.

In summing up these introductory remarks about the relationship between biopolitics and Arendt's philosophy of natality, we can say that Arendt's multifaceted notion of natality provides an alternative account to Foucault and Agamben of the dangers that biopolitical normalisation poses to human agency and democratic plurality. While Foucault does not have Arendt's and Agamben's detailed accounts of either totalitarianism or the racism inherent in biopolitics, Agamben's biopolitics of 'bare life', unlike Foucault and Arendt, fails to address in detail the nuanced operation of discrimination within normalising biopolitics in liberal democracies. Moreover, unlike Foucault and Agamben, Arendt's approach provides us with the means of showing how biopolitics, working in tandem with political theology, sexism and racism, targets women's reproductive self-determination as biopolitical threats to democratic plurality in general intensify. Hence, Arendt's philosophy of natality facilitates our diagnoses of interconnections between three dangers that biopolitics still poses within some Western democracies: the erosion of democratic plurality, the rise of elements of 'totalitarianism', and restrictions to women's reproductive self-determination. Equally important for current political and feminist theory, Arendt's philosophy of natality includes a powerful account of agency, freedom and action, which provide a means of countering the negative effects of biopolitics in ways usually downplayed or ignored in biopolitical theory. Indeed, the key feature of Arendt's conception of the political that sets her apart from Foucault's approach to biopolitics and from liberal political theory is, as Dana Villa notes, the 'central place [she gives] to action' in politics (Villa 1999: 114). Although the importance of action has been frequently noted in Arendt scholarship, this book expands this discussion by exploring in some depth how the concept of action applies to political alliance, political hospitality, responsibility and narrative, indicating their relevance for feminist and political theory. There are two related themes regarding Arendt's concept of action that we address in these analyses. One is working out exactly what Arendt means by (political) action, given that she rarely spells it out beyond the basic criterion that action begins something new in the world, which entails engagement with other actors, publicity and significant impact (action must be consequential and public to count as political action). The second theme involves taking up

Arendt's concern about how to temper the unpredictable and potentially boundless consequences of action with the political need for some social stability and endurance of human beings and their worlds. The issue is how to temper the insecurity of unpredictability without suppressing natality.

Understanding what Arendt means by action and why and how biopolitical government suppresses natality in discriminatory ways while also soliciting the complicity (coordination) of the wider population requires showing how Arendt's philosophy of natality supports her unique notion of human agency and her political ontology. By 'political ontology' we mean something more general than Heidegger's focus on the ontological character of *Dasein* (put simply, *Dasein* 'is' understanding the meaning of being as being-in-the-world-with-others arising from being 'thrown' into the world not of one's making). Our analysis does include attention to the 'being' or existence of the human political actor from this perspective of concern for one's own being, but in terms of how being-toward-birth structures both agency and one's 'biography' ('life story') in relation to others and a world. But Arendt's idea of the disclosure of natality between human actors also heralds a new political ontology in a broader sense that includes revised understandings of the character or 'reality' of human collectives, of the 'common world' into which we are born, of the role of relations of 'exteriority' within inter-relationality in general, and of human agency, which together redefine the province and character of 'the political' beyond representative government.[15] It is this field of interaction that is erased or suppressed by all the forms of biopolitics and normalisation mentioned above. By the end of Chapter 1, we have outlined what we see as the key features of Arendt's political ontology that support diagnoses of threats to democratic plurality posed by some forms of biopolitics. We find her political ontology unique in the way it emphasises not just speaking out in contestation of the status quo but also collective *action* and *interaction*. And we find the normative basis of Arendt's political philosophy lies in the responsibility of all of us to keep open the space for the revelation of the 'unique distinctness' and the 'capacity' of natality of all persons. When we turn our attention to how biopolitics suppresses natality, in Chapters 2 and 3, what emerges is a feature of Arendt's philosophy of natality that sets it apart from other biopolitical theory – it is especially conducive to a diagnosis of not only the racism embedded in biopolitical government, but also the patriarchal basis of biopolitics. Indeed, it is the potential application of Arendt's philosophy of natality to a feminist politics that guides the book's focus through Chapters 3 to 5. We gradually develop Arendt's action-based model of politics as a means of countering the deleterious effects of biopolitics, especially in Chapter 3, through two examples of political alliances among women pitted against the biopolitics of women's reproductivity, in Chapter 4, with an account of how Arendt's notion of political inter-relational action extends responsibility to include responsibility for others and for the world, and in Chapter 5, by developing the political and the aesthetic aspects of Arendt's notion of narrative. These analyses yield an important alternative to liberal notions of citizenship and to the logic of sovereignty.

While the approach taken in the book is largely philosophical, employing conceptual analysis and argument, the book also follows Arendt's mixed methodology of historical (genealogical) and comparative analysis of events, concepts and thinkers combined with engagement with contemporary political issues and events. Rather than providing an exhaustive account of

Arendt's political philosophy, our conceptual analyses draw out those concepts most relevant to our themes regarding the relationship between natality and biopolitics. This also guides our choice of thinkers who we bring into conversation with Arendt: we engage those feminist, political and Continental philosophers whose insights are most conducive to expanding any elements of Arendt's philosophy of natality that may need adapting to shifts in the biopolitical milieu since Arendt's lifetime. Even though the contemporary political issues and events we engage are drawn mainly from the US and Australia, they aim to resonate with similar trends in Continental Europe and the UK. We do not, however, undertake a detailed genealogy of any particular example of how biopolitics suppresses natality (such as Arendt has provided with totalitarianism). To provide a genealogy of biopolitical regulation of immigration, for instance, would not help our conceptual analysis of the biopolitical restriction of democratic plurality in general, given the enormous diversity in political approaches to immigration across different nation states. These differences pertain, in part, to differences in notions of (national) identity and citizenship and differences in the historical impetus for, and impact of, waves of migration to 'settler' nations such as the US and Australia compared with migration to the UK from its 'colonies' following the breakup of the so-called British Empire, and compared with patterns of migration across Europe beset by an altogether different set of historical factors to do with war and imposed border changes during the twentieth century. While it would be a mistake, then, to generalise from any particular example regarding illiberal attitudes toward immigration or any example of a perceived threat to democratic plurality, we engage with particular examples of biopolitics for three reasons: to challenge any biological or essentialist understandings of human identity, difference and citizenship that may underpin the political reality portrayed by the example; to illustrate as we draw out and expand Arendt's non-biological understanding of the human condition and of democratic plurality; and to test our own conceptual analyses and interpretations of both biopolitics and non-biological understandings of human existence and inter-relations that the concept of natality underpins.

This methodology and use of the example are consistent with what Arendt means by freedom and responsibility with regard to critical thinking, judgement and politics. It is also how Jacques Derrida (2002) describes freedom and responsibility in relation to the generation and critique of scientific knowledge of the human being in his discussion of the ethics of the project to map and derive patents from the human genome. As Derrida writes, 'freedom and responsibility are incompatible with the mere reporting of the existence of a norm, a normative reality', such as in the project mapping the human genome (Derrida 2002: 200). While freedom and responsibility require taking into account the scientific, hence biopolitical, conceptions of such reality, they also require, most fundamentally, that examples of those descriptions and the norms they harbour are subjected to rigorous critique, genealogical or otherwise. Contesting (interpreting, judging) biopolitical accounts and regulation of reality aims at reopening reality and biopolitical conceptions of the human to what Arendt calls natality and Derrida (possibly following Arendt) here calls the 'who', not only regarding the 'who' (plurality) of the 'human species', but also the '*who* of this *we*' undertaking the critique (Derrida 2002: 207). This means that our critical interpretations of examples of biopolitical suppression of natality, including parts of Arendt's genealogy of totalitarianism as well as contemporary examples, are aimed not only at challenging the discriminatory and potentially dangerous casuistry of those examples but also at testing Arendt's and our alternative conceptions of the human condition in order to avoid any dogmatism that may arise from our own adherence to the conceptual traditions (scientific, biopolitical, philosophical and political) that we have inherited.

In Chapter 1 we draw out accounts of the unique notions of inter-relationality, the historicity of the self, agency and 'political community' arising from Arendt's philosophy of natality. This reveals not only what is suppressed or normalised by biopolitics, but also what Arendt's action-based politics aims to keep open. The focus initially is on how these political concepts tie in with Arendt's discussions of the disjunctive temporality (the 'gap between past and future') that characterises the event of natality and the disclosure of natality to, and by, others through speech and action. We also examine how the event of natality differentiates Arendt's idea of the political from concepts central to classical liberalism (such as difference, diversity and sovereignty). At the same time, we show how Arendt's philosophy of natality transforms or prefigures other approaches to the political that we engage through the book (for example, those of Foucault and Jean-Luc Nancy). Filling out Arendt's concept of political action involves explaining how Arendt's political ontology transforms usual notions of 'power', 'freedom' and 'alliance' into notions of open-ended inter-relational action. The final section of Chapter 1 distinguishes Arendt's notion of the political (which is based on 'birth', understood as the 'new beginning') from what she views as politics based on 'death' (apparent in Hobbes's political philosophy and in the racism and imperialist tendencies of emergent nation states) and from a politics of 'life' (that is, biopolitics formulated by Arendt as the 'rise of the social').

Chapter 2 examines Arendt's analyses of the dangers to natality and hence to democracy posed by what she formulates as the 'social' precursors of totalitarianism and 'totalitarianism' itself. The analysis, firstly, reframes Arendt's accounts of the 'rise of the social' and the emergence of precursors of totalitarianism as pre-empting Foucault's definition of biopolitics, understood as state-centred control of the power over 'making live' and 'letting die' through the 'regularisation' of the biological life of the population. This involves explaining Foucault's definition of biopolitics, including its inherent racism and other normalising tendencies, and providing some preliminary comparison of, and contrast between, Arendt and Foucault with regard to their approaches to the impact of (bio)power on the body in the biopolitical suppression of natality. The analysis then focuses, secondly, on how biopolitics, by suppressing the event of natality, can, in the extreme, transform one pole of biopolitics, the power to 'let die', into totalitarianism and a politics of 'making die' or of (living) death. We argue that Arendt's analysis of the key 'elements' of totalitarianism shows, contrary to Agamben's subsequent account and as if a forewarning of the politics of the early twenty-first century, that the normalising biopolitics within democracy (discussed in the first half of the chapter) can morph into the totalitarian politics of (living) death without recourse to the state exercise of sovereign power. We explain the power at work in totalitarianism in terms of a combination of the normalising biopower apparent in the precursors of totalitarianism and Arendt's unique idea of totalitarian 'power' as the 'force of movement' (within her formulation of 'total terror') that closes the temporal gap between past and future characteristic of the event of natality. The chapter closes with an account of how totalitarianism forecloses natality in the target groups by stripping people of their inter-relational agency, worldly attributes of identity and 'political community', thus reducing them to 'abstract nakedness' (which Agamben subsequently calls 'bare life') before further reduction of these bodies to 'living corpses' in the death camps.

In Chapter 3 we address the other pole of biopolitics – the biopolitics of 'making live' – through analyses of the relationship Arendt sets up between two orders of natality: the appearance of the new beginning through human birth and the new beginning characteristic of the political order of inter-relational speech and action. Our focus is on the most ignored implications of Arendt's philosophy of natality for feminist approaches to women's reproductivity and birth control. The central argument is that the event of natality that is integral to political action and inter-relational agency *is dependent upon* ensuring that women's inter-relational agency with regard to the first order of human birth is acknowledged and preserved. After discussing critical approaches to Agamben's and other biopolitical theorists' neglect of this issue we use a US case study (of religious opposition to abortion during the 2012 presidential election) to examine how the convergence of biopolitics with 'political theology' (*à la* Carl Schmitt), by attributing the birth of new life to God or the sovereign, closes down political agency in general. The focus in the second half of the chapter is on reversing this erasure of political agency by expanding Arendt's notion of collective action or 'alliance', first in the context of an unlikely political coalition that formed in Australia in 2005 to fight for the licensing of RU486 (the 'home abortion pill') at a time when government was intent on securing the 'life' of the population in general at the expense of democratic plurality. The second example of alliance is women of colour fighting for 'reproductive justice' in the US, which highlights the racism at the centre of reproductive biopolitics and both enacts and transforms the scope of political coalition. The overarching argument of the chapter is that these coalitions enable the public 'appearance' of women's inter-relational agency with regard to the first order of birth, and this 'appearance' is a prerequisite to achieving the general equality of unique distinctness and 'freedom' that Arendt sought through her action-based notion of politics.

Chapter 4 explores the inter-relation of the three orders of natality that Arendt distinguishes in *The Human Condition*: the 'private' sphere of intimate relations, the realm of work, and the birth of new beginnings within politics. We examine the impact of biopolitics across the three realms, this time in terms of political hospitality and responsibility, politics and ethics. In turning to the motif of hospitality, the analysis follows the way Arendt connects all areas of human activity to the *welcome* of the beginner who enacts new beginnings. First, with some reference to Derrida and Levinas, we engage Arendt's principle of political hospitality in a broader analysis of the relationship between the failure of political hospitality at the level of the nation (manifest, for example, in erecting barriers to refugees and immigrants), increased biopolitical regulation of human plurality and sexuality in 'private' or domestic realms, and the deregulation of labour in the sphere of 'work'. The analysis expands the theme of the impact of the foreclosure of natality on the body, temporality and affectivity as a means of explaining not only *how* biopolitics can normalise a population in an apparently robust democracy to dampen 'action', but also how action can be provoked and re-emerge from such malaise. We draw on several of philosophies of embodiment and temporality for this purpose. But also we engage Arendt's later work on responsibility, where she examines in some depth the same issue, although in terms of the dampening of 'conscience' (independent judgement of right and wrong) and hence of action that she witnessed during the rise of Nazism. With some reference to Nietzsche's similar idea of conscience, the analysis shows how, for Arendt, conscience is tantamount to the experience of natality working against a morally bankrupt politics. Hence, in an account that has much relevance to contemporary struggles against the rise of right-wing 'popularism' and the erosion of democratic plurality, Arendt links responsibility to the maintenance of human plurality (or equality of distinctness) that contests and undermines biopolitical normalisation. This allows reconsideration of the relation between personal responsibility and political responsibility, between ethics and political action.

Chapter 5 builds on Arendt's unusual claim that it is actions, rather than individuals, that create politically relevant stories. The analysis consists in reconstructing the role of narrative in sustaining the politics of natality against the negative effects of biopolitics. Although Arendt herself does not give us a coherent and well developed theory of narrative, we adapt her philosophy of natality to argue that any narrative created by action is also an act in its own right, which enables a new beginning. This new beginning can be understood in multiple ways: as a new interpretation of actions, as a new interpretation of historical events, or as the very capacity to create a new beginning through language. Second, such narrative discloses the uniqueness of actors. And finally, stories produced by action retrospectively reveal its meaning and this implies a crucial role of memory. By forming and contesting the politics of commemoration, narratives preserve and renew the effects of action into the future. This narrative supplement of action not only expands its meaning but also offers, in addition to promising, another 'remedy' for the fragility of action, a remedy important for counteracting the biopolitical suppression of natality. Consequently, a narrative capable of manifesting natality negotiates between seemingly incompatible tasks: it at once participates in the politics of commemoration and constitutes a new event; it negotiates between the singularity and plurality of actors; and it contests determinations of history and the erasure of the events from the past. A narrative in this sense departs from the politics of representation or the legitimation of the dominance of history, or the ideology of aesthetic realism, and foregrounds instead discontinuous temporality between past and future and the key role of reflective judgement and art in renewal of the world. Taking a range of elements of the narrative into account, we develop what Kristeva and Cavarero and other feminist scholars have called in different ways an ontological dimension of storytelling, namely, the creation and preservation of human life as a narratable *bios*. This concept of *bios* based on action and narrative provides an important alternative to the liberal notion of citizenship, biopolitics and the logic of sovereignty.

Notes

1   For a summary list of Trump's Executive Orders up to October 2017 see Avalon Zoppo, Amanda Proença Santos and Jackson Hudgins, 'Here's the full list of Donald Trump's executive orders', *NBC News online*, 14 February 2017, updated 17 October <http://www.nbcnews.com/news/us-news/here-s-full-list-donald-trump-s-executive-orders-n720796> (last accessed 30 November 2017).

2   This Memorandum was signed on 23 January 2017. For a summary of
    the background and impact of this anti-abortion "rule" that the Memor-
    andum reinstated see Molly Redden, "'Global gag rule" reinstated by
    Trump, curbing NGO abortion services abroad', *The Guardian (Australia)*,
    24 January 2017 <https://www.theguardian.com/world/2017/jan/23/
    trump-abortion-gag-rule-international-ngo-funding> (last accessed on 15
    February 2017).

3   Indeed, three months later, on 13 April 2017, Trump (quietly) signed
    legislation allowing US states to deny federal funds to Planned Parenthood
    and other organisations that provide abortions.

4   Throughout we note the page numbers of the two different editions of
    On Revolution (OR) presently in circulation: first, the page numbers of
    the original edition, published in 1963 by Faber and Faber but no longer
    in print; followed by the page numbers for the Penguin edition, first
    published in 1977.

5   Benhabib reaches a similar conclusion in her longer analysis of Arendt's
    notion of the 'right to have rights' in *The Reluctant Modernism of Hannah
    Arendt* (Benhabib 1996: xxxiii).

6   Emphasis in the original, as is the case with italics in quotes throughout,
    unless otherwise stated.

7   An early exception to the absence of discussion of Arendt's philosophy
    of natality in biopolitical theory is Miguel Vatter's (2006) convincing
    argument that natality should be considered in the biopolitical framework
    as a counter to totalitarianism. Catherine Mills's recent book *Biopolitics*
    (2018) is notable for including a chapter on the contribution of Arendt's
    discussion of totalitarianism to biopolitical theory. While the timing of the
    release of Mills's book did not allow its consideration in our analysis, we
    refer to her earlier critique of Agamben in Chapter 3.

8   By contrast, Thomas Lemke (2011), while claiming that the notion of bio-
    politics has a 100-year history and that he provides an overview of the most
    salient approaches, mentions Arendt only once, and not as a key figure
    in the field. Equally puzzling is that the only woman Lemke counts as a
    major thinker of biopolitics is Agnes Heller, whose sole contribution is a
    1994 book (co-authored by Ferenc Fehér) that (inappropriately, according
    to feminist scholars in this field) attacks feminist 'politics of the Body',
    the peace movement and French post-modernism for furthering harmful
    biopolitics by valuing 'difference' and 'life over freedom' (Lemke 2011: 79).

9   Consistent with her concept of natality, Arendt finds the French Declara-
    tion of the Rights of Man problematic because it itemises a list of rights said

to be 'inherent in man's nature, as distinguished from his political status', whereas she favours the American 'Bill of Rights because it emerged from the political process (of interactive speech and action), and so it remains contestable, and because it was aimed at instituting 'permanent restraining controls upon all [state] political power' (OR: 104–5/98–9). As Lisa Disch (2011) explains, Arendt favours the American Revolution over the French for similar reasons.

10 Hamacher (2004) provides a particularly informative history of the 'right to have rights' that is indebted to Arendt and Marx and focuses on the relationship between politics, the rise of the nation state, notions of 'human being' and Christianity.

11 Indeed, Penelope Deutscher, in *Foucault's Futures: A Critique of Reproductive Reason* (2017), finds Foucault's work particularly conducive to analysing the biopolitics of human procreation. While Deutscher's book appeared too late to be considered properly in our analysis, in Chapter 3 we include discussion of her earlier critique of Agamben on the biopolitics of reproduction. Jemima Repo goes further in adopting Foucault's philosophy of power for a thoroughgoing genealogy of the biopolitics of, not just reproduction or race, but gender per se. She argues that, since the mid-1950s, *gender* has emerged as the primary 'apparatus of biopower' for 'normalizing, disciplining, and governing sex' (Repo 2016: 2).

12 Rose's position has come in for some criticism of late, especially for implying that, as Claire Blencowe puts it, 'specifically *biopolitical* racism is a thing of the past' (Blencowe 2012: 127). Blencowe devotes an entire chapter of her book *Biopolitical Experience* (2012) to an enlightening critique of Rose for this and other aspects of his approach to biopolitics.

13 'Biological citizenship' is a term coined by Rose (for example, Rose 2007: 6), which he appears to have borrowed from Adriana Petryna's (2002) book on the topic. As Torsten Heinemann points out, while 'biological citizenship' is meant to denote new forms of 'subjectivation and collective action on the basis of shared biological traits' (for example, agitation for access to medical treatment or welfare services) it has just as easily become the basis for 'exclusion and restriction of citizenship rights' (Heinemann 2015: 1). This sort of discrimination and normalisation is why Arendt and Foucault object to the biopolitical practice of identifying persons in terms of supposedly shared biological traits.

14 This abdication of political action and absence of dissent is apparent, for example, in bipartisan and popular support in Australia for policies that hold asylum seekers in 'inhumane' conditions in off-shore detention centres; in

the rise of right-wing 'popularism' across Europe, and in majority support in Turkey in a referendum in April 2017 for a return to centralised authoritarian government on the (hollow) promise of economic empowerment, certainty, and security.

15 For a comprehensive definition of what is meant by the term 'political ontology' along these lines, as well as an enlightening analysis of why it has become a focus of political philosophy in recent decades, see Hay (2009).

1

Natality Reframing the Meaning of Politics

Arendt's notion of 'natality' as the event of a new beginning signals her novel understanding of three aspects of the political – human agency, plurality and uniqueness of persons (unique distinctness) – and, when considered in terms of our 'second birth' into public life, the event of natality also provides the basis for explaining how the self and the world we share are transformed within a democratic polity. These considerations consist in Arendt's unique approach to phenomenological attempts to forge a path between determinism and notions of absolute and individual freedom. This path can be summarised as follows: the disclosure and welcome of 'natality', of the beginner beginning something anew and the beginner as unique distinctness, is, for Arendt, the meaning and purpose of human existence in general, and is what distinguishes human existence from the determined existence of 'nature' and machines, on the one hand, and from the absolute disembodied 'worldless' freedom of gods, on the other. Together, the life of the body (*animal laborans* or 'labour') and the 'work' (*homo faber* or fabrication) and 'action' (*vita activa*) of those who come before us provide the social, material and meaningful world that we share (the common world) and in which we appear. On the one hand, human beings, 'no matter what they

do, are always conditioned' by 'everything they come in contact
with', by 'the conditions under which life is given' on earth as
well as by the conditions they 'constantly create' (HC: 9). On
the other hand, these 'conditions of human existence – life itself,
natality and mortality, worldliness, plurality, and the earth – can
never "explain" what we are or answer the question of who we
are for the simple reason that they never condition us absolutely'
(HC: 11). The formula that Arendt adds to political philosophy
to explain this play of the conditioned and unconditioned is the
disclosure of natality between human beings: through activities that
begin something anew, activities that impact others in being acknowledged and accepted *as* a new beginning originating from a
human agent (a beginner) (that is, actions that 'establish relationships' – HC: 190), not only are we opened to an undetermined
future (that is, we retain our 'who-ness' or unique distinctness)
but also we alter the conditions of our existence and thereby
keep the world that we share open as the 'potentiality in being
together' (HC: 201).

This idea of the disclosure of natality to and by other human
actors, we argue, grounds a new political ontology consisting
of revised understandings of the character of human collectives,
inter-relationality and human agency, which together redefine
the dominion and nature of 'the political' as well as the relationship between political agents and the common world.[1] While it
is clear that Arendt remains opposed to ontological individualism, she does not spell out her model of inter-relationality
except in terms of the space of the political. Hence, in this
chapter we draw out the notion of inter-relationality implied in
Arendt's references to the disclosure of natality between human
agents (through speech and action) and between the agent and
the world. This is necessary in order to account for Arendt's

repeated claim that action is quashed and the event of natality is foreclosed by various kinds of government, particularly what is now called normalising biopolitics and its extreme deviation into totalitarianism. For example, Arendt's claim that 'bureaucracy is a form of government in which everybody is deprived [. . .] of the power to act' (OV: 81) indicates that in this case (but not always) the notion of 'action' carries special (political) significance, although what that entails is rarely spelt out. More generally we show how, by mobilising this idea of natality to link politics to a particular idea of historicity of the self and of the 'common' world, Arendt revises concepts of the political beyond those of liberalism, communitarianism and Marxism without reliance on conventional notions of a human essence based on, for example, a specific human aptitude such as the capacity to reason. The analysis also considers how Arendt's notion of the disclosure of natality between agents provides a 'principle' of sorts for democratic political community.

This multifaceted analysis includes, first in section I, preliminary accounts of the notions of 'agency', plurality, 'political community' and transformation of the 'common' world that emerge from Arendt's accounts of the *disjunctive temporality* (the 'gap between past and future') inherent in the disclosure of natality through speech and action. After discussing, in section II, criticisms of Arendt's apparent adherence to the public/private distinction and her approach to embodiment, in section III we explore how Arendt's notion of natality and her implicit model of inter-relationality compare with other ideas of the political that we engage in later chapters: with the notions of identity and difference of classical liberalism; with Foucault's idea of the 'event' of the new that disrupts tradition and normalisation and underlies his approach to biopolitics; and with

Jean-Luc Nancy's idea of inter-relationality as 'exposure' to, and the 'sharing' of, 'singularity' in community (being singular-plural) that he describes, more explicitly than Arendt, as the principle of democracy. In section IV we outline the way that Arendt's characterisation of human inter-relationality in terms of the disclosure of natality transforms the meaning of conventional political concepts of power, freedom and collective political action (solidarity or alliance). By way of introducing our specific focus on biopolitics in Chapters 2 and 3, the final section of this chapter explains how Arendt poses this notion of the political based on the disclosure of natality against biopolitics as Foucault later defines it, that is, both politics based on 'death' (exemplified by Hobbes) and politics of 'life'.

I. Natality and Human Agency: Temporality, Action and Politics

The *first* point to note about the event of natality is that it saves human existence from the determinism and necessity brought on by some kinds of biopolitics by *historicising or temporalising* 'life', although neither arbitrarily nor by virtue of any human aptitude. Rather, natality refers to the way that the very 'appearance' of human beings in a world temporalises (interrupts) what Arendt, echoing Aristotle, describes as the cyclic time of 'nature' (*zoe*) and, following Augustine, the passing of linear (historical and biographical) time (*bios*) (HC: 96–8). As Agamben has made this distinction between *zoe* and *bios* significant in his biopolitical theory, it is worth saying more about how Arendt approaches these spheres of life, with special regard to temporality. She is clear that, by 'life', she does not mean a substrate of 'flux' of materiality or organic or biological processes. Rather, as she says, 'life' has 'an altogether different meaning if it is related to the world and meant to designate the time interval between birth and death' (HC: 97). On the one hand, this 'life' as *zoe* (nature or biological life) is conventionally said to be governed by cyclic and repetitive temporality in several ways. Human biology is subject to: nature's 'cyclical movement' of growth and decay, the 'circular movement of bodily functions', and the repetitive flow of human reproduction and manual labour (HC: 98). (Unusually, Arendt's formulation of manual labour, as well as labour in the sense of giving birth, borrows from Locke's sense of the 'laboring body' ministering to 'the necessities of life' [*animal laborans*] and is distinguished from the creative, fabricating activity of 'work', which gives nature some permanency in the form of things – HC: 79–80, 98.) *Zoe* is also the mode of life characteristic of the conventional (Aristotelian) 'household' or the private sphere and is the form of life that humans share with other living things. The key point at this stage of our account is that, in Arendt's genealogy of political ontology with regard to temporality, *zoe*, driven by necessity and the 'motor of biological life', is a determined mode of 'life'.

On the other hand, human 'life' is also partly *bios*, which is governed not by 'necessity' but by what Aristotle called 'praxis'. For Arendt, *bios* refers to human existence as *political life* emerging through speech and action. Rather than adhering to a pattern of repetition through time, *bios* is that aspect of human life characterised by dynamic historicity: the 'chief characteristic of this specifically human life [. . .] is that it is itself always full of events which ultimately can be told as a story, establish a biography' (HC: 97). We discuss biography with regard to natality and action further in Chapter 5. For now, it is notable that Arendt does not conclude from this point about the temporality and historicity of the self that, as a series of 'events', *bios* is driven by a free human agency as if we are free to transcend time or be fully self-present. On the contrary, as the term 'biography' implies, our life stories are told by others, conditioned by cultural heritage, as well as by the personal history of both actors and storytellers: human life as *bios* is 'worldly' rather than free in the usual sense (HC: 95). Hence, while human life is never mere *zoe*, human life as *bios* is never free in the usual sense underlying ontological individualism: *bios* and the self-image that we develop through speech and action witnessed by others are conditioned and can fall into habits and 'patterns of thoughts' and a continuous existence that, as a life story, seems to follow a linear temporality 'no matter how accidental or haphazard the single events and their causation may appear to be' (HC: 95, 97). This worldly aspect of *bios* provides human life with some stability and is not necessarily a problem. Crucially, while apparently linear and process-like, *bios* is not determined: the point about the temporality of both *zoe* and *bios* is that, as aspects of *human* life, they are, for Arendt, necessarily punctuated by the event of natality, which gives human existence its futural undetermined directionality.[2] Arendt's worry throughout her political philosophy is that the repetitive or linear temporality said to be characteristic of 'biological' and/or 'natural life' can be transformed into the equally deterministic linear 'life process' when public life is dominated by what she refers to in *The Human Condition* as 'labouring activity' in its wider sense of repetitive work, bureaucracy, technocracy or predictive science (HC: 47), which is the kind of biopolitics that is the focus of that book. We discuss this worry further in the final section of this chapter and in subsequent chapters.

How, then, does the event of natality temporalise human life against cyclic repetition, linearity, historical necessity and determinism of any kind? In her later works, *Between Past and Future* (BPF: 6–15) and *The Life of the Mind* (LM I: 202–13) Arendt formulates the temporality of natality more clearly, by distancing notions of the historicity of the self from any notion of cyclic or linear time. She emphasises the operation of natality in reflective thinking and judgement rather than just praxis through speech and action (*bios*) and she simply sets aside the question of the temporality of *animal laborans*, biology and nature (*zoe*). Nevertheless, as Dianna Taylor argues, while Arendt reformulates her notions of judgement in her later work in terms of Kant's philosophy of mind, she 'does not depoliticize' the notion (Taylor 2002: 153). Hence, what Arendt says in these works about temporalisation of human life through thinking, willing and judgement is important for understanding how her political ontology in *The Human Condition* forges a path between determinism and absolute freedom. In *The Life of the Mind* and *Between Past and Future* Arendt suggests that 'the insertion of man' into a world, through reflective thinking and judgement, disrupts the present, 'breaks up the unidirectional flow of [historical] time' between birth and death (LM I: 202–13; BPF: 11–12). Her account of the historicity of the self borrows from Nietzsche's concept of time in *Thus Spoke Zarathustra*, 'The Vision and the Riddle' (Nietzsche 1978: 155–60), as well as Kafka's short parable 'He'. Against notions of both cyclic time and linear historical time Nietzsche, via Zarathustra, formulates time in terms of two paths extending from the present gateway called the 'moment' in which human beings stand, one toward the past and the other toward a future that contradicts the past. For Nietzsche, the practice of critique (which he variously refers to as the 'revaluation of value', critical history and genealogy) opens this gateway or momentary gap between past and a divergent future. Kafka emphasises 'He's' *experience* of this temporal interval as a battleground between the forces of past and future clashing with each other. Adapting both Nietzsche and Kafka's approaches to time, Arendt argues, with reference to Kant's notion of judgement, that it is the path paved by reflective thinking and the act of judgement that marks this gap between past and future, this disruption of linear historical time between those two exemplars of human finitude, the moments of birth and death. Only a finite being can inherit a tradition of concepts, laws and norms, but in inheriting a tradition that would determine the path one takes, trains of thought, that is, remembrance and anticipation, open an undetermined future. Nietzsche's moment of contradiction and Kafka's conflictual interval represent, for Arendt,

> [t]he path paved by thinking, the small inconspicuous track of non-time beaten by the activity of thought within the space-time given to natal and mortal men. Following that course, the thought-trains, remembrance and anticipation, save whatever they touch from the ruin of historical and biographical time. This small non-time space in the very heart of time, unlike the world and the culture into which we are born, cannot be inherited and handed down by tradition. (LM I: 210)

Here Arendt is suggesting that reflective thinking paves the way for a gap to open between the past and future such that past and future appear as infinite and contradictory forces that are transformed as they impact upon and condition the 'self' in the present. This moment of rupture of linear time, historical progress and cyclical time is not itself part of the common world we inherit; nor is one's 'insertion' into a (public) world 'forced upon us by necessity, like labor', or 'conditioned by' others (HC: 177); nor does the *content* of the thought or judgement bring on the rupture. The *act* of reflective thought itself clears away established universals so as to judge particulars anew and so breaks with tradition and the past. While Arendt sometimes implies that this rupture or event of natality originates within the self, significantly, this thinking and judgement must 'appear', or are expressed, *to* others for this gap to open (the thinker is inserted into the world and 'appears' to others as a beginner beginning something anew).[3] Moreover, witness to the judgement is also paramount (it must be disclosed *by* others): while Kafka's 'He' desires to be his own witness, Arendt notes that only an omnipotent (read 'totalitarian') god could be witness to its own uniqueness.

While there is much debate about Arendt's approaches to thinking and judgement,[4] we take her basic point regarding temporality and natality here to be twofold. First, thinking draws on the meanings (or sense) of the world we have inherited and share, and it involves personal remembrance of the past, but also, simultaneously, the act of judgement or decision involves anticipation, which is futural and therefore breaks with the past. The acts of reflective thinking and judgement thus transform the tradition we have inherited and our biographical narrative, both of which condition us, thereby propelling us into an open future (LM I: 210). But, second, and we emphasise this, others play a crucial role in calling us to think and judge in the first place, such that we are futural beings. As Arendt's implicit model of inter-relationality in *The Human Condition* suggests, only if others appear as natal and distinct beings are we propelled to think and speak and, conversely, only if the person is revealed and welcomed as the beginner of the new does this gap between past and future open. And in *The Life of the Mind* (LM I: 207–8) Arendt suggests that it is a person's 'insertion' into the world *per se*, an appearance that is revealed *to and by* others, which 'deflects' cyclic and linear historical time by introducing a 'difference between past and future' into 'everlasting change'. The point for now is that this gap between the no longer and an undetermined future, which thinking opens and judgement and action make manifest, constitutes the self's futurity. In ways we will discuss in subsequent chapters, it is this futurity, inherent to the event of natality, that can be suppressed by biopolitics and foreclosed by totalitarian government. This also destroys human plurality in general.[5]

This brings us to the *second* crucial point to note about the event of natality, aside from its temporalising aspect: the disclosure of natality through *public action and speech* reveals the fundamental *unique distinctness of each person and the plurality* of human existence. That is, in public life we appear to each other as unique and distinct beginners of something new. This emerges from Arendt's alternative explanation of how natality temporalises life besides through reflective thinking and judgement. Reading her discourse on temporality in *The Life of the Mind* back into her account of the political in *The Human Condition* we can say that what opens a gap between past and future is the disclosure of natality, not in the first instance through thought and reflective judgement, but more so through action and speech. Although, crucially, in *The Human Condition*, even though Arendt largely ignores reflective thinking and judgement, she does conclude that action must be 'thoughtful' to count as action, meaning that action must be well considered and worldly rather than rule-bound, introspective and detached from the reality (the 'common world') that we share (HC: 324–5; also BPF: 14). With regard to the direct relation between the event of natality and politics, participation in public action and debate (which Arendt describes in *The Human Condition* as a 'second birth' – HC: 176) is how the speaker and actor begin something new in the public world, which is coextensive with the political as Arendt understands it. As Dana Villa suggests, there is no overstating the significance of this revision of the notion of the political: basing the political on 'initiatory action in the context of a robust, talkative human plurality' is a radical departure from the Western tradition of political theory (Villa 2000: 11). Arendt's account of the disclosure of natality through public action and speech revolutionises notions of the political in two ways: it revises the usual notion of agency as a sovereign individual being in control of their thoughts and deeds; and, second, it also revises the usual notion of the democratic political space as the parliamentary meeting of individual minds elected to represent diverse interests with the view to reach consensus about the common good. With regard to *agency*, Arendt's emphasis on public action and speech challenges the notion of human agency based on individual sovereignty and on the assumption of a faculty (such as will or reason) considered essentially human that precedes and directs the action or speech. Instead, as Bonnie Honig argues, in her chapter entitled 'Arendt's accounts of action and authority' (Honig 1993: 76–125), which entails a particu-larly interesting reading of Arendt's idea of action and its role in continually reconstituting the political, agency for Arendt, as the 'capacity' of beginning something new, is 'performative' (Honig 1993: 87). As Arendt puts it, public action 'disclose[s] the agent together with the act' (HC: 180). Even though in *The Life of the Mind* Arendt might seem to follow Kant's view that there are different faculties of mind (willing, thinking and judgement) and in *Between Past and Future* she acknowledges that 'motives and aims' are 'important factors in every single act', she also insists that they 'are not determining factors, and action is free to the extent that it is able to transcend them' (BPF: 151). If an action counts as beginning something *new*, it cannot be a sign of a pre-existing inner thought or reasoning process as it is for Descartes. In *Discourse on Method, Part V*, Descartes famously posits creative language use and versatile action as tests for the presence of reason and thinking, which for him constitute the inner essence of human being. In implicitly critiquing this Cartesian model of the relation between the human agent and action and speech, Arendt is in agreement with Nietzsche's dictums that there is no 'I' behind and the cause of thinking (Nietzsche 1973: 27–8) and there is no 'doer' behind 'the deed' (Nietzsche 1967a: 45). Honig (1988) argues convincingly that even in *The Life of the Mind, Volume II: Willing*, Arendt, while entertaining the idea of the will as a mental faculty, retains her view that there is no inner self or 'free will' prior to political action that is its cause. Rather, the will is the organ of 'spontaneity' (LM II: 109–10), in the sense that it makes 'action, a beginning, possible' by turning the 'mental self' away from its concern with itself outward toward the world (Honig 1988: 80–1). Just as the will is not determined by any other mental faculty, nor is action. Nor should human action be interpreted as a sign of 'behaviour' (which implies a pre-existing disposition determining action) or as an expression of an inner feeling. As we will see in Chapter 2, understanding human action as a sign of behaviour or an expression of inner identity is one way that biopolitics strips human action of its natality. Nor can the action be guided by a rule if it is the event of natality, the beginning of the new or a break with tradition.

43

Indeed, for Arendt, instead of preceding action, *agency* is *human action that presents the person as a source of initiative*, as an actor who makes a difference to the world, whose appearance through action opens a gap between past and future. In sum, for Arendt, public action realises or actualises agency by actualising *natality*, that is, action discloses the actor as an agent in the sense of a unique beginning (HC: 178).

Speech is a crucial partner to action. Arendt goes on to suggest that the actor, appearing as a moving body, could be perceived as a non-human 'robot' (here Arendt suffers a bit from Descartes's doubt that the moving body can signify humanness without other proof of the presence of a *person*). Hence, for public action to count as *human* agency it needs to be accompanied by speech or some other indicator of the presence of an *initiator* who begins something new: 'the action he [*sic*[6]] begins is *humanly* disclosed by the [. . .] spoken word in which he identifies himself as an actor, announcing what he does, has done, and intends to do' (HC: 179). As we discuss below, there are some difficulties in the reason Arendt gives for positing speech as a necessary supplement to action: because a moving body is an insufficient indicator of human agency. For now, it suffices to say that the content of any intention declared in the spoken word is not what matters to the disclosure of natality, only that the spoken word presents the actor as a beginner in the sense of another agent distinct from oneself. Nor is having the *faculty* of speech the key to being a political agent; rather, it is having access to 'a way of life in which [public] speech makes sense' (HC: 29). Speech reveals the actor as a 'who', not a 'what' (HC: 179), that is, not an entity with attributes of identity or an inner being that is known or knowable, and not in terms of content (not as this or that sort of person or 'character' – HC: 181).

Instead, speech discloses a person per se, that is, as 'unique dis-tinctness' (HC: 207), a perpetual beginner of both a change in the world and a change to 'who' they appear to be. So, while public action as 'beginning' is 'the actualisation of the human condition of *natality*', speech 'is the actualisation of the human condition of *plurality*' (HC: 178, emphasis added). This form of participation in public life implies a specific kind of relation-ality that ideally should apply in all spheres of human life. With regard to politics, Arendt's general point is that, together, public speech and action not only signify human agents' willingness to engage in collaborative, collective transformation of the world and, simultaneously, of themselves, but also actualise that trans-formation.

The *third* point we wish to emphasise regarding this political ontology that the notion of the disclosure of natality allows (besides disjunctive temporality and agency) is its *communal* aspect: that is, for Arendt, *being-with-others is crucial* for the dis-closure of natality and therefore for agency and politics. While at times Arendt may seem to emphasise the self-animating disclosure of uniqueness *to* others (the 'expressive' component of action) this is also always the (multidirectional) disclosure of natality *by* others (action is 'communicative'): as Maurizio Passerin D'Entrèves suggests, plurality is an essential condition of (political) action because it 'confirms the reality of the actor and his or her deeds' (D'Entrèves 1994: 70, 84), but also the mutual disclosure of natality engenders relationality and political 'bonds', as it transforms those in relation and the world they are acting through. This latter point in particular marks out Arendt's notion of the political from liberal political thought and from aspects of Kant's philosophy, with which she increas-ingly engages in her later works. For Arendt, the public 'space of appearance' (HC: 198–9), the space of the disclosure of natality, does not consist in a collective of different self-contained individuals coming together for the sake of formulating laws and public policy (although it includes such activities); rather, the very uniqueness of actors and speakers, their mutual disclosure as initiators or beginners, happens *through* 'human togetherness' (HC: 180). Moreover, '[a]ction and speech go on between men [*sic*], as they are directed toward them, and they retain their agent-revealing capacity even if their content is exclusively "objective", concerned with matters of the world' (HC: 182).

So, *political community* as the public world has *two aspects* (HC: 50–3). *First*, it is the space of appearance or 'publicity' of everything everyone says or does (HC: 50), the intangible 'in-between' that Arendt also describes as the '"web" of human relationships' consisting of the disclosure of natality and plurality (HC: 183). Implicit in this notion of human togetherness is a model of inter-relationality that sets her apart from other phenomenologists such as Heidegger, especially in the way she focuses on the political dimensions of human relations. It is difficult to judge the extent of the kinds of interactions Arendt would count as political. Sometimes she uses the phrase 'acting in concert' (for example, EU: 334), which implies a gathering of people (often spontaneously and often short-lived) for a shared and explicitly political purpose of acting, for example to oppose war and violence – as in the Greenham Common Women's (anti-nuclear) Peace Movement of 1981–2000 – or to overturn their oppression – as with, for example, the Black Lives Matter movement that began in the US in 2013. Importantly, 'acting in concert' does not mean acting in agreement or unity. On the contrary, while people 'act in concert as equals' with a common purpose, it is always with a plurality of dissimilar perspectives that are initiated within the assemblage of actors (EU: 334). On the other hand, as Arendt also describes the public world in terms of the space of appearance of everything that everyone says and does, then presumably her notion of acting in concert, consisting of the disclosure of natality and plurality, applies to human inter-relationality in general. So, while Arendt's examples are mostly of revolutions or popular uprisings, the model of mutual disclosure of natality and plurality also applies to all sorts of gatherings, large and small (local community forums, research workshops, policy round-tables, a gathering at a homeless drop-in centre), even if the purpose of the gathering is not overtly political and the extent of publicity and unpredicted consequences of the attendant actions are modest. The size of the gathering does not necessarily matter providing there is sufficient diversity within the assemblage to initiate new beginnings and the 'performance' is 'broadcast' in a way that impacts the wider world. Hence, in recent decades Arendt's notion of initiating new beginnings by acting in concert has morphed into a variety of forms of participatory democracy, including the development of the notion of 'mini-publics' to agitate for changes to public policy on particular issues.[7]

The *second* aspect of the public world that Arendt notes (HC: 50–3) is that it is 'reality', the world that is 'common to all', not 'earth or nature' but world as 'human artifact' built partly through 'fabrication' (work) (HC: 52), partly through cultivating 'culture' (BPF: 211–12) and by introducing laws that 'hedge in', and are nurtured by, the 'new and unpredictable' (OT: 465),[8] and partly by the dynamic in-between that speech and action actualise and through which we 'sense' our own reality and that of the common world (HC: 208).[9] In 'Truth and politics' (BPF: 227–64), as James Phillips (2013) explains, Arendt argues that this

47

'common world' is a shared reality consisting of 'factual truths' that are based on multiple opinions of community members, which have been tested and debated to a point where we can just trust in the reality of the world we share.[10] But as this world is under constant revision and contestation through the event of natality, the world is not 'common' in the sense of common interests or values that are shared, static or reached by consensus. On the contrary, it is common in the sense that: 'the world, like every in-between, relates and separates men at the same time' (HC: 52). As Arendt puts it in *The Promise of Politics*, this world is a conglomeration of 'standpoints' of people 'who stand in some particular relationship with one another' (PP: 176), hence a conglomeration of standpoints undergoing transition. Similarly, 'common sense', as Arendt defines it in *The Human Condition*, is the sense we have of this reality (the common world), the sense by virtue of which 'the other sense perceptions [. . .] disclose reality' (HC: 209) and by virtue of which we are 'fitted' into the world (HC: 283), again not by consensus but by participating in its dynamism. Or, as she formulates 'common sense' in her later works and partly following Kant's notion of the communicability of aesthetic judgement (which we discuss in more detail in Chapter 5), thinking and judgement that manifest in the political must transcend the individuality of speculative reason (which Arendt often says has no place in politics): this thinking 'cannot function in strict isolation or solitude; it needs the presence of others "in whose place" it must think', not in the sense of thinking on behalf of others, but thinking that refers to others 'whose perspectives it must take into consideration, and [most crucially] without whom it never has the opportunity to operate at all' (BPF: 220–1). By contrast, 'alternative facts', 'ideology' or 'organised lying', where meaning is imposed upon the public world without being open to contestation, undermine the reality of the world we share, destroy this 'sense by which we take our bearings in the world' (BPF: 257) and condemn people to 'isolation' and 'loneliness' (OT: 474–5). This is also the effect of some forms of biopolitics, as we discuss in Chapter 2.

It is because Arendt understands 'action' in terms of her implicit model of inter-relationality within a common world, that is, in terms of action and speech disclosed by others as originating with a unique human agent, that she can claim that to be without this web of the 'in-between' of the disclosure of natality, hence, 'to be isolated is to be deprived of the capacity to act' in a way that is unpredictable and consequential (HC: 188). Arendt seems to use this notion of being 'deprived of the capacity to act' in three different senses: the *experience* of one's actions having no impact on a situation (for example, the experience of being caught in a treadmill and thwarted by bureaucratic processes); lacking the impetus to initiate anything, that is, to act spontaneously *against* the norm because one has been rendered compliant; and being deprived of a political community in which one's actions are recognised as the actions of a beginner (an agent) beginning something new, which is a key feature of totalitarian biopolitics. In subsequent chapters we examine how biopolitics can deprive people of the 'capacity to act' in all these senses.

The insight about reliance of the event of natality and hence plurality on human inter-relationality and vice versa distinguishes Arendt's understanding of the operation of democratic plurality from that of liberalism and communitarianism in two ways. First, Arendt's political community is based neither on mutual recognition of sameness (such as everyone having the same capacity to reason), nor on sharing a common language, or 'values', but on the disclosure of the uniqueness of each to the other. Indeed, for

Arendt, the notion of community based on this assumption of sameness, shared interests or a common good in the government of a nation is a 'communistic fiction' (which she explicitly, and ironically, attributes to liberal economics rather than Marxism) that is an anathema to democratic plurality (HC: 42–6). Political community is not a substance to which individuals belong. Rather, the dynamic space of political community *is,* or consists in, the disclosure and welcome of natality through the action and discourse of each of us. Second, while Arendt's human agent is exposed as unique and distinct *through* community, the liberal individual is supposedly already constituted as autonomous and distinct prior to coming together with others.

Arendt's idea of the relation between the event of natality and plurality is also different from other ideas of being–with–others in the phenomenological tradition, including that of Heidegger. The crucial difference between Arendt's and Heidegger's ontology, aside from Arendt's focus on the political, is that, for Arendt, the disclosure of uniqueness through community is made possible by the socio-political significance of birth of the newborn in two ways beyond concern for one's being. First, the signification of the political actor as a beginner of the new beginning (the disclosure of natality within political community) borrows from the shared significance of the first-order 'fact of birth', where the newborn 'appears' *to* others as 'unique', a new beginning (HC: 178). Second, from the perspective of the newborns, once they perceive others as separate (opaque and distinct) beings, this fact of their own birth as distinct beings propels them (to act and speak) *toward others*, a leaning toward others that is reinforced, rather than emergent, in mature political actors' retrospective being-toward their *own* birth. (As we will see, this idea that, from our earliest years, being-toward the unknowable exteriority of others is a crucial aspect of being-with is emphasised further by thinkers such as Jean-Luc Nancy, with added benefits for an Arendtian diagnosis of the harms of biopolitics.) For Heidegger, on the other hand, it is being-toward-*death* that discloses *Dasein*'s uniqueness, not to others but to *oneself* in a way that distances human being from being-with-others: the realisation that death cannot be shared exposes human being to the singularity and uniqueness of one's own becoming and this being-toward-death makes one responsible for one's *own* potentiality for existence. Indeed, in 'What is existential philosophy?' (EU: 163–87), Arendt is explicitly critical of Heidegger for privileging concern for one's *own being* and a kind of self-mastery and solitude in being-toward-death: for Heidegger, '*Dasein* could be truly itself if it could pull back from its being-in-the-world into itself [. . .]', but this leads to 'alienation' and hence '[o]nly at death, which will take him out of the world, does man have the certainty of being himself' (EU: 179).[11] Arendt's notion of the political is equally concerned with restoring responsibility but to the realm of the political rather than just oneself. For her, though, as we argue in Chapter 4, responsibility is based on the disclosure of natality within a collectivity or the togetherness of community. We say more in the final section of this chapter about the significance for politics of this shift away from being-toward-death.

II. Critical Reflections

Before we move on to discuss specific political concepts arising from Arendt's philosophy of natality, there are two aspects of Arendt's political ontology that require critical attention in the interests of facilitating diagnoses of threats posed by *contemporary* biopolitics. Because of her worry about the reduction of the temporality of human existence to necessity, which the suppression of natality entails, Arendt, in *The Human Condition* at least, tends to leave in place the distinctions between 'biological life' and political life, private and public life, presumably to protect political life from the force of necessity.[12] She also leaves aside the question of the role of the body in political life throughout and under-appreciates the affective dimension of human inter-relationality.[13] Both tendencies have attracted criticisms, which call for provisional consideration.

First, the usual criticism of the conventional distinction between the public and the private realms in political theory is that it involves excluding various kinds of people, on the basis of sex, race, class, religion, age and so on, from participation in public affairs. The distinction also plays a role in determining what activities count as political and what escapes public attention (and so escapes both the law and public resources). For example, it remains the case that violence against women continues unchecked so long as it is categorised as 'domestic'. Of particular concern is also that isolating the 'private' and the 'social' from the political sets aside questions pertaining to workplace, economic and reproductive justice, issues we pursue in later chapters. It is true that in her detailed genealogy of the distinction between the public and the private realms in *The Human Condition* (HC: 22–78), Arendt does seem to leave in place the conventions about what activities should be excluded from public affairs, even though she may not share all of the historical ideas she describes in this account. The simplest defence of the criticism that she leaves the distinction and the inequities in place is to say, as Mary Dietz (1995) does in her insightful defence of Arendt, that, in *The Human Condition*, Arendt analyses three (not two) realms of human activity – labour (including 'biological life'), work (the fabrication of things) and action (political life) – all involving beginning something anew (HC: 9). While inequities, subjection and exclusions may feature in the realms of labour and work, Dietz argues, Arendt's notion of the political devoted to the mutual disclosure of natality enables the means of countering such inequities. We discuss some examples in later chapters. Moreover, and crucially, her salient understanding of the public realm is that it is not a place as such; as we have indicated, the public disclosure of natality is Arendt's description of the fabric of the 'in-between' of public interactions rather than a sphere or an institution that endures beyond that interaction: the political 'does not survive the actuality of the movement which brought it into being' (HC: 199). In the same vein, but conversely, labouring and work activities can be considered 'private' in Arendt's political ontology, in the sense that, as D'Entrèves suggests, 'they can be carried out in isolation from others' (D'Entrèves 1994: 35), although, as we argue in later chapters, this ignores the notion of inter-relationality consisting of the mutual disclosure of natality, which arguably underscores all activities, as Arendt at times suggests, even if the person appears to act alone.

In the context of the understanding of 'public' as the sphere of publicity of expressions of natality, Arendt points to a notion of the 'private' that is essential to the human condition and for good reasons must be preserved. This is the 'who' of the person, which is private in the sense that 'who' we are remains an enigma; we are not transparent to ourselves or to others because 'who' we are depends on ongoing witness, by others, of our uniqueness, as distinct beginners of the new. It is this kind of privacy (or non-transparency) that totalitarian biopolitics, by rendering everything transparent, seeks to destroy and it is precisely the kind of 'privacy' Arendt's philosophy of natality aims to defend. This notion of 'private' also suggests that Arendt must assume a notion of inter-relationality where ideally we treat each other as beginners of the new irrespective of whether the activities and actions in which we are engaged could be considered political and public or private in the usual sense. On the other hand, Arendt clearly reserves the notion of the political for speech and *action that is consequential* (has an unpredictable impact) and this seems to assume a *public* space of appearance in a conventional sense. As Peg Birmingham points out, it is not enough for Arendt that a person is just welcomed or acknowledged as a beginner with the capacity to begin something new: 'significant speech and action [. . .] can only occur in a political space' where one is able 'to initiate action in concert with others' (Birmingham 2006: 59). We note that advances in digital media do complicate what is meant by public (versus private) 'appearance', such that a minor event of natality can be shared widely and gather together an assemblage of actors with significant consequences. We go on in later chapters to broaden Arendt's notion of political action to include a variety of ways of countering biopolitical foreclosure of natality.

The second (and related) potential problem implicit in Arendt's distinction in *The Human Condition* between public action and the ('private') activities of labouring bodies (*animal laborans*) is her apparent assumption that the body, biology and (most) feelings present a danger to public affairs. She does seem to hold that pleasures and pains that are unrelated to political action (OR: 59/55), as well as the 'bodily part of human existence' and other 'things connected with the necessity of the life process' (HC: 72), including various intimate relations, should remain private in the usual sense. 'Love', for example, while vital for the way it bypasses objectification of a person in aiming for the 'who', is inappropriate for politics insofar as love, 'by reason of its *passion*, destroys the in-between which relates us to and *separates* us from others' (HC: 242, emphasis added). Even 'compassion' can present a danger to politics by destroying this 'worldly space' and unique distinctness between human beings (OR: 81/76). In her later 'On humanity in dark times' (MDT: 3–31), Arendt does acknowledge the importance of *political passions* that 'transmit reality' and that encourage action, such as outrage against domination of any kind and anger against exclusions from the world (MDT: 6–13, 21). But these comments are rare. Birmingham (2006: 70–93), in a careful and innovative reading of Arendt's non-political works, specifically her engagement with Augustine (in LSA) and her writing about Jewish identity, in 'The Jew as pariah' (RLC: 69–90) and *Rahel Varnhagen: The Life of a Jewess* (RV), draws out an account of both the embodied aspect of the event of natality and the 'animating affection' that propels us to act with and toward others. In Birmingham's account, this 'animating affection' arises from the political actor's internal self-relation; specifically, it is a kind of 'gratitude' for one's 'givenness' and one's birth, an idea from which Birmingham develops (with some reference to Kristeva's reading of Arendt) into her own notion of 'the ethical-political imperative of gratitude for the foreign, the alien, and the given in a world that has undergone the death of God' (Birmingham 2006: 123), which she adapts for an account for the affective dimension of 'common responsibility' (125–30).

More often than not, though, Arendt seems to take for granted that biological processes and some types of bodily

activities erase the disjunctive temporality and unique distinctness that are characteristic of the public disclosure of natality.
As Bonnie Honig argues, for Arendt, the 'human body is [. . .]
a master signifier of necessity, irresistibility, imitability, and the
determination of pure process' (Honig 1995: 138), both in *The
Human Condition* and in later works such as *On Revolution* (for
example, OR: 59/55). As a thinker of biopolitics Arendt is not
wrong about the power of affect and biologism to erase the
disjunctive temporality of natality and reduce the distance and
hence difference (as uniqueness) between people and she has
good reason to steer politics away from biologism, which would
reduce human affairs to determined existence characteristic of
'life process'. But biologism is a scientific and political *perspective*
and approach to the human body, which itself is irreducible to
biology, certainly from a phenomenological (and Foucauldian)
perspective. Also, Arendt neglects consideration of the affectivity underlying the mutual disclosure of natality and, arguably,
by seemingly equating the human body with the biological, she
goes too far at times in her own judgements of what counts as
efficacious (political) action.

Arendt's hesitation about the role of the body in politics is
apparent in her discussion of this disclosure of natality to and by
others in terms of revealing the 'personal identity' or the 'who'
of the person as opposed the 'what' a person might be. The issue
regarding the body here is this: even though the person necessarily appears to others as an acting body, Arendt says explicitly
that an acting body does not reveal the 'who' of the person, only
their 'physical identity' (HC: 179). This distinction between
'personal identity' ('who') and 'physical identity' is reminiscent
of Locke's distinction between the 'personal identity' and the
identity of the 'man' (bodily identity), a distinction that persists

in contemporary discussions of personal identity within liberal empiricism.[14] But it would be a mistake to make that correlation, given that Locke's notion of personal identity is about consistency of the same person over time and is decidedly devoid of the event of natality inherent in relations with others. Still, Arendt's distinction between 'personal identity' (the 'who') and physical identity (the 'what') is behind her comment, already mentioned, about the need to supplement action (a moving body) with speech to signify the presence of a person (a beginner) rather than a robot (HC: 179). Hence, in 'acting and speaking men show who they are, reveal actively their unique personal identities' and this 'disclosure of the "who" in contradistinction to "what" somebody is – his personal qualities, gifts, talents, and shortcomings – is implicit in everything somebody says and does. It can be hidden only in complete silence and perfect passivity' (HC: 179). While we fully endorse Arendt's position that a person is 'unique' per se and that 'who' a person is cannot be reduced to either physical characteristics or behaviour or skills, we contend that uniqueness cannot be disclosed without some implicit interpretation of 'ontic' characteristics of the acting body, or worldly aspects of what-ness (Arendt does this herself when discounting certain labouring activities as involving actions that initiate something new). As human interaction is informed by the meanings embedded in the common world in which we appear, every disclosure of the 'who' of another must be accompanied by an interpretation of their 'what-ness' (that is, socio-historical significances of different kinds of bodies along the lines of gender, race, age and so on, as well as socially informed evaluation of 'what' the person does and how they do it), even though those meanings are challenged and transformed through the interaction.

57

Insisting that the 'who' of the person is disclosed *as a moving body* without the need for speech and that the 'who' co-appears with the 'what' according to others' interpretations has a twofold purpose consistent with Arendt's aims.[15] First, it explains how prejudice and discrimination happen within biopolitics and in everyday interactions: while in theory no one is excluded from participating in the public disclosure of natality, exclusions do arise, arguably because of the way different body markers (of sex, race, gender, age, ability and so on) signify unevenly such that not all speech and action will make sense in specific public arenas and not all action will be 'read' as originating with a beginner of the new (a human agent). Ideally, and second, bodily markers of difference can just as easily accentuate rather than erase 'uniqueness' and 'who-ness', providing that we treat each other as beginners of new beginnings whatever our bodily markers imply. If we allow that we encounter another's uniqueness as it breaks through interpretations of 'what' they appear to be, this opens the possibility not only that bodies and actions that seem out of place or persons whose speech we do not understand (that is, those who consequently appear 'passive' and/or 'mute') are disclosed as unique and human but also that those prejudicial interpretations of who the other is will be challenged and transformed in the process, along with the common world that joins and separates us.

Arendt would no doubt agree with this qualification about the interplay of the 'who' and the 'what' in the disclosure of natality, even if she does not spell it out herself in these terms. She hints at it in noting the frustration we experience in being unable to 'say *who* somebody is' without being led 'astray into saying *what* he is' (HC: 181). Not just a source of frustration, this interplay of the 'who' and the 'what' in human inter-relationality is also the interplay of the unconditioned and the conditioned aspects of human existence, and is central to Arendt's descriptions of the common world and 'every in-between [as that which] relates and separates men at the same time' (HC: 52, 242). Arendt's key point about 'personal identity' is that, because 'natality' is disclosed through the 'flux of action and speech', a person's identity, 'who' they are, is always undergoing transformation. That is one aspect of 'agency' – 'who' a person is changes, not through their own volition, but *through* interaction *with others* and disclosure of their 'who-ness' *by* others.[16] Hence, every self-relation is mediated by reference to interpretations by others and the socio-historical meanings that inform those interpretations. The second aspect of agency follows from the first: the *publicity* of the person's action and speech also transforms 'reality' or the 'common' world through which we appear, but, again, only by virtue of the reception of the actor by others as a beginner of the new. This is Arendt's criterion for 'political' action: that it begins something new in the public 'space of appearance' impacting the common world in ways that are 'unpredictable' and 'boundless' (HC: 191).

The point in raising the role of the moving body in signifying political action without the need for further indications of agency or uniqueness is to suggest that people may gather in public without the specific or shared intention to effect change in the world or to alleviate their oppression but can set off new beginnings of some efficacy precisely because they publicise types of bodies and activities that are usually hidden in 'private'. In *Notes Toward a Performative Theory of Assembly*, Judith Butler (2015) lays out several contemporary examples of this kind of 'acting in concert' by people living 'precarious' lives, examples of collective action that Butler rightly claims as political but that Arendt may categorise as the kind of 'acting from necessity' that introduces violence into the political realm (OR: 112–14/107–9; Butler 2015: 46). There was a gathering of homeless people in Martin Place, in Sydney central business district, in the winter of 2017 that well illustrates much of Butler's astute analysis. What began as the usual smattering of individuals sleeping rough in covered alcoves of the office towers and sandstone legal and banking institutions that line this plaza gradually morphed into a lively tent-village complete with its own soup kitchen and serviced by several NGOs that attend to the medical and other needs of the homeless. The participants were 'acting in concert' in the sense of treating each other as agents, beginners of the new, actors who gradually came together, not for the purpose of protest, nor out of 'necessity' in the sense of determinate need, but for a range of reasons to do with comfort, security, shelter, company and so on. The world of the participants was transformed by virtue of the gathering itself. But the 'common' world of the city was also altered because this assembly of bodies coincidently displayed, in public, their (usually private) plight. This was an example of bodies acting in public as an '*assembly* [that] *is already speaking before it utters any words*' (Butler 2015: 156, original emphasis). The growth of the assembly was witnessed by the thousands of office workers and shoppers who traverse Martin Place every day, many donating tents, conversation and other means of support and participating in the mutual disclosure of natality accordingly. The assembly became expressly political in attracting the attention of TV cameras and then politicians from the state government and the city council (all housed nearby). The gathering thus exposed the poverty, homelessness and inequality underlying a relatively affluent city and prompted city officials to do something about it, at least in the short term. What this example illustrates is, firstly, that the 'appearance' in public of bodies acting against the grain of the public/private distinction can itself be political action that contests the conditions of one's existence without express intention or being driven by necessity. Second, it also suggests that the onus is on the privileged and those with political power to witness the natality of the event, treat these bodies as human agents and respond to the call (implicit in the publicity of the event) to alter those conditions.

We will have more to say in subsequent chapters about these distinctions between the labouring body and action, private and public, and whether Arendt entrenches them or, as we are inclined to argue, provides the conceptual means for diagnosing and addressing the political effects of their endurance in Western democracies. We are also inclined to agree with Roberto Esposito's claim that Arendt's 'blind spot' consists in equating genuine politics with what is understood conventionally as the public realm, which tends to rule out the possibility of political action emerging from activities where 'the materiality of life unfolds' (Esposito 2008: 150).

III. Difference, Event, Singularity

To better appreciate the contribution of Arendt's notion of natality to rethinking the impact of biopolitics on democratic plurality, and to avoid confusion with the Lockean notion of personal identity, it helps to examine briefly how the event of natality differentiates Arendt's political ontology from the notions of difference and diversity implied in contemporary identity politics based on classical and neo-liberalism. We will also distinguish Arendt's idea of natality from Foucault's idea of the 'event' that disrupts tradition in preparation for integrating their approaches to biopolitics. How Arendt departs from both these ideas of difference and a new beginning rests on her idea that natality is disclosed in and as (political) community. Hence, we will also demonstrate how Arendt's notion of the mutual disclosure of natality pre-empts Jean-Luc Nancy's idea of singularity 'shared' in community (that is, 'being singular-plural'). This is significant insofar as Nancy, by refiguring the notion of being-singular-plural into a *principle underlying* democratic plurality, rather than a model of the political per se, provides a way of understanding that maintaining the mutual disclosure of natality through action at *all levels* of society is the key to achieving justice throughout.

Arendt's departure from Locke's notion of personal identity signals her divergence from contemporary neo-liberal politics of identity and difference. As we discuss in more detail in Chapter 2, Arendt argues in *The Origins of Totalitarianism* that the trend (since the late nineteenth century) toward self-identification as a member of a social group or rank, in conjunction with biopolitical regulation and classification of static, reified social identities (especially racial, cultural, religious and sexual identities, such as Jewishness and homosexuality), is tantamount to erasing the event of natality from public life and from the historicity of the self. This kind of identity politics serves as a form of normalising biopolitics and a potential precursor to totalitarianism. According to Arendt, basing politics on biological or socially static identity tends to convert the dynamic in-between of human inter-relations (consisting in the disclosure of natality and the unknowable 'who' to and by others) into a relationality based on identifying oneself as sharing (fixed) features with a group (a 'what'). This is also true of some kinds of neo-liberal identity politics (especially arising from Locke's classical liberalism), which assume that one's identity is based on a self-relation that comes *before* and apart from relations with others and that differences and similarities are derived by contrast and comparison of already constituted identities. On the basis of this notion of identity and difference, politics of equality is about striving to give each identity type equal *opportunity* to achieve public recognition of equal worth. By contrast, for Arendt, 'personal identity' is socio-historical, the dynamic, ongoing *accomplishment* of human inter-relations, which leads to a different kind of politics of equality.

Arendt distinguishes between this basic liberal empiricist notion of identity, difference and equality from her own understanding of plurality as follows. Human plurality, she says, 'has the twofold character of equality and distinction' (HC: 175) where equality is understood in terms of equality of *'uniqueness'*, or equality of the 'capacity' of natality, rather than as a precondition of socio-economic equality of different types. She explains what she means by human 'uniqueness' by distinguishing it, first, from the notion of 'otherness', 'alterity' or abstract difference between entities, the kind of distinctness that we share 'with everything that is', including *inanimate objects* – a medieval notion of alterity that 'transcends every particular quality' (HC: 176). Second, Arendt distinguishes her notion human uniqueness from distinctness based on 'variations and distinctions' (presumably observable qualities) apparent in all *organic life* that enable one to distinguish even members of the same species. So, while humans can be differentiated from each other in both these ways, human distinction (and hence human plurality) rests on the *uniqueness* of each human being that is 'communicated' and *revealed*, not through knowledge of the person's characteristics or disposition or behaviour, but through the sheer 'initiative', natality or the 'who' disclosed to and by others through public speech and action (HC: 176). If human beings were not distinct in this special way of appearing in the world as unique 'beginners' of something new, 'they would need neither speech nor action to make themselves understood' – their 'identical needs' would be immediately communicated by mere sound (HC: 175–6). Moreover, only human beings 'can express this distinction', this uniqueness, by the communication of the *self* as a human being, a person, rather than some*thing* (HC: 176); identity, the 'who' of a person, is an existential issue, not a question of 'substance' (EU: 177). And, crucially, this uniqueness is disclosed only to and by other *human* beings: speech and action are 'the modes in which human beings appear to each other, not as physical objects, but *qua* men [i.e. human]' (EU: 177).

Still, there is a problem with condemning identity politics on the basis of assuming that self-identifying in terms of attributes and qualities shared by a group amounts to reducing identity to 'what-ness' at the expense of expressing uniqueness or 'who-ness'. Arendt at times leans this way and was criticised in her lifetime for insisting that her identity as a Jew was a matter of historical fact (and, hence, irrelevant to public interactions) and she has been criticised by some feminist scholars since for not taking up feminist identity politics.[17] In response to criticisms regarding her approach to her own Jewish identity, Arendt clarified her position in a way consistent with her thesis on the dynamic character of the 'who' as it is lived through and contested in the common world we share with others (and so can be political). She says that when living under Nazi domination, 'I considered the only adequate reply to the question, Who are you? to be A Jew. That answer alone took into account the reality of persecution' (MDT: 17). As she argues, in times of 'defamation and persecution', the important principle of action is 'that one can resist only in terms of the identity that is under attack' (MDT: 18).[18] As discussed in section I, we argue that 'facticity' or attributes of 'what-ness' and their meanings are inseparable from the common world we share and transform and are shaped by power relations of race, gender, division of labour, ethnicity, age, nationality, occupation, religion, sex and so on, as well as all kinds of affiliations and actions that we undertake. As feminist and critical race theorists have argued in different ways since Arendt, these attributes are relational, imbricated in patterns of power and knowledge, caught in hierarchies or exclusions, and reshaped by the struggles against such exclusions. As identity formation is inter-relational and 'who' we are at any time carries aspects of 'what-ness' and, as definitions of 'what-ness' emerge from within the differential relations of power, then there is arguably no escaping objectification, discipline and normalisation entirely. The political challenge is to ensure that the unknowable 'who-ness' and uniqueness of persons is not erased in the process. Such erasure of natality is how some forms of biopolitics tip conditioning into discrimination, subordination, domination and exclusion from public affairs.

On the basis of Arendt's novel understanding of difference as 'unique distinctness' she adds a different idea of equality to political philosophy. *Political equality*, for Arendt, is not about treating everyone as the same or giving each different group identity equal public recognition or the same socio-economic resources. The equality that Arendt champions is a *precondition* to this liberal notion of equality based on equal rights and the Marxist notion of material equality based on just distribution of material resources according to need.[19] The more fundamental political equality that is Arendt's focus is paradoxically and 'necessarily an equality of unequals', in the sense of an *equality of unique distinctness per se* beyond any comparison of identity or of observable characteristics (HC: 215). Political equality is precisely about providing the conditions where human beings are considered of *equal worth as natal beings*, as initiators or beginners, whatever their characteristics or the content of their speech and actions, and this can happen only through the welcome and disclosure of this uniqueness in the web of human relations.[20] Conversely, equality of 'sameness', says Arendt, pertains only to *mere life*, to the 'experience of life and death', which occurs only to a life deprived of the means of disclosing this uniqueness, a life of 'utter loneliness, where no communication, let alone association and community, is possible', which is a 'dead' life (HC: 215); 'it has ceased to be a human life because it is no longer lived among men' (HC: 176). In Chapter 2 we discuss this idea of a 'dead life' engendered by totalitarian biopolitics and how it anticipates Agamben's notion of 'bare life'. But, as we will see, Arendt also applies this idea of equality of sameness to '*animal laborans*' more generally and is part of her formula for what Foucault refers to as the 'regularisation' of biological life by normalising biopolitics. Equally, we show in later chapters how Arendt's contrasting understanding of equality of unique distinctness underscores her notions of the 'moral person', responsibility and the normative dimension of her understanding of the political.

That coexistence as plurality is crucial for political action as the expression of agency or the uniqueness of the beginning of something new is what distinguishes Arendt's notion of 'event' from some other biopolitical theorists such as Foucault. In his initial discussion of 'event' Foucault explains 'agency' and the emergence of the new not in terms of being-with-others but in terms of 'accidents' that happen to bodily beings and a critical history (genealogy) that discerns these accidents so that the changes they effect to the self and to culture can endure. This idea of event is central to his reading of Nietzsche in 'Nietzsche, genealogy, history' (Foucault 2000b: 369–92), where Foucault links the emergence of new concepts through the practice of genealogy to the emergence of new ways of living through transformation of bodily being (Foucault 2000b: 377). Genealogy, he says of Nietzsche's 'method', is a kind of 'historical philosophizing' that retrieves the 'singularity of events' from 'the world of speech and desires' (Foucault 2000b: 369). This is to study the 'origin' of something new not as *Ursprung* ('origin' as essence or cause) but in terms of its surprising *emergence* from struggle ('origin' as *Entstehung*) (Foucault 2000b: 376–8) and its heritage or its *decent* ('origin' as *Herkunft* or birth) (373–5). The point of this kind of practice of critical history is to identify the 'accidents that accompany every beginning' or 'the errors [. . .] that gave birth to those things which continue to exist and have value for us' (Foucault 2000b: 373–4). So, like Arendt, Foucault challenges the idea of history as a continuous linear progress of the self and a culture and, like Arendt and Nietzsche, Foucault formulates the 'event' in temporal terms, as a moment between the past and a divergent future. But in contrast to Arendt, for Foucault, at least in this earlier work, the event of the new is a consequence of *accidents emerging from conflict and struggle* rather than from human inter-relations and political action, the initiative of which is revealed to and by others. Also, again in contrast to Arendt, Foucault places more emphasis on the role of the body as the site of the battle between the continuity of tradition and the event of the new. For example, he says that the 'body is the surface of the inscription of events' (Foucault 2000b:

375). 'The body manifests the stigmata of past experience' (for example, in the form of socially conditioned habits) but also it 'gives rise to desires, failings, and errors' (Foucault 2000b: 375). More in accord with Arendt is Foucault's (and Nietzsche's) idea of genealogy by which identification of new beginnings (in bodies, practices or discourses) through 'historical philosophiz- ing' (Nietzsche's term) does as much to bring about change as the beginning itself: '[h]istory becomes "effective" to the degree that it introduces discontinuity into our very being' (Foucault 2000b: 380).

In Chapter 2 we discuss some benefits of Foucault's focus on the body as the site of both action and subjection for explaining the suppression of the event of natality by biopolitics. For now the point about his claim that the emergence of events or new beginnings is accidental presents a problem for political action. Without the benefit of Arendt's claim regarding the centrality of the presence of others to the event of the new beginning, Foucault does not envisage a collaborative political practice as a means for opening new and multiple ways of thinking and living. In *The History of Sexuality, Volume I* he simply suggests that new ways of being emerge from 'bodies and pleasures' that have somehow escaped normalising mechanisms of biopolitical and disciplinary government (Foucault 1980a: 143, 157). This problematic idea of a pre-social level of affective corporeality seems to be the basis of Foucault's formula for a counterforce to subjection and normalisation apparent in his proposal that wherever there are relations of power, there is also 'a multiplicity of points of resistance' (Foucault 1980a: 95) or 'antagonistic' 'points of insubordination' and 'means of escape' (Foucault 2002: 346). So, while Foucault accounts for 'struggle' at the site of the event of the new beginning and occasionally acknowledges the importance of collective struggles (such as feminism) for opposing subjection (for example, Foucault 2002: 329–30) his solutions to suppression of the event tend to be individual *techniques of self* or 'practices of freedom' that, while considerate of others (including non-human 'others'), are primarily self-directed and not reliant on the presence of others.[21]

Arendt's insight that the event of natality is disclosed as and through political community has been extended in Jean-Luc Nancy's subsequent elaborations of the relation between 'singularity' ('unique distinctness' in Arendt's terminology) and community. While Nancy names Heidegger as his primary influence and there has been little comment on the possible debts Nancy's idea of 'inoperative community' owes to Arendt's notion of the space of the political, the similarities are palpable.[22] For our purposes, what Nancy adds to Arendt's political ontology is a less hesitant account of the *embodied* character of inter-relationality applicable to political action and a way of understanding the disclosure of natality more explicitly as a normative *principle* of democratic plurality. For Nancy, community is 'inoperative' in the sense that it consists in the 'sharing' of singularity' (Arendt's disclosure of natality) but without unity as the outcome; it is 'community without communion' and always in the process of undoing itself (Nancy 1991: 144). This is not unlike Arendt's idea of political community variously formulated as: the space of appearance, power as the 'potentiality in being together' (HC: 201), and the in-between world that we constitute and hold in common that both 'relates and separates men at the same time' (HC: 52). Indeed, Nancy seems to take up Arendt's idea of the political as the 'space of appearance' in describing community *as* 'exposition' of the 'unheard', the exposure of uniqueness or singularity *through* sharing (Nancy 1991: 26; Nancy 1993: 204).

He later summarises the notion of human existence implied in this idea of inoperative community as 'being singular plural'.

One obvious difference between the two conceptions of inter-relationality based on the 'sharing of singularity' lies in the way that Nancy views the body of the actor as a primary site of singularity or uniqueness and for the 'taking place of sense' within human inter-relations (Nancy 1993: 204). We have already alluded to some of the advantages of this sort of adjustment to Arendt's notion of the political agent (the homeless gathering in Martin Place count as political agents actualising natality). For Nancy, the acting living body *itself* signifies the existence of an agent in the sense of 'another access to the world', another 'origin' of a world (or another source of new beginnings, in Arendt's terminology), another access to 'sense' (meaning), another 'manner' of existence, besides one's own (Nancy 2000: 14–15). As with Arendt, Nancy insists that this other 'access to a world' is unique, 'singular' and inaccessible: 'each child that is born has already concealed the access that he is', not because the person or the agent's intentions are hidden inside an acting body, but because the other 'manner, the turn of the other access, [. . .] conceals itself in the very gesture wherein it offers itself to us – and whose concealing *is* the turning itself' (Nancy 2000: 14). Hence, for Nancy, this acting body is itself the 'who' of the person and, because the other is 'exposed' (disclosed) as 'exteriority', they appear as 'strangeness' (2000: 14). Where Nancy is in full agreement with Arendt is in his claim that this 'singularity' appears only through 'sharing': '[c]ommunication consists before all else in this sharing' whereby human being 'is what it is, singular being (singularity of being), only through [. . . exposure] *to an outside* [which is] nothing other than the exposition of another [. . .] singularity' (Nancy 1991: 28).

A second (related) difference between Arendt's and Nancy's conceptions of (political) community and inter-relationality is that Nancy provides an explanation of the animated directionality underlying this sharing of singularity that characterises human inter-relations and our 'feeling' for the world we share while maintaining the separation between bodies. As discussed in section II, Arendt occasionally refers to emotions accompanying our regard for others, including 'compassion' for and 'fear' of others (MDT: 11–16) and she talks of the 'public happiness' of acting and talking together (OR: 119–25/114–20) as well as noting 'our feeling for reality' (HC: 51), which thinkers such as Birmingham and Kristeva have worked into accounts of the 'animating affection' behind action that propels us toward others. But this does not account for what it is about the *other* that might prompt a person to engage them in the first place: what is it about another person that inspires or motivates disclosure, perception, or interpretation of them? Nor does Arendt account for the directionality of 'bonds' with others, of the in-between of potentiality, beyond or before specific emotions or stated intentions (even though the feeling is undoubtedly there). Nancy goes some way toward providing an account without relying on a notion of pre-social corporeal affectivity to explain the event of the new, as Foucault is inclined to do.[23] For Nancy, what characterises this inter-relation between bodies (and what cannot be assimilated or known in any terms) is a directional, affective *leaning-toward* or 'unidentifiable' *inclination* ('*clinamen*') toward others (Nancy 1991: 6–7), which is not self-generated. What engenders this inclining, and co-appears with the inclination, is others' singularity or 'strangeness', or what Nancy also describes as the other's *unidentifiable inclination toward* other others and toward the world. In other words, for

Nancy, 'natality' or the beginning of something new 'appears' as a body uniquely inclined toward a world (and toward others) and, because we cannot know what that inclination consists in, this not-knowing inclines us toward that inclination. Insofar as 'inclination' can be understood as being tantamount to the 'appearance' of action in the movement toward another body, it provides a formula for the disclosure of natality to and by another that may compensate for Arendt's neglect of the body in her political ontology.

Nancy's ultimate interest in theorising the operation, the 'exposition' or 'exposure' of uniqueness (singularity) between humans is, like Arendt, political: he is concerned with the political erasure of this sharing of singularity in its contemporary forms – genocide, mass deportations, and other extreme forms of what we refer to as biopolitics. In his later work, such as *The Truth of Democracy* (2010), Nancy becomes more intent on spelling out how politics might prevent this erasure. To this end he drops the term 'community' but keeps the schema of the sharing of singularity and distinguishes it from politics as such. In a way that would position the disclosure of natality as a normative principle of human interaction, Nancy refers to the sharing of singularity as the *principle* of democracy (rather than the space of the political or politics per se). His point about the centrality of being-singular-plural to the human condition is this: what opens us to ourselves, to each other and to 'potentiality' is the 'sharing (out)' of the 'incalculable', unique 'sense' of each and all together, or the 'affirmation' of the 'uniqueness' of each of us in all our relations (Nancy 2010: 24). This sharing is not itself politics because (contrary to Arendt's idea of the *public* space of the disclosure of natality) it happens everywhere in all sorts of private and public encounters. The role of politics, including the role of government, is to make this sharing of singularity possible (Nancy 2010: 26), not to shut it down, as in some forms of biopolitics. As we will discuss further in Chapter 4, Arendt has a similar notion in the form of political responsibility as a kind collective responsibility of all of us for maintaining the conditions that make possible the equality of unique distinctness and the disclosure of natality through action and speech.

Arguably, Nancy's idea of being-singular-plural highlights the 'deconstructive' aspect of basing human interaction on the disclosure of the beginning of the new, what Arendt describes as the 'unpredictability', 'irreversibility' and 'boundlessness' of action that is tempered or stabilised by contestable law, flexible promising, a forgiveness (HC: 236–46). The problem with emphasising the destabilising effect of the event of natality is that it risks idealising unpredictability and instability, and ignores the political realities of lives lived under the state institutions that govern human inter-relations. The biopolitical theorist Roberto Esposito (2013), for instance, criticises Nancy (and other deconstructionists) for abstracting community, as a schema of inter-relation, too far away from lived relations and actual politics. Hence, while Nancy's concept of community (*communitas*) emphasises one side of being-in-common – '*cum*' or 'with' – Esposito, on his own account, emphasises the other side – '*munus*' or gift – the duty or responsibility that accompanies being-with-others (Esposito 2013: 84). He brings politics back into the centre of schemas of human inter-relation, but in the form of *bio*politics. He thus returns us to Arendt's concerns, although, because he does not view biopolitics as entirely negative, he finds solutions to totalising politics within its bounds. Esposito reworks Nancy's concept of community (and, implicitly, Arendt's idea of inter-relationality) by introducing the notion of 'immunity' (in both the legal and the medical-biological senses) into his model of human interaction. If 'community' (as the mutual disclosure of natality though collective action or as the 'sharing' of singularity) 'breaks down the barriers of individual [or group or national] identity, immunity is the way to rebuild them, in defensive and offensive forms, against any external element that threatens it' (Esposito 2013: 85). What Esposito does in effect is bring together Arendt's three spheres of the disclosure of natality (labour, work and action) and the two orders of the birth of the new (birth of the newborn and political birth of new beginnings) under the umbrella of biopolitics without assuming that natality is erased as a consequence. His point is that biopolitics (which he defines more loosely as the *intersection of law and biology*) is inescapable and it does both harm and good – it provides stability and saves lives, but can also normalise and totalise. In sum:

> Although immunity is necessary to the preservation of our life, when driven beyond a certain threshold it forces life into a sort of cage where not only our freedom gets lost but also the very meaning of our existence – that opening of existence outside itself that takes the name of *communitas*. (Esposito 2013: 85)

In Chapters 2 and 3 we examine how Arendt's notion of the disclosure of natality within human inter-relations deals with this struggle between freedom, normalisation and domination in the context of biopolitical regimes. And in Chapters 4 and 5 we discuss different ways of maintaining stability without erasing natality. Before that, in the next section, we introduce Arendt's novel idea of freedom among other revised political concepts.

IV. Power, Freedom, Alliance

Aside from providing the basis for developing a notion of demo-cratic politics based on the 'sharing of singularity', Arendt's ideas of agency and inter-relationality based on the mutual disclosure of natality also give us revised notions of power, freedom and collective political action (solidarity and alliance).

Arendt's idea that natality is disclosed as such only to and by others, and most effectively in public, forms the basis of a unique account of *power* that she sketches in *The Human Condition* (HC: 199–206) and develops further in *On Revolution* and *On Violence*. In *The Human Condition* Arendt defines power as 'potentiality in being together' (HC: 201), that futurally oriented 'in-between' consisting of the disclosure of natality to and by others that characterises the togetherness of public life: 'Power is what keeps the public realm, the potential space of appearance between acting and speaking men, in existence' (HC: 200). Arendt's notion of 'potentiality' should not be confused with that tied to Aristotle's metaphysics of 'substance' or with any notion of an ideal actuality that a person could become.[24] Rather, power *is* potentiality per se, a 'power potential' that 'springs up between men when they act together and vanishes the moment they disperse' (HC: 200). It is potentiality as change through beginning anew, futurity per se opened through the disclosure of natality between actors or speakers. Arendt's idea of potentiality has more in common with Heidegger's idea that *Dasein is* potentiality or being-possible rather than *Dasein has* the potential to become a particular (Heidegger 1962: 182–7). Following Arendt, Nancy mobilises this idea of potentiality explicitly when describing the 'sharing of singularity' as the principle of democracy. Mirroring Arendt's concerns (but without mention of her work) Nancy refers to 'potentiality' as a key factor in the continuing project of overcoming democracy's failure to save itself from tipping into totalitarianism: democracy must recognise itself as 'potential of being' that is also the 'disruption' of historical time progressing toward a *particular* future; this is democracy as 'true possibility of being *all together, all and each one among all*' (Nancy 2010: 13–14). Similarly, if understood as a *principle* of democratic plurality, Arendt's notion of power as the 'potentiality in being together' (the power potential inherent in the disclosure of natality through speech and action) can also be understood as the factor that would work against normalising biopolitics and prevent democracy from tipping into totalitarianism. While Nancy's use of the motif of potentiality is close to Arendt's, as we will see, Arendt is more cautious regarding the possible negative effects of pure potentiality, that is, the negative consequences of endless instability and unpredictability.

Arendt's idea of power as 'potentiality of being together' characteristic of the space of appearance (HC: 199) also prefigures Foucault's ground-breaking idea of power that is productive rather than simply prohibitive, power as a 'field' of relations that produces subjects rather than simply represses action (for example, Foucault 2002: 340–2). As Amy Allen argues, Arendt's and Foucault's ideas of productive power are similar insofar as they are directed against what Foucault calls the juridical and sovereign models of power that pervade liberalism and that '[t]his [juridical] model equates power with the rule of law and pre-supposes that the paradigmatic power relation is that by which a sovereign imposes his will on his subjects' (Allen 2002: 132). On these conventional models, power is viewed as a commodity that some agents possess and use to repress others who do not have power. In contrast, Arendt says explicitly that power, as it pertains to acting together, is independent of material resources and cannot be 'possessed like strength or applied like force' (HC: 201). Where Foucault and Arendt differ is on the *purview* of productive power. As we will discuss in Chapter 2, because Foucault thinks that disciplinary power and biopower are 'productive' in the sense just outlined, this means that *power is also normalising* (it can suppress the 'event') by 'producing' a subject with capacities that comply with existing laws and norms and economic systems. Arendt, on the other hand, reserves the term 'power' (at least in *The Human Condition*) for the positive side of the political; that is, 'power' is the space of 'appearance', the 'in-between' where the natality is disclosed through action and speech, which is precisely what, for her, *thwarts the forces of normalisation.*

> Power [as 'potentiality in being together'] preserves the public realm and the space of appearance, and as such is the lifeblood of the human artifice, which, unless it is the scene of action and speech, of the web of human affairs and relationships and the stories engendered by them, lacks its ultimate raison d'être. (HC: 204)

Also, unlike Foucault, who says there is no outside of power (for example, Foucault 1980a: 95), Arendt contrasts this productive power as potentiality with 'force' and 'violence' (HC: 202–3). Force and violence destroy power as potentiality by destroying the relationships essential for the expression of natality. In *The Human Condition* Arendt defines 'force' as the subjection of one will by another (HC: 203), which is what Foucault would call 'sovereign power', and in *On Violence* she equates violence with any will to domination, including the 'rule of law' (OV: 36) (which Foucault calls 'juridical power'). For Arendt, force and violence destroy power insofar as citizens are rendered 'impotent' and 'have lost their capacity to speak and act together' (HC: 203). This could also occur at a more local level as a consequence of treating a person as a thing (or a pure 'what') rather than a 'who'. However, as we argue in Chapter 2, Arendt's notions of force and violence are not exactly the same as Foucault's accounts of sovereign power, insofar as in *The Origins of Totalitarianism* she claims that totalitarian biopolitics relies on 'an entirely new and unprecedented concept of power': 'Power, as conceived by totalitarianism, lies exclusively in the force produced through totalitarian organization', that is, the force of 'movement' (OT: 417–18). What she means by force produced through organisation will become clear in Chapter 2. For now, it suffices to say that power reduced to 'force' involves suppressing the event of natality by achieving total domination of a population and isolation of people from the common world; this is biopolitics in the extreme. Crucially, though, Arendt insists that violence, force and political tyranny can never completely destroy power as potentiality (HC: 203); the expression of natality is never eliminated entirely, which leaves open the door for agency, creativity, cultural renewal and political renaissance.

By the time she published *On Revolution* in 1963, Arendt had reformulated her idea of the public sphere as the 'potentiality of being together' into a new idea of *freedom*, where the 'idea of freedom and the experience of a new beginning should coincide' (OR: 21–2/19). Here, and in an earlier essay entitled 'What is freedom?' (BPF: 143–72), Arendt distinguishes her idea of freedom intertwined with the disclosure of natality through action from the liberal idea of negative freedom and the Marxist notion of liberation as the 'revolutionary overturning of history' through the universal class struggle.[25] With regard to the liberal notion of negative freedom, Arendt agrees that liberation from external force, including from sovereign rule and liberation from 'unjustified restraint' that deprives people of basic 'rights' (life, liberty and property), and liberation from the 'necessities of life' (BPF: 148), that is, negative freedom in all its facets, is a 'condition of freedom' (OR: 22/19). But this does not mean that liberty 'leads automatically to' freedom (OR: 22/19). The problem as Arendt sees it is that, besides making the error of the 'identification of sovereignty and freedom' (HC: 234), philosophy has moved on from the assumption that liberation entails freedom to transposing the 'idea of freedom such as it is given in human experience [. . .] from its original field, the realm of politics and human affairs in general, to an inward domain, the will, where it would be open to self-inspection' (BPF: 145).[26] As her political ontology has done away with the idea of this 'inward domain' of a 'doer behind the deed', freedom, for Arendt, is not about free will. Indeed, she argues that the move to equate freedom with inner freedom is illegitimate if for no other reason than the very *experience* of 'freedom or its opposite' arises through 'our intercourse with others, not in intercourse with ourselves' (BPF: 148). Equally, then, the accomplishment of freedom requires engagement with others. Once Arendt takes that step, freedom is no longer about protecting one's life, enacting an intention formulated by oneself, imposing one's will upon the world, or choosing between (good and bad) acts (BPF: 151). Rather, freedom is about acting (where the I-will and I-can coincide – BPF: 159) and specifically *acting with others*. That is, freedom is about beginning something anew, making a difference, affecting the course of events, and this is achieved only by acting with other agents who are thereby affected by the action and who treat the actor as a beginner of the new (an agent) and the act for what it is: the event of natality.

This is not 'positive freedom' as defined by Isaiah Berlin in his celebrated 1958 essay 'Two concepts of liberty': the freedom of self-determination or having the means of reaching one's full potential. On the one hand, Arendt's idea of positive freedom is less presumptuous than Berlin's: there is no goal to freedom (such as self-realisation) beyond the act that actualises it. Freedom is no more than its performance: it is 'a demonstrable fact' (BPF: 149). On the other hand, Arendt's idea of freedom is in another way more grandiose than Berlin's: freedom is about participation in human affairs, not for the sake of furthering one's own interests, but for the sake of enriching the world. The performance of freedom ('for to *be* free and to act are the same' – BPF: 153) enriches the world in a particular way: in acting in the world the people participate together in the disclosure of natality, the welcome of the new and of the uniqueness of others, and thereby in the creation of 'worldly reality' at the same time as keeping at bay the 'automatism' that is a feature of normalising biopolitics (BPF: 154, 168). So, this 'living space of freedom' (OT: 466) is the same as what Arendt had described in *The Human Condition* as the space of the political, 'power' as 'potentiality of being together'. By equating freedom and politics, Arendt sought to counter what she saw as a dangerous trend in public affairs (which we are witnessing again now, in the early twenty-first century) where freedom is equated with individual sovereignty and *against* politics. Freedom in the neo-liberal state has become freedom from interference in all activities (economic, educational, cultural), including 'freedom *from* politics' (BPF: 149). The danger in equating 'political freedom with security' or with freedom from harm to individual sovereignty or to one's life is that politics becomes thereby equated with government of this freedom – either government takes on the protection of life (which, as we will see in Chapter 2, is biopolitics) or it leaves life entirely alone to 'follow its own inherent necessity' (BPF: 150). In either case there is no space left for freedom as the equal participation of all in the disclosure of natality.

Arendt's suggestion that freedom '*should* coincide' with the experience of a new beginning indicates that, for her, freedom is the *aim* of politics rather than an actuality. Freedom therefore operates as a normative ideal in Arendt's philosophy of natality: 'The *raison d'être* of politics is freedom, and its field of experience is action' (BPF: 146). There are two points to note for now about this account of freedom. First, entailed in Arendt's notion of freedom is a particular idea about the limits of freedom. Arendt is aware of the need to limit the unpredictable consequences of action to ensure some social stability and certainty about the future but without eliminating the event of natality. As she has redefined the field of freedom as the experience of natality through action within the *togetherness* of human affairs (that is, freedom is the 'potentiality of being together'), then limiting the unpredictable consequences of action is the same as limiting the consequences of freedom as pure potentiality. But instead of limiting freedom by imposing laws to restrict individual action (which is where classical liberalism takes us), for Arendt, limiting freedom must involve actions with the same *collective* character integral to freedom as she understands it, if natality is to be preserved. As we will see, Arendt elects promising as the appropriate collective action for limiting freedom; not promising by an isolated individual, but promising dependent on 'plurality, on the presence and acting of others', which thereby limits unpredictability without eliminating natality or new beginnings (HC: 236–7). The second (related) point about Arendt's notion of freedom and its connection to politics is that

81

it instigates a different understanding of the nature of solidarity for the purposes of political action. This brings us to Arendt's concept of alliance.

What gathers the plurality of unique and heterogeneous political agents for specific actions are *alliances* made by mutual promises. We could say that the alliance is a dynamic and open-ended political association necessary to assemble participants for the purpose of action. As Arendt puts it, alliance is the very 'grammar' of action and the 'syntax' of power – 'the grammar of action: that action demands [. . .] a plurality of men; and the syntax of power: that power [. . .] applies solely to the worldly in-between space by which men are mutually related, combine [. . .] by virtue of the making and the keeping of promises' (OR: 175/167). As the words 'grammar' and 'syntax' suggest, alliance introduces into the intangible web of human relations a minimum of articulation, which keeps the participants of action together, despite the frailty and the unpredictability of their interactions. Such a minimal organisation is created by nothing more and nothing less than by mutual promises. Because a promise is an act in its own right, it can 'combine' people together for the joint action while respecting their plurality and uniqueness. This performativity of promise generates a dynamic and interactive political organisation assembling actors together even though they do not know themselves, or the consequences of their actions.

The key feature of political alliance in Arendt's sense is that it does not presuppose that participants share a common origin, or common past, as assumed in the notion of nationality, for instance. Furthermore, since action depends on agents' unique-ness and plurality, which includes but nonetheless exceeds gender, race, ethnicity and class differences, political alliance does not presuppose a common identity or common interests. Even the pragmatic goals of collective action do not precede but are generated by an alliance and remain contestable (OR: 168–72/158–63). Nor does the formation of an alliance for the purpose of action presuppose the equality of actors; instead, the alliance *creates* political equality through the act of reciprocal promises and pledges. Thus, although participation in existing democracies is limited by multiple subjugations, as the history of political protests and struggles demonstrates, marginalised and subjugated groups can, by contesting injustice, violence and oppression, create equality among themselves in the process of collective action, regardless of whether or not they succeed in transforming oppressive relations on the institutional level. This has been the case with alliances such as the international Occupy Wall Street movement and the Black Lives Matter activist network, first mobilised by the Afro-American community in the US in 2013 to fight racism and police brutality and to demand justice.[27]

Because Arendt's notion of political alliance does not pre-suppose a shared identity or common history, it is especially important for feminist and post-structuralist critiques of the political, which, as Judith Butler (1992), among others, points out, are often criticised for failing to formulate political agency or provide the basis for political organisation.[28] It is also important to note that, in *On Revolution*, Arendt distinguishes her notion of political association from both religious notions of the biblical covenant and from the secular contract theory, both of which are based on the consent to be governed by external authority (OR: 172/162). Arendt criticises the principle of consent as insufficient basis for political coalition, arguing that the secular liberal notion of consent, in Locke's contract theory for example, involves 'surrendering rights and powers to either the government or the community' (OR: 168/160), which limits the power of political actors. By contrast, a 'covenant', pledge or agreement underlying political 'alliance' *generates power* through the very process of 'combination' (OR: 170/162). This is 'power as potentiality', to use her terminology of *The Human Condition*. Furthermore, consent engenders a vertical relation of subjection to external authority, rather than a mutual relationality among unique members of the alliance.

Despite Arendt's explicit critique of social contract theory in *On Revolution* (OR: 168–72/158–63), even sympathetic readers of Arendt, like Antonio Negri, often confuse it with her notion of alliance. For instance, Negri acknowledges that the radicality of Arendt's thought lies in her discovery of a 'constituent' power, or the power to create new political forms 'grounded on nothing more than its own beginning' and 'its own expression' (Negri 1999: 16). However, he misreads her critique of contract theory in going on to argue that Arendt fails to sustain the most radical insights of her discovery because, he claims mistakenly, for her, alliance amounts to 'contractualism' (Negri 1999: 18). There are three key differences between the notion of a social 'contract' and Arendt's notion of alliance. First, forming alliances with others, whether for the purpose of specific concrete actions or constituting new political bodies, is enabled by the fact that we are relational beings from the start, rather than the isolated, sovereign individuals presupposed by contract theory and liberalism. The second fundamental difference is that, in contract theory, the consent to be governed leads to isolation and the loss of power of each member of the body politic, whereas the members of the alliance gain power and community. Third, contract theory, by formulating the transfer of political power to the sovereign or the state in return for protection, treats power as a transferable commodity. By contrast, the kind of power (as potentiality) at work in alliance is creative and generative – it augments or creates new power.

In contrast to contract theory or impersonal institutional structures that do not depend on political participation, alliances based on promises and mutual commitments might seem precarious: by gathering strangers for the purpose of joint action, promises provide merely 'a guidepost' in 'an ocean of uncertainty' (HC: 245). In terms of the traditional political vocabulary, alliances seem to be groundless. That is why alliances can be dispersed by violence, as we have witnessed in 2016–17 in Syria and Ukraine, or dissipate from within when the participants are driven apart by internal conflicts or sheer indifference to one another. Conversely, as we discuss further in Chapters 2 and 4, alliances and the promises that keep them together can become petrified, through biopolitical normalisation or if propped up by an external authority, into formations that are self-defeating because they predetermine the future. Nonetheless, despite their seeming precariousness, such dynamic, participatory and plural political associations are precisely what generate power as potentiality. And if, after specific collective action, such power is preserved through continuous commitments and mutual promises, it leads to the enduring transformation of political bonds, institutions and relations. Because it is so closely intertwined with action, generation of new power and participation, Arendt's theory of political association provides an alternative to the anarchy of sovereign individuals vying for dominance, on the one hand, and government by impersonal political structures, on the other hand.

V. Against Politics Based on Death, Violence or the 'Life Process'

As discussed in the previous section, Arendt's idea that freedom is the experience of natality arising from inter-relational action (rather than the protection of sovereignty or freedom from interference) shifts the focus of politics away from preservation of existing norms and laws, of national identity, or of 'life'. This shift indicates why and how Arendt's philosophy of natality alters the meaning of the political: by challenging the usual notions of finitude it refigures the role of birth, life and death in politics. It is well known that Arendt departs from the tendency in philosophy to limit finitude to mortality, or being-toward-death, by including in finitude the principle of natality and being-toward-birth in the sense of the new beginning: 'natality, and not mortality, may be the central category of political [. . .] thought' (HC: 9). And as we have discussed throughout this chapter, this principle of natality revises the meaning of politics by signifying the centrality of being with others in the world (human plurality) and the possibility of a new beginning in the polis. To this we add the claim that politics based on the principle of natality offers an alternative to the binary governing philosophical and political thought between a political ontology centred on death (from Hobbes to Freud) and different versions of a philosophy of life, from Darwin to Bergson and the politi-cisation of biological life through what has become known as biopolitics. In this section, we provide a provisional examination of Arendt's critiques of both kinds of politics.

Arendt's critiques of the uses of death in politics and in political philosophy arose within a historical context that included: the convergence of imperialism and racism; the genocidal politics of totalitarianism (which we discuss in more detail in Chapter 2); and the atomic bomb explosion that ended the Second World War and opened the unprecedented prospect of the destruction of the planet, with all its life forms. As Arendt also explains in the preface to *On Revolution*, the possibility of nuclear warfare ending in total annihilation makes the moral choice of death for the sake of freedom or for the sake of the protection of others a slogan of bad faith. Our focus here is on the two key aspects of Arendt's subsequent general critique of politics based on death: first, her analysis of the role of death in the political structure of the bourgeois state and sovereignty envisaged in Hobbes's political philosophy; and second, her account of the persistence of the fratricidal or patricidal violence in the explanations of the foundational beginnings of new political bodies. In both these instances Arendt accounts for the political of power of death in terms of the destruction or negation of natality.

In her interpretation of Hobbes in *The Origins of Totalitarianism*, Arendt reads his *Leviathan* as the political theory of the nascent bourgeois state that explains its subsequent drive toward imperialism (OT: 139–44). For Arendt, Hobbes is the first political philosopher to provide (*avant la lettre*) a trenchant account of the function of death in the imperialist bourgeois state driven solely by private interests and the accumulation of capital rather than by the political bonds of equality and freedom, as Arendt understands these concepts. The bourgeois commonwealth 'acquires a monopoly on killing and provides in exchange a conditional guarantee against being killed' (OT: 141). Consequently, both the individual and the state are characterised by their ability to kill (OT: 143) and on the basis of this threat of death Hobbes defines the role of the state in terms of protection on behalf of the private economic interests of the growing bourgeoisie for the purposes of facilitating the limitless accumulation of capital. In the political structure of this capitalist state, freedom is either downgraded to apply to the accumulation of property or associated with the natural capacity to kill and equality is reduced to the equal distribution of this capacity. Arendt's main point here is that the bourgeois state, subordinated to the endless accumulation of capital, has to remove freedom, action and equality to the pre-political sphere of nature and to elevate the competition of economic interests and the accumulation of capital to the highest public good. In the process, the state 'acquires a monopoly on killing' (OT: 141), the state exercise of the power to kill that, as we will see in Chapter 2, had been transformed into one pole of biopower by the end of the nineteenth century – the state-centred power to 'let die'. By interpreting the state of nature in terms of the structural requirements of the bourgeois state, Arendt reverses the dominant interpretation of Hobbes's account of the fear of death in the formation of Leviathan. According to Arendt, rather than beginning with his pessimistic picture of human nature as essentially violent and motivated by fear as a means of explaining the formation of the Commonwealth, Hobbes begins with the political structure of the bourgeois state and then describes what kind of members such a state requires (OT: 140–1). Arendt insists that the formation of such a state is from the outset subordinated to class interests: it 'corresponds to the new needs and interests of a new [bourgeois] class' (OT: 143).

Arendt's often overlooked critique of the bourgeois state, the coincidence of the accumulation of capital and state accumulation of power to kill, and imperialism shows that all three of these formations are antithetical to the politics of natality. In Hobbes's picture of the capitalist and imperialist state there are no public commitments, bonds or obligations to others, and no human rights. The only notion of the 'common' is the shared interest in 'security' and the protection of private property and one's own life against the violence of others (OT: 141). Indicative of the lack of communal bonds in this state is that, for Hobbes, once the state fails to provide security, everyone is free to rebel against the state and resort to violence. Under such conditions, the only kind of organisation Hobbes 'foresees and justifies' is in the form of 'a gang of murderers' driven by violence (OT: 142). In the absence of any communal bonds Hobbes's bourgeois state reveals itself to be 'built on sand': by keeping individuals isolated and in the grip of fear, the state is internally fractured and, as each particular state is pitted against each other, it maintains the natural '"condition of the state of war" of all against all' (OT: 142). Hence, the bourgeois state contains the principle of its own dissolution. We can interpret this dissolution of political bonds as the symbolic work of death, antithetical to natality, which underscores the inter-relationality characteristic of Arendt's 'potentiality of being together' and the forming of alliances for the purpose of acting in concert. '[O]nly by extending its authority' and by the 'never-ending accumulation of power necessary for the never-ending accumulation of capital' can this state remain stable, Arendt argues (OT: 142–3). Hobbes thus foreshadows the rise of imperialism in the nineteenth century and the export of violence to the colonies (OT: 143–6). What Arendt finds in Hobbes, therefore, is the first philosophical diagnosis of power understood in terms of 'dynamic' political organisation capable of generating endless violence. At the stage where the accumulation of power and capital overflows national boundaries into imperialism, Arendt finds one of the precedents of the endless force of movement, which, as we will discuss in Chapter 2, is characteristic of the 'power' of totalitarian biopolitics.

Arendt's second critique of the political uses of death is also significant, as it contests the widespread conviction that both the mythical stories of origins and the revolutionary beginning of political bodies are accompanied by seemingly unavoidable murderous violence: Cain slaying Abel, Romulus killing Remus in biblical and classical stories of new beginnings, or the modern fable of the primal horde of brothers killing and devouring their father in Freud's *Totem and Taboo* seem to imply that 'violence was the beginning and [. . .] no beginning could be made without using violence' (OR: 10/10). Similarly, historical revolutionary acts of founding new political structures evoke the spectres of 'extraordinary' murderous violence, in order to justify their revolutionary dictatorships. In *On Revolution* Arendt attempts to answer the question as to why there is such persistent association of the beginnings of political assemblages with crime and violence (OR: 10–11/10). Arendt argues that it is 'in the very nature of a beginning to carry with itself a measure of complete arbitrariness' and novelty, 'as though the beginner had abolished the sequence of temporality itself, or as though the actors were thrown out of the temporal order' (OR 207/198). Yet, the 'curious fact' is that, in Western political traditions, there is a persistent need to 'explain' completely new beginnings, usually in terms of an 'absolute', in order to establish legitimacy (OR: 207/198). As recourse to God to explain and justify the 'absolute' break with the old is not available to modern revolutionaries, they tend resort to violence in fact or in theory. Consequently, Arendt argues that politics based on violence and death stems from the crisis of legitimation of the new beginning, which either breaks from, or appears to be prior to, any tradition.

Arendt analyses various ways that Western political theory has explained or resolved the death and violence associated with the lack of legitimacy of the new foundation. Of interest to our analysis is the way Western philosophy has explained the arbitrariness of new beginnings by appealing to a transcendent source of authority (God or nature) or its own versions of secular authority, such as the 'reasoning capacities of man', the will of the nation, or natural law, to legitimate the absolutely new beginning (OR: 207–8/198–9). For instance, secular national sovereignty can occupy the place of the absolute (interpreted as the immortal legislator), bestowing legitimacy on the new law. Arendt's diagnosis of secular solutions to legitimating a new beginning by appeal to a transcendent absolute is an indirect reference to Schmitt, who famously analyses the theological foundations of the secular sovereignty in his *Political Theology*.[29] Contrary to Schmitt, however, Arendt rejects the binary options of the use of death and violence to legitimate the new beginning and the political theology of sovereignty and points instead to a third option, her own notion of freedom based on the mutual disclosure of natality through collective (inter)action. Under the principle of natality, the actions of a plurality of beginners carry the principle of the new beginning within those actions, which means the new beginning those actions bring about is self-legitimating and requires no violence or external authority. Or, as Arendt puts it:

> What saves the act of the beginning from [any violence associated with] its own arbitrariness is that it carries its own principle within itself [. . .]. The absolute from which the beginning is to derive its own validity and which must save it, as it were, from its inherent arbitrariness is the principle which, together with it, makes its appearance in the world. The way the beginner

starts whatever he intends to do lays down the law of action [the principle of natality] for those who have joined him in order to partake in the enterprise and to bring about its accomplishment. As such, the principle inspires the deeds that are to follow and remains apparent as long as the action lasts. (OR: 213–14/205)

In 'democratic' revolutions, the act of foundation reveals the principle of action based on mutual promises and deliberation. Arendt points out that the notion that the beginning and the principle of natality co-appear in the act is inscribed in both the Greek and the Latin etymology of the word 'principle'; the Latin *principium*, for instance, means both the beginning and the principle (OR: 214/205). Common worlds built from collective actions in which the principle and the beginning are coeval have no need for violence or external authority to maintain themselves because they remain contestable, open to diverse re-interpretations, augmentations and amendments. Arendt thereby opposes the political ontology of violence and death with her political ontology of natality. We could say that Arendt's entire philosophy of natality, understood as the capacity to begin with others something new, is directed against these explanations of political beginnings in terms of death and violence.

Arendt's philosophy of natality is also, we argue, posed against politics that engages the 'life' of the population. While Arendt shifts politics away from this cult of death by basing the political on the disclosure of the birth of the new beginning, this does not mean that she bases politics on the preservation or administration of (new) *life*. On the contrary, Arendt's main target in *The Human Condition* is precisely this sort of politics where various forms of the administration of what are taken as the 'life process' take the place of what she considers to be genuine politics. She refers to this trend as the 'rise of the social'. As we argue more fully in Chapter 2, her diagnosis of the rise of the social amounts to a diagnosis of emergence, by the early twentieth century, of biopolitics as the dominant mode of governmentality in liberal democracies. As the 'rise of the social' has been one of the most debated aspects of Arendt's thought, we close this chapter with an interpretation of Arendt's distinction between the social and the political and some provisional comments about its connection to biopolitics.

Part of the controversy over Arendt's distinction between the social and the political is that her definition of 'the social' or 'society' seems to shift, even within *The Human Condition*. Sometimes Arendt speaks as if 'the social' is equivalent to the private sphere, or the Aristotelian notion of the 'household'. But then she also explicitly says that the 'emergence of the social realm is neither public nor private' (HC: 28). Most commentators agree that the social is not a space per se between public and private (like civil society as we define it now), or a class (such as 'high society', although she does lean toward that idea in the *Origins of Totalitarianism*).[30] While we agree with that claim, we disagree with the conclusion of some commentators that, for Arendt, society is therefore more like an *attitude or mentality* (for example, Wolin 1977: 95) where, through repetitive work and bureaucracy, we approach public life as merely about the satisfaction of need (this is 'labour' in the widest sense that Arendt uses the term). Certainly 'society' as Arendt understands it involves a mentality that focuses on process, but we also claim that this is a *govern*-mentality: that is, society for Arendt is a mode of organisation of public life where the opportunity for beginning something new (agency in Arendt's sense) is limited or is not disclosed by others or welcomed as the new beginning enacted by a beginner. This is an organisation of relations between people where speech and action are replaced by other kinds of activities, by labour in its widest sense. In her initial brief account of the rise of the social in *The Human Condition*, Arendt mentions various forms that 'society' can take: the domination of public life by bureaucratic administration, by mechanistic technology, utilitarian principles, consumerism, economic concerns and the reduction of action to the model of making, and so on. While Arendt's critique of the rise of the social attracted much criticism in the 1970s and 1980s from political theorists concerned by how this seemed to exclude a focus on achieving economic or social equality, we go on to show why that criticism is hasty.

Arendt provides three key definitions of the social in Chapter 2 of *The Human Condition* that together help explicate the concept.[31] The first is the Roman (Latin) definition of *societas*, which departs from the ancient Greek idea of the polis that Arendt tends to favour. *Societas* means an 'alliance between people for a specific purpose, as when men organize in order to rule others or commit a crime' (HC: 23). There are two reasons why Arendt has a problem with this idea of society being equated with the political. First, quite apart from any intention to commit a crime, a form of organisation aimed at facilitating *rule over others* implies violence and domination, which, as already discussed, is contrary to the principle of natality underlying political action. The second reason she rejects the Latin definition of society as a model for politics is more novel: Arendt objects to group activity aimed at a particular *predetermined goal* or that assumes a stable *group identity or common interest* (which is also a feature of the 'consent' said to underlie the social contract). Such aims and assumptions preclude uniqueness, beginning something new, and, hence, the form of association is normalising. This is typical of the modern liberal democratic nation state that justifies government policy in terms of the 'national interest', a development that Arendt describes as the 'complete victory of society' over politics involving the 'communistic fiction' of the 'harmony of conflicting interests' (HC: 43–4). As discussed in section I, this is a feature of liberal societies (not communism) where the assumption of shared interests and 'values', the invisible guiding hand of the market and a burgeoning bureaucracy contribute to the emergence of the 'rule of no-body' (HC: 40–5). The 'rule of no-body' is a principle of normalisation not unlike Heidegger's concept of *das Man*, the One, or the dictatorship of the 'they'.

Arendt's second key definition of 'the social' refers to the form of association that results when public life becomes dominated with activities traditionally associated with the private sphere or, more precisely, with the (Aristotelian) household where living together is said to be driven by 'wants and needs' of biological 'life itself' (HC: 30). This, says Arendt, is characteristic of the modern political form of the 'nation-state', where 'we see the body of peoples and political communities in the image of a family whose everyday affairs have to be taken care of by a gigantic nation-wide administration of housekeeping' (HC: 28). Society modelled on the household can take many forms – for example, a society of property owners (Locke) or 'a society relentlessly engaged in a process of acquisition' (Hobbes) or a 'society of jobholders, as in our own society' (HC 31). None of these schemas of society, based as they are on 'mastering the necessities of life' through competitive and contractual interrelations, are conducive to the kind of action and debate that Arendt thinks fosters beginning the new. But also, characterising political relations on these notions of human nature as they play out in either nature or the household leads to a reductive understanding of freedom that Arendt rejects: freedom to pursue one's own needs. When 'freedom is located in the realm of the social' in this way it 'justifies the restraint of political authority' (HC: 31).

A second point to note about this second definition of the social (and most significant for a diagnosis of biopolitics) is Arendt's objections to the way that care of the 'biological life process' (HC: 37) that characterises the business of the private sphere becomes the model for administration in public life. This is where household administration meets the problem of the assumption of common interest in the rule of nobody. The modelling of public life on the 'necessity' of biological processes involves the expansion of 'labour', understood as the proliferation of repetitive work requiring rule-following behaviour, rather than contesting the status quo (HC: 46–7), and the domination of public life by economic concerns (HC: 41). Arendt even criticises Marx's notion of labour for contributing to this tendency; she claims that his idea that labour is the source of all values is based on the idea of 'man's metabolism with nature', where whatever 'labor produces is meant to be fed into the human life process' (HC: 98–9). Hence, in *On Revolution* Arendt claims that Marx, wrongly, puts the 'life process of society' at the 'centre of the human endeavour' (OR: 59/54). In these ways politics, according to Arendt, has been reduced to the management of the (biological or just unquestioned) needs of the masses and is thereby driven by imperatives of production and consumption and making rather than acting. Another key way that 'life process itself [. . . gets] channeled into the public realm' (HC: 45) to become the focus of politics is through the combination of the increasing reliance on population statistics in social analyses and the dominance of behaviourism geared toward 'leveling out of fluctuation' in these statistics (HC: 43). 'Statistical uniformity is by no means a harmless ideal': it encourages conformism and 'automatism in human affairs' (HC: 43). This is a clear early formulation of what Foucault will later call *biopolitics*, which we discuss in more detail in Chapter 2. The danger of biopolitics so understood is that it involves the 'substitution of behavior for action and [. . .] bureaucracy, the rule of nobody, for personal rulership' (or personal responsibility), which risks reducing 'man as a whole, in all his activities, to the level of a conditioned and behaving animal' (*animal laborans*) (HC: 45).

The third definition of society in *The Human Condition*, which Arendt only touches on briefly, is society (or community) based on a normalised and normalising group identity, a single shared interest, or social rank (HC: 39–41). Her point about this is that such 'society' remains modelled on the family and hence remains prone to the same kind of conformism and suppression of natality as any rigid group identity. But what distinguishes this notion of society from the other two is the way politics of 'equality' became based on its notion of sameness of a static identity. It is the basis of a form of biopolitical normalisation apparent in the rise of Nazism, where lacking a preferred identity justifies exclusion from the category of human with the 'capacity' to begin the new. This is an aspect of the 'rise of the social' that Arendt highlights in *The Origins of Totalitarianism* as one precursor of totalitarianism and we this take up again in Chapter 2. In summary, her objection is to the way political equality is depoliticised into a 'mundane fact' about social identities that are no longer contested or formed within the public space of appearance in the presence of other agents. When depoliticised in this way, the social notion of equality is normalising (and forecloses the event of natality) because it is likely to be 'mistaken for an innate quality of every individual, who is "normal" if he is like everyone else and "abnormal" if he happens to be different' (OT: 54). Moreover, 'equality based on the conformism inherent in society [is] possible only because behavior has replaced action as the foremost mode of human relationship' (HC: 41).

What all these ideas of society share is what connects them to what has become known as biopolitics: 'Society is the form in which the fact of mutual dependence for the sake of life and nothing else assumes public significance and where the activities connected with sheer survival are permitted to appear in public' (HC: 46). This is politics geared toward the state management of biological life that Arendt opposes as vehemently as she opposes politics based on death, violence and sacrifice. Her primary objection is that both kinds of politics suppress collaborative action and debate and hence the event of natality, or new beginnings. They eliminate the disjunctive temporality necessary to keep human existence and the world open to potentiality rather than determined by biological, historical or political necessity. As mentioned in the Introduction, Foucault's classic definition of biopolitics also covers both kinds of politics that Arendt's critiques target: biopolitics, on Foucault's definition, refers to state control over life and death, or more precisely biopolitics is *state-centred power over the right to foster life or let die*. What we set out to show in Chapters 2 and 3 is that Arendt's philosophy of natality makes a unique contribution to diagnoses of both arms of biopolitics because, unlike Foucault, she insists that while the birth of the new beginning in political life may depend on action and speech in the company of other agents, any event of natality depends of the worldly 'fact of birth' of human existents.

Notes

1   We agree with Anya Topolski (2015) that the key feature of Arendt's political ontology is her notion of inter-relationality, a point rarely made in Arendtian scholarship. Topolski's focus is a comparison of Levinas's and Arendt's models of relationality that shows how Levinas's notion of 'alterity', which 'inspires' the ethical relation, can be brought together with Arendt's notion of 'natality' at the heart of the political in order to 'sketch a post-foundational political ethics of relationality' (Topolski 2015: 179). We similarly argue in Chapter 4 for a normative principle underlying both politics and ethics, although in the context of examining the relation between personal and political responsibility.

2   In *The Human Condition* Arendt has not yet fully formulated the temporality of the event of natality in terms of instituting a gap between past and future. Hence, she tends to describe the historicity of the political 'self' (or *bíos*) in terms of linear temporality even though she wants to distinguish this temporality from the idea of 'life process'. Maurizio Passerin D'Entrèves provides an insightful account of Arendt's apparent 'ambivalence' toward 'process' depending on whether it is with regard to 'biological life', 'making' or 'action', arguing that she never resolved this tension (D'Entrèves 1994: 53–8). Along with O'Byrne (2010) we go on to argue that the temporality of 'natality' goes some way to explaining this apparent tension in HC and, beyond O'Byrne, we mobilise Arendt's later insights about judgement and natality to explain the difference between 'process' as described by the biological sciences and the temporality arising from the disclosure of natality through action.

3   Arendt elaborates the role of others in thinking and judgement in terms of communicability and publicity in her lectures on Kant (LKPP: 38–40). As Rodolphe Gasché suggests, Arendt reformulates Kant's reflective judgement as a kind of internal deliberation with others, which is, therefore, communicable from the start (Gasché 2013: 112–14). In Chapter 4 we add another dimension to this account by noting that the unique distinctness of others prompts us to think and speak and is therefore a precondition to this internal dialogue.

4   Insightful interpretations of Arendt's approaches to thinking and judgement that we have found helpful include Richard Bernstein (2000), D'Entrèves (1994), Max Deutscher (2007), Gasché (2013) and Taylor (2002).

5   Elizabeth Frazer provides a particularly astute account of three kinds of plurality in Arendt's work associated with our 'political capacity', all

of which are also noted in this paragraph of our analysis of natality and temporality: a plurality of spheres of activity dependent on each other, a plurality of radically distinct beings in relation with each other, and distinctions within the self that allow the self-relation necessary for thinking and judgement (Frazer 2009: 208). In our book, when we use 'plurality' as shorthand, we usually mean the second kind of plurality. The main point for now is that it is because of the dependence of the plurality of the self-relation on the plurality of human inter-relations (the disclosure of natality to and by others) that biopolitics can destroy our 'political capacity' and humanness in general.

6   Consistent with academic conventions of her time, Arendt uses 'man' and masculine pronouns throughout her work to refer to human being. Henceforth, when quoting Arendt, we remain faithful to her text in this regard but we do not endorse equating the human with 'man'.

7   For a recent overview of different approaches to 'mini-publics' see Grönlund et al. (2014).

8   In *The Origins of Totalitarianism* Arendt says '[p]ositive laws in constitutional government are designed to erect boundaries and establish channels of communication between [people] whose community is continually' de-stabilised by natality, by 'new beginning[s . . .] born into it'. If laws bring stability while allowing 'the potentiality of something entirely new and unpredictable [. . . then] they guarantee the pre-existence of a common world, the reality of some continuity which [. . . also] absorbs all new origins and is nourished by them' (OT: 465).

9   Arendt uses the term 'common sense' to refer to this sense we have of both 'one's own identity' and of 'reality' (HC: 208). As Marieke Borren suggests, there is some debate about whether, for Arendt, 'common sense [is] a given faculty or a socio-cultural achievement' (Borren 2013: 226). Borren argues that, for Arendt, common sense is *both* the pre-reflective understanding of meanings we have inherited and share *and* what 'emerges in the space between a plurality of actors and spectators, in our perpetual interaction with the common world, and which maintains this common world at the same time' (Borren 2013: 248). We also note that Arendt's scant reference to 'common sense' in HC is explicitly tied to Whitehead's notion rather than Kant (for example, HC: 283). For Whitehead, 'common sense' arises in the context of his speculative philosophy where experimental thinking is grounded in 'common sense' understood as dynamic sense experience. See Birmingham (2006: 62–9) for an informative account of Arendt's more Kantian notion of 'sensus communis'.

10 Phillips (2013) provides an insightful account of Arendt's discussion of fact, opinion and truth in her challenging essay 'Truth and politics'. By careful analysis, Phillips explains how, for Arendt, opinion is converted to factual truth through political (collaborative) action. Hence factual truth is both 'the limit and condition of possibility of action' and change (Phillips 2013: 97). Lisa Disch (1993) also provides an insightful account of Arendt's distinction between truth and fact, but this time with regard to Arendt's approach to storytelling as a 'spontaneous but principled response to the phenomenon of total domination', a response that is neither subjective nor objective but consists in 'critical understanding from experience' (Disch 1993: 666).

11 This is not to say that Arendt's understanding of the schema of political action departs far from Heidegger's descriptions of being-*toward-the-world* in his analytic of *Dasein*. Arendt does soften her stance on Heidegger in her later work, including admitting her debt to Heidegger's 'The Anaximander fragment' toward the end of *Life of the Mind II*. Peg Birmingham (2013) argues that *The Human Condition* also owes a debt to Heidegger's 'The Anaximander fragment' in the idea of 'Being as potentiality' rather than 'actuality' and the idea that the 'self [. . .] is both singular and plural, both unique and in a relation of belonging-together in being-with' (Birmingham 2013: 158–9). Still, as we go on to show, especially in Chapter 3, the way Arendt ties the event of natality back to the fact of human birth having the socio-historical significance as the event of natality (rather than just the basis of an internal relation to one's own birth) makes her work particularly suited to a diagnosis of the rise of biopolitics in ways that Heidegger's philosophy is not.

12 From among the many critiques of Arendt's use of the public/private distinction, we single out Sarah Sorial's (2006) sympathetic approach as one that accords with ours.

13 See Linda Zerilli (1995) for an early feminist critique of Arendt's neglect of embodiment in her theory of action. Kathryn Gines (2014) is also critical of Arendt partly on this basis, but from the perspective of the politics of race and racism.

14 Locke outlines his model of personal identity, which relies on the distinction between personal and bodily identity, in 'Of identity and diversity', Chapter 27 of *An Essay Concerning Human Understanding*. As Arendt engages with Locke's political philosophy throughout *The Human Condition*, including discussion of his account of the labouring body, it is easy to assume that her account of personal identity is also informed by

Locke. The danger in assuming this connection is that Locke's is a (legal) notion of *constant, individual* identity that forms the basis of current ways of attributing responsibility and culpability to a person. Locke thus envisages a core to the self that, through reflection and memory, attributes different actions and states of consciousness to the same self over time. While this idea of personal identity is different from Arendt's notion, her use of the distinction between physical and personal identity opens the possibility for misunderstandings, especially for readers from a liberal empiricist tradition.

15 For a detailed account of this thesis about the role of the moving body in the mutual disclosure of the 'personhood' of the person, see 'Performing body identity through the other' in Diprose (2002: 59–74).

16 O'Byrne (2010) puts Arendt's point succinctly: 'The temporality of natality is such that I am with others before I can grasp that I am and who I am as a finite being. The origin from which I am removed is certainly mine, but it also belongs in an important sense to others' (O'Byrne 2010: 106).

17 Bonnie Honig (1995) provides an excellent explanation and partial defence of Arendt's refusal of (feminist and other) identity politics in the context of Arendt's debates with her contemporary critics, her performative (and, hence, transformative) models of action and personal identity, and her 'agonistic' politics, which, in Honig's account, involves interrupting established identities.

18 Arendt's relation to Judaism and the cultural, religious and political aspects of Jewish identity is complex and a subject of much debate, to which we cannot do justice here. For illuminating discussions in this regard, see Richard Bernstein (1996) and recent essays collected in Roger Berkowitz et al. (2010).

19 For a succinct definition of the Marxist idea of equality see Fetscher (2001: 177–8).

20 Although, as Birmingham and others argue, enjoying this basic respect for one's uniqueness (and, hence, the right to have rights) 'requires the accompanying rights to the fulfillment of vital needs such as food, shelter, health care, and education' (Birmingham 2006: 61).

21 For Foucault's answer to the question of the place of others in his ethics of 'care for the self' see, for example, 'On the genealogy of ethics: an overview of work in progress' (Foucault 2000a: 253–80) and 'The ethics of the concern for the self as a practice of freedom' (Foucault 2000a: 281–302).

22 A notable exception is Dorota Glowacka (2006), who uses both Arendt and Nancy in a compelling analysis of 'community-in-conflict: the

Polish-Jewish community' (n.p.n.), where she not only credits Nancy's reading of *The Origins of Totalitarianism* (mentioned briefly in Lacoue-Labarthe and Nancy 1990: 293) for his move away from Heidegger's emphasis on being-toward-death, but also she argues that 'Arendt's comments on the role of death in the community' and her analysis of the biopolitics of 'death in the concentration camps seem to anticipate Nancy's ideas on death and the community' (Glowacka 2006: n.p.n.). Mustafa Dikeç (2015) provides an interesting comparison of Arendt's and Nancy's (and Rancière's) political thinking in terms of the aesthetic premises underlying each, arguing that their conceptions of politics depend on their understanding of the construction and apprehension of worlds through spatial forms and distributions. O'Byrne considers both Arendt's and Nancy's different approaches to 'natality', although without direct comparison beyond claiming that, in contrast to Arendt, who, as a consequence of being 'troubled by the threats of racist biological determinism, could not give the material world its due', Nancy considers 'material being and embodiment [. . .] central and unavoidable' (O'Byrne 2010: 107).

23 Nancy's acknowledged debt to Heidegger includes critical appropriation of his notion of 'mood' underlying being-with-others-in-the-world, although Nancy emphasises the *toward-others* component of this schema rather than the anxiety-prone concern for one's *own* being. Arguably, Nancy, in his idea of 'inclination', also borrows from Levinas's idea of 'desire' for 'alterity' (the absolutely other) that inspires the 'bond' of sociality (discussed, for example, in 'Meaning and sense' – (Levinas 1987), although Nancy does not to our knowledge acknowledge any debt to Levinas and would reject (as would Arendt) Levinas's idea that desire for the other, or the disclosure of natality, is one-way.

24 In contrast to Arendt, 'potentiality' for Aristotle (as outlined in *Metaphysics* 1046a–50b) is the capacity of matter to change into a different state or form or substance by either a change in the quantity of matter or a change in how it is put together (form) (Aristotle 1976).

25 For a discussion of the Marxist notion of freedom as 'revolutionary over-turning of history' see Balibar (1995: 36–9). For Balibar, Arendt criticises Marx for basing 'free' action on making, that is, giving priority to poesis (making) over free praxis. Balibar criticises this interpretation of Marx by arguing that, for Marx, 'effective freedom' represents the unity of poesis and praxis, making and acting (Balibar 1995: 41).

26 Or, in the case of Marxism, Arendt claims that philosophy has substituted

the 'mastery' of making (HC: 222) for freedom of a new beginning, manifesting itself in acting in concert (HC: 222–30).

27 For excellent accounts of the formation of new anti-racist movements in the US, such as Black Lives Matter, see, among others, Taylor (2016: 153–220) and Davis (2016: 13–40). The unarmed victim of the shooting that sparked the formation of that movement was seventeen-year-old Trayvon Martin, killed in Florida in 2012.

28 For Judith Butler's interpretation of Arendt's notion of alliance and the space of appearance as a key idea informing Butler's own performative theory of assembly, see Butler (2015: 44–6, 76–80, 174). As indicated in section II of this chapter, Butler also shares our key criticisms of Arendt's lack of account of the body in her theory of action.

29 Arendt's condemnation of Hobbes can also be seen as an indirect reference to and critique of Schmitt, who praises Hobbes for the preservation of personal sovereignty (Schmitt 1985: 33–4). For a lucid analysis of Arendt's relation to Schmitt see Benhabib's (2010) account, which stresses the incompatibility between Schmitt's friend/enemy distinction and Arendt's notion of democratic plurality.

30 See Hanna Pitkin (1995) for a useful and thorough account of Arendt's various definitions of the social.

31 Sheyla Benhabib (1995) also discusses three meanings of the social but her categorisation differs from Arendt's three definitions. Benhabib's three categories of the 'social' are: commodification, mass society, and a form of sociability that Benhabib favours based on the bonds of conversation and friendship within the feminine space of the salon.

2

Natality, Normalising Biopolitics and Totalitarianism

In Chapter 1 we have elaborated how Arendt's philosophy of natality refigures political concepts such as agency, power and freedom, as well as the notion of the political itself. The discussion concludes with an account of the two forms of politics that Arendt, in *The Human Condition*, pits her notion of the political against: a politics of death, violence and expansion based on sovereign power (exemplified by Hobbes's conception of the political); and a politics of 'life', a form of biopolitics that Arendt describes in terms of the 'rise of the social'. In this chapter, we develop these critiques of the politics of death and life in terms that position Arendt as the first substantial thinker of biopolitics. With a focus on her earlier work, *The Origins of Totalitarianism*, we examine in more detail the damage that biopolitics can do to natality in the following inter-related manifestations: the public appearance of a new beginning as the uniqueness and plurality inherent to the human condition; the natal 'capacity' to create a new beginning in history; and 'political community', consisting of the inter-relationality and potentiality of being-together, characterised as the mutual disclosure of natality through speech and action. In this chapter we leave aside the question of how biopolitics impacts the event of natality in the first order of human birth, but we address this in Chapter 3. Here we examine how, according to Arendt, biopolitics in the extreme form of 'totalitarian domination' (in the special sense Arendt uses this term) forecloses natality and hence eliminates the disjunctive temporality (the gap between past and future), the historicity and the potentiality characteristic of both human coexistence and the 'reality' (the 'common' world) that we share. Arendt's diagnoses in these terms of how natality is eliminated in totalitarian biopolitics remains unsurpassed (even by Agamben) for the way it exposes the essential 'elements' of totalitarianism while issuing a warning about what comes of a governmentality that treats people as mere 'life' devoid of natality.

However, this analysis of the key elements of totalitarian biopolitics is not where we begin. As our ultimate concern is with how some modes of contemporary biopolitics pose a threat to human existence and democratic plurality, Arendt's analyses of the historical *precursors* to Nazism and Stalinism (to her mind the only examples of pure totalitarianism as she defines it) are equally important for revealing what totalitarian elements may be present in liberal democracies now. So we also examine some aspects of Arendt's accounts of preconditions to totalitarianism that are uncomfortably similar to our times, from the spectacular mass displacement of peoples in Europe by the 1920s that rendered them 'right-less' (OT: 297–300) to the seemingly banal 'normalisation' apparent in aspects of European society from the late nineteenth century, which morphed into anti-Semitism, racism, homophobia and other kinds of '*dumb hatred*' *of difference* (OT: 301, emphasis added). This is not to assume a direct causal link or equivalence between these trends in normalising biopolitics of the late nineteenth century or in contemporary liberal democracies and full-blown totalitarianism, which

Arendt explicitly denies in response to reviews of her book.[1] As she explains in her 'Reply to Eric Voegelin' (EU: 401–8), the word 'origins' in the book's title, *The Origins of Totalitarianism*, is perhaps misleading if understood in the usual senses (as root causes, for example); by 'origins' Arendt means 'essence' (as in, say, Heidegger's 'Origin of the work of art', although she is not explicit about this connection). And in examining the precursors of totalitarian biopolitics Arendt says she provides not an account of its continuous historical development but 'a historical account of the *elements which crystallized* into totalitarianism' (EU: 403, emphasis added). Nor is our examination of some precursors of totalitarianism meant to underplay the unimaginable scope of the death and destruction inflicted by Soviet and Nazi totalitarian regimes, which Arendt says explicitly were 'unprecedented' (for example, OT: 417; EU: 405).[2] Rather, like Arendt, we juxtapose the two forms of biopolitics and make conceptual links between salient elements of each to reveal what is wrong with, and reasons for acting against, the normalisation and regularisation in some forms of contemporary biopolitics whether or not these are destined to tip into 'totalitarian domination'.

In juxtaposing the normalising and discriminatory biopolitics characterising the 'rise of the social' with the key elements of the thanato-biopolitics of totalitarianism we are linking Arendt's analyses not initially to Agamben's subsequent account of biopolitics in terms of the reduction of 'political life' to 'bare life', as is the more usual practice, but to Foucault's definition of biopolitics as involving two inter-related aspects. *First*, for Foucault, biopolitics involves the emergence in liberal democracies by the late nineteenth century of a new operation of political power in the government of life and death: *biopower*, whereby the state takes up the right to *foster* life or *disallow* it (instead of the more explicit sovereign right to kill or let live, which remains apparent in Hobbes's political philosophy). *Second*, for Foucault, the target of this political power is the *biological life of the population* rather than individual subjects: biopower targets 'problems posed to governmental practice by phenomena characteristic of a set of living beings forming a population: health, hygiene, birth rate, race . . .' (Foucault 2008: 317). As we will discuss in more detail below, in Foucault's account biopolitics involves a combination of these two defining features of biopower, which together '*regularise*' the 'life' of the population (biopower aims at eliminating the unpredictable and unviable from biological processes). In addition, biopolitics '*normalises*' individuals: by linking up with disciplinary and other modes of productive power operating in individualising and subjectifying governmental practices, biopolitical practices that aim at maximising the biological life of a population rely on social norms of viability in determining what forms of life, biological processes, desires and so on are to be fostered. Political 'power over life' in liberal democracies, therefore, consists in a network of relations extending toward 'two poles', with the individual body at one end and the 'biological processes' of the population at the other (Foucault 1980a: 139; Foucault 2003: 242–3). While aimed at maximising life, biopolitics is also potentially *lethal* (as biopolitics regulates the emergence of the anomalous, the new and the unpredictable in biological life, it implicitly consists in the political regulation of the life and death of people). Moreover, and crucially, in liberal democracies biopower *hides itself* in institutions and practices of care: as biopower does not often appear publicly as a form of state-centred political power over life and death, the discriminatory and potentially lethal elements it may harbour are difficult to expose and therefore to counter.

Arendt's account of the 'rise of the social' in *The Human Condition*, discussed in Chapter 1, can be reframed in terms of the normalising feature of biopolitics that Foucault describes. In this chapter, though, we show that Arendt's analysis of the normalising precursors of totalitarianism similarly pre-empt both the normalising and the regularising aspects of Foucault's definition of biopolitics. Her account of the essential elements of totalitarianism, however, reveals more explicitly than Foucault's how normalising biopolitics, understood as the (hidden) exercise of state power over life and death, also aims at eliminating natality. While showing how Arendt's approach to biopolitics anticipates Foucault, we also compare their approaches to the impact of (bio) power on the body, indicating how Foucault reveals techniques of power that may explain the material suppression of natality outside of the brutalisation of bodies in totalitarian death camps. Again, this is not to downplay the scope of that brutalisation or the importance of Arendt's identification of the unique form of power that underscores (or is equivalent to) totalitarianism, but to point to less explicit mechanisms of the suppression of natality that are operational within some kinds of contemporary biopolitics and that pose a threat to democratic plurality in ways that Arendt's philosophy of natality explains.

Exploring how Arendt's accounts of the suppression and elimination of natality by normalising and totalitarian bio-politics address both Foucault's and Agamben's concerns is not the only point of this chapter. We also examine the ways that her approach to biopolitics yields important insights that Foucault and Agamben fail to develop. Unique and particularly enlightening is Arendt's account of what is involved in the mutation of one pole of normalising biopolitics, the power to 'let die', into totalitarianism and its thanato-biopolitics of 'making die' or of (living) death. We argue that Arendt's analysis of this shows, contrary to both Agamben's and Foucault's subsequent accounts and as if a forewarning of aspects of the biopolitics of the early twenty-first century, that normalising biopolitics within democracy can harbour elements of, or crystallise into, totalitarian politics *without recourse to the exercise of sovereign power* by the state or its political leaders. According to Arendt, totalitarianism can emerge from its precursors yet be unprecedented because 'what is unprecedented in totalitarianism is not primarily its ideological content, but the *event* of totalitarian domination itself' (EU: 405), which involves a new kind of (bio)power. That is, 'totalitarian domination' and its thanato-biopolitics is an unpredictable event of natality that brings together pre-existing elements into a power 'structure' that forecloses the event of natality for all. We outline the key elements of this structure of totalitarian domination in sections II and III of the chapter. The analysis reveals that at the centre of the event of totalitarianism is Arendt's formulation of total terror and what she describes as an *unprecedented kind of 'power'* as the 'force of movement', which eliminates the disjunctive temporality characteristic of natality within human existence and political community (democratic plurality) such that human existence and 'reality' both appear to be determined by force of nature or history.

A final preliminary remark about Arendt's terminology in *The Origins of Totalitarianism*: she does not use the term 'natality' in that work; instead, she refers to the suppression or elimination of action, uniqueness, individuality and 'spontaneity' in public life. 'Spontaneity' is a term she also uses in her later work *The Life of the Mind*, where she describes 'the will' as the organ of 'spontaneity' (LM II: 109–10) in the sense that it opens the possibility of action or a new beginning by turning thinking away from its concern with oneself outward, toward the world. While the meaning of 'spontaneity' varies a bit throughout *The Origins of Totalitarianism*, it does line up with this idea of unpremeditated action or acting and thinking in unexpected ways. This, in turn, is consistent with the various meanings of 'natality' in *The Human Condition*, specifically, the 'capacity' to begin something new and the notion of the 'appearance' of a person as a beginner (an agent) rather than an automaton that is reacting to, or resisting, the actions of others. For instance, toward the end of *The Origins of Totalitarianism* Arendt defines 'spontaneity [as] man's power to begin something new out of his own resources, something that cannot be explained on the basis of reactions to environment and events' (OT: 455). 'Individuality' and 'uniqueness' appear to hold a similar meaning within this work. And while Arendt has not yet refined the idea that natality is disclosed to, and by, others within the 'togetherness' of human affairs, the notion of spontaneity in *The Origins of Totalitarianism* contains as its condition some sense of acting *with* others. So, for example, she says that in destroying spontaneity, totalitarianism destroys 'the space of freedom', understood as a special dynamic quality of the space *between* natal or spontaneous beings (OT: 466). We will return to discuss the full impact of totalitarianism on natality in section III. The point for now is that we use the terms 'spontaneity' and 'natality' interchangeably for the purposes of this analysis. We also import into the analysis of totalitarianism Arendt's later refinements regarding the disjunctive temporality characteristic of natality, which we have detailed in Chapter 1.

I. Arendt and Foucault on Normalising Biopolitics

Just to reiterate in what sense Arendt's account of the 'rise of the social' in *The Human Condition* is an account of biopolitics in Foucault's sense: 'society' is a mode of governmentality and social organisation that treats public life as a kind of 'life process' requiring streamlining, normalising and so on. Arendt's concern in both *The Human Condition* and the work that precedes it, *The Origins of Totalitarianism*, is with the way the political has been gradually subsumed by the social since the late nineteenth century at the expense of democratic plurality. On the one hand, '[s]ociety is the form in which the fact of mutual dependence *for the sake of life and nothing else* assumes public significance and where the activities connected with sheer survival are permitted to appear in public life' (HC: 46, emphasis added). On the other hand, the focus on 'behaviour', mundane work and the preservation and reproduction of human 'life' is normalising in the sense of fostering conformity and limiting the capacity of beginning something new. This, in turn, can destroy personal responsibility, agency and political community by 'reduc[ing] man as a whole, in all his activities, to the level of a conditioned and behaving animal' (*animal laborans*) (HC: 54). In elaborating the connection Arendt hints at here between the 'rise of the social' and biopolitics, as well as examining the consequences of this trend, our focus will be on Arendt's analysis in *The Origins of Totalitarianism*. Arendt's analysis there is of the rise of the social with regard to anti-Semitism, homophobia and racism in general in late-nineteenth-century Europe. Her account contains some important insights about the emergence of the more lethal kind of normalisation inherent in the biopolitical operation of power in liberal democracies. This is where biopolitics entwines with an emphasis on individual social 'identity' such that decisions about what kind of 'life' should be fostered and what should be 'left to die' are tied to norms of viability and of social or biological identity, a dangerous trend that in Arendt's account forecloses the disclosure of natality characteristic of human agency, action and genuine politics. Significantly, her diagnosis provides an account of normalisation that precedes Foucault's diagnoses of normalisation of individuals by disciplinary power and 'regularisation' of the biological life of the population by biopower.

Arendt's analysis of this aspect of normalising biopolitics is woven throughout her account of three preconditions of totalitarianism that, together with other preconditions (such as nineteenth-century imperialism and a massive displacement of people across Europe before and after the First World War), came together to tip Germany's fledgling democracy into totalitarianism, with the implicit consent (or at least the apparent indifference) of much of the population. These social preconditions can be summarised as: first, the transformation of the political notion of equality into a social notion of the 'normal' versus 'abnormal' (OT: 54); second, the subsequent emergence of notions of innate inner identity (aligned with, for example, culture, race, religion, nationality or sexuality) that are increasingly understood as individual, fixed, biological and non-volitional; and third, the transformation of the concept of crime into the notion of a vice belonging to particular social identities. Closer examination of each of these trends helps explain how the rise of the social as a precursor to totalitarianism amounts to a genealogy of the emergence of the biopolitical suppression of what Arendt refers to in *The Origins of Totalitarianism* as 'spontaneity' or 'individuality' (natality and uniqueness) in public life. Hence, Arendt's analysis is tantamount to an account of the threat that this kind of normalising biopolitics poses to the disclosure of natality whereby others are acknowledged as human agents, which, in turn, undermines the principle of democratic plurality.

The first aspect of the rise of the social that Arendt analyses does not seem to be at first glance particularly dangerous for democratic plurality, let alone a precondition of totalitarianism: the *perversion of a politics of equality* into a social process of normalisation. But her key insight about this is crucial to understanding the hidden danger that normalisation presents to natality and the human condition of plurality: the 'more equal conditions are the less explanation there is for the differences that actually exist between people; and thus all the more unequal do individuals and groups become' (OT: 54). This claim is reminiscent of Nietzsche's infamous criticism of the doctrine of equality of classical liberalism on the grounds that it is really about producing sameness among the 'herd'; a politics of equality amounts to normalisation that erases, covers over and/or denigrates differences (for example, Nietzsche 1968: 91). While in agreement with Nietzsche's main point, Arendt provides a more considered account of how processes of normalisation transform equality into sameness (in terms of a norm understood as an innate quality) and difference into abnormality. She argues that discourses of equality become normalising when they move out of the political sphere of struggle for justice into the realm of 'the social' struggle for status on the basis of (racial, sexual, class or other) identity. As she explains later in *The Human Condition*, and as discussed in Chapter 1, in the realm of the political, identity is always contested and under the process of transformation within the in-between of public activities where the disclosure of natality always keeps both personal identity (the 'who' of the person) and our shared reality (the 'common' world) open to potentiality and an undetermined future (HC: 175).

The problem that Arendt highlights in *The Origins of Totalitarianism* is that when the demand for equality is depoliticised into a 'mundane fact' about social identities, it is normalising in both senses of demanding conformity and demonising difference as abnormal. Social equality is thus likely to be 'mistaken for an innate quality of every individual, who is "normal" if he is like everyone else and "abnormal" if he happens to be different' (OT: 54). Normalisation separated from political community, collective action and political struggle is necessarily discriminating against those who do not fit the 'norm'. At worst, this process of normalisation becomes lethal. As Arendt puts the point, the

> perversion of equality from a political into a social concept is all the more dangerous when a society leaves but little room for special groups and individuals, for then their differences become all the more conspicuous. (OT: 54)

As Arendt goes on to show, these conspicuous differences within the social are not necessarily vilified; they may fascinate when viewed as 'exotic', as was the case with some stand-out homosexuals and the 'exception Jews' in the nineteenth century, such as Disraeli, who used their difference to their advantage (OT: 68–72). But in a racist and/or homophobic society, achieving equal social status as an exception amounts to moving from 'pariah to parvenu' (OT: 56), which leaves the lowly status of the (different) minority race in place and bolsters the 'normal' (white, heterosexual, male, Christian and so on) identity toward which one aspires.[3] Equally, the perversion of difference into abnormality means its elimination can become easily justified.

How this happens requires examination of the second precondition of totalitarianism that Arendt proposes.

The second aspect of the rise of the social that Arendt examines as a precursor to totalitarianism is more obviously biopolitical: the emergence of the notion of an *innate inner identity* that defines a person (as a 'what' rather than a 'who'). Susan Bordo (1987) traces this notion of the individual inner self back to Descartes's *cogito*, although the *cogito* is not yet a personal identity in the sense of personality or character. Foucault argues in *The Order of Things* that the notion of an inner self truly takes hold in the late eighteenth century with Kant's philosophy, which, for Foucault, paved the way for the emergence in the nineteenth century of the sciences of 'man', where the individual inner self becomes the subject and object of knowledge (Foucault 1970: 344–87). Arendt's claim is that what changes during the nineteenth century is that the inner self of the Enlightenment, which was characterised by the general capacity to think, becomes an inner personality or a 'type' that not only categorises the particular person but does so in terms of an essence. The 'identity' of the person is increasingly understood in natural or biological terms, outside of the person's control, and untouched by their engagements with others in the human world. Arendt notes that this turn to a notion of innate identity was most manifest as a growing obsession in European 'society' in the nineteenth century with the 'exotic, abnormal, and different as such' that replaced the 'Enlightenment's genuine tolerance and curiosity for everything human' (OT: 68).

There are two key points Arendt makes about this trend toward categorisation of persons in terms of innate identity that are relevant to a diagnosis of the harms of biopolitics. First, the phenomenon whereby many 'exotics', especially among those 'assimilated' into European 'society', embraced their respective identities as a matter of pride in 'blood and race' (OT: 74–5) illustrates that the turn toward categorisation of people by type of inner identity relied on the intertwining of a process of self-identification with processes of external identification by the political operation of biopower and other processes of normalisation. When he began to outline the operation of bio-politics in *The History of Sexuality, Volume I*, Foucault described this intertwining as the 'truth effects' of power that operate through the techniques of 'confession' and 'surveillance' (for example, Foucault 1980a: 53–73). Arendt's observation about the tendency toward individual self-definition foreshadows Foucault's account of the two-sided process of subjection within normalising society described in summary form in 'The subject and power' (Foucault 2002: 326–49).[4] According to Foucault, normalising techniques of power (including both discipline and biopower) are dispersed through the human sciences and state institutions that attend to our health and welfare and thereby regulate biological life. These techniques of power are both 'individualising' and 'totalising' in that they target people as in-dividuals but also as sets of biological processes while measuring them (at both levels) against various social norms in relation to the whole of the population. Moreover, the individual 'subjects' are produced through this operation of power in two senses: they are *subjected* to the actions of others and are thereby 'subject to someone else by control and dependence'; and second, they attain individual identities as *subjects* through subjectify-ing practices of 'confession' and self-identification in terms of the norms of identity and behaviour that pervade these human sciences and governmental practices that attend to the health and welfare of the population (Foucault 2002: 331). Hence, the

117

same processes of biopolitical and disciplinary government that reduce us to objects of political power (which, for Arendt, would suppress the event of natality) also aim at modifying conduct to align with norms of behaviour. Similarly, Arendt's account of the increasing practice of self-identification in terms of innate identity is a vehicle for explaining in part how individuals can become unwittingly complicit in their own subjection and in the surveillance, normalisation and subjection of others.

Arendt's second point about the trend toward categorising according to inner innate identity is that the practice was part of a wider trend that subsumed the political under the 'social', although distinguished by the way it involved aligning group identity with biological markers such as race or ethnicity 'separated from action' and 'other ties with the common world' (OT: 240–1). This also marks the rise of biopolitics insofar as people's 'private lives', including their apparently immutable identities that are supposedly continuous with the givenness of 'life', become the target of political power (OT: 83–4). While 'exception Jews' and other so-called 'exotics' could take advantage of any 'morbid lust with the exotic' in late-nineteenth-century society, unassimilated Jews and other groups of people who fell outside the social categories deemed 'normal' suffered negative consequences of this turn to innate identity as a means of categorising the different as 'abnormal'. The danger of the whole trend lay in the increasing lack of flexibility in self-definition beyond biological or essential terms. Indeed, in time, once an implicit norm of innate identity has captured enough of a population it becomes the core identity to which mass society clings. Under such circumstances, those who are 'different' are considered 'abnormal' and are more likely to be condemned as such. This is particularly so if identity is viewed as innate and immutable. We are witnessing a similar problem now, in liberal democracies, where, after the events of 9/11 2001, so-called 'people of Middle-Eastern appearance' and Muslims have been increasingly marked out in alarming ways as a threat to security and to (mythical) national 'values'. These beliefs that identity is innate and that identities that are deemed to be different to the norm are a threat to social stability and security allowed the Nazi regime to generate, through propaganda, fear of those 'abnormal' others (Jews, drug 'addicts', homosexuals, communists, intellectuals and so on) who appeared to threaten the 'normal' identity by seemingly 'living against the eternal laws of nature and life' (OT: 345). Arendt traces how, in combination with the depoliticisation of equality, the Nazis transformed this notion of a 'normal' innate identity into the promise of a stable, consistent, homogeneous 'people's Community' or *Volkgemeinschaft* 'of all Germans' (OT: 360).

Whether embracing the notion of innate social identity (implicitly measured against an unspecified 'national identity') can have these negative and even lethal effects depends on the *third* element of the rise of the social that Arendt describes as a precondition to totalitarianism: a trend since the early twentieth century to attach criminality to individuals deemed 'abnormal' in the form of a 'vice', that is, an immoral tendency of particular types or identities (OT: 80–1). In other words, once a dynamic sense of self is detached from collective or individual *action* and is viewed, instead, as a stable inner identity it may be embraced as a virtue, but just as easily it can take on the character of a vice (OT: 83). Significantly, by 'assimilating crime and transforming it into vice, society denies responsibility and establishes a world of fatalities in which men find themselves entangled' (OT: 80–1). Arendt's main point (and she later uses the anti-black racism of

1950s America as her example) is that once identity is viewed as innate (rather than an ongoing process of inter-relationality and the mutual disclosure of natality) and a particular identity gets associated with social corruption or a vice, it is impossible to escape the surrounding racism, 'dumb hatred' of difference, 'mistrust, and discrimination' (OT: 301) because the people who are the target of this hatred and mistrust cannot escape their (supposedly essential) 'given' identity (OT: 301). Again, Arendt insists that this tendency to characterise inner identity as a virtue or vice could happen only 'when society had emancipated itself completely from public concerns, and when politics itself was becoming part of social life' (OT: 80). The crunch comes when crime is seen not as an act of will but as a tendency arising from one's 'inner life' or nature.

> If crime is understood to be a kind of fatality, natural or economic, everybody will finally be suspected of some special predestination to it. [. . . And] in a moment it can switch to a decision to liquidate not only all actual criminals but all who are 'racially' predestined to commit certain crimes. Such changes take place whenever the legal and political machine is not separated from society so that social standards can penetrate into it and become political and legal rules. (OT: 81)

The 'social standards' Arendt is referring to here that would legalise liquidation of criminal types are those social 'norms' of a 'criminal' society imbued with violence, racism and homophobia. What is particularly disturbing about this part of Arendt's genealogy of totalitarianism is that this criminalisation of particular so-called 'deviant' identities was happening in a fledgling democracy – 1930s Germany – and it is a kind of biopolitical normalisation of identity that happens in relatively robust democracies today.

To reiterate, there are two features of these precursory 'elements' of totalitarianism that Arendt's analysis of the rise of the social is designed to explain. First, under certain forms of normalising biopolitics operative within liberal democracies, individuals may be conditioned and subjected to a point where they are not only inadvertently complicit in their own subjection, but also those individuals not directly targeted as 'abnormal' may end up tacitly condoning, or remaining indifferent to, the rejection, eviction or elimination of the so-called 'abnormal' from 'society' or the nation. Second, Arendt's analysis explains how this normalisation is tantamount to the biopolitical suppression and eventual destruction of 'spontaneity' or the elimination of the disclosure of natality from human activities. In *The Human Condition*, Arendt describes this destruction of natality in terms of 'force and violence' working to eliminate power as 'potentiality in being together' (HC: 199–206), which, we recall, is a generating energy consisting of the mutual disclosure of natality characteristic of public debate and action that opens human existence and the 'world' as unpredictable and boundless transformations. In contrast, force and violence destroy power of action by destroying the disclosure of natality, or what Arendt also calls 'spontaneity'. We examine in sections II and III below how totalitarianism destroys the event of natality through a new form of 'power' specific to totalitarian organisation (which Arendt calls the 'force of movement'). The point we make here is that in Arendt's account of the rise of the social discussed so far she has provided an insightful account of how seemingly banal forms of biopolitical normalisation can display elements that can be seen in retrospect as preconditions for totalitarianism. Less apparent here is any account of the *mechanics of the kind of normalisation producing conformity* prior to the emergence of techniques of terror and explicit violence. In Chapter 4 we discuss further how Arendt explains this kind of normalisation or 'coordination' of the population in her later work on conscience, moral judgement and responsibility. For now, we turn to Foucault's accounts of normalisation and regularisation through disciplinary power and biopower. The primary difference between their accounts is that, because for Foucault there is no 'outside' of power, he does not have recourse to Arendt's idea of 'spontaneity', natality or power as 'potentiality of being together' as an explanation for how normalisation in both senses can be thwarted through political action. As we will see, while his accounts of normalisation and regularisation fill in some of the gaps in Arendt's political ontology, he fails to pick up on some of her crucial insights about how some forms of biopolitics can lead to totalitarianism and genocide.

While Foucault does not acknowledge any debt to Arendt, his idea of disciplinary power and his account of the operation of biopower develop elements and themes central to some of Arendt's work. As discussed in Chapter 1, an obvious advantage of Foucault's account of disciplinary power, over those implied in Marxist and liberal political theory, is that he explains how subjection can occur without recourse to sovereign power, explicitly repressive techniques of government, obvious propaganda or explicit violence. His analysis thereby clarifies the kinds of political power involved in the two new mechanisms of normalisation that Arendt charts in her accounts of the rise of the social and pre-totalitarian biopolitics: the normalisation that produces conformity and the kind that singles out the so-called 'abnormal' for correction or worse. Also, we will show how Foucault spells out forms of power implicit in the phenomena that Arendt diagnoses where regulation of the 'life process' comes to dominate public life. Putting aside the differences between Foucault's notion of 'the event' and Arendt's idea of 'natality', which we discussed in Chapter 1, Foucault's discussions of power help to explain how political power mediates and can suppress 'the event' (in the sense of both the emergence of a new beginning and the mutual witnessing of unique distinctness of each other as human beings). In Foucault's account, this occurs not through prohibition of speech and action but through normalisation of bodies (through disciplinary power) and regularisation of biological 'life' (through biopower). This, according to Foucault, is how human beings can be conditioned and normalised by political power and social norms without us noticing, such that we participate in the subjection of others without necessarily meaning to.

Foucault takes up the first aspect of this account in *Discipline and Punish* (1979), where he explains in detail how surveillance and disciplinary techniques of power (operating throughout social and state institutions such as the home, schools, hospitals, the workplace) individualise human bodies, rendering them 'docile' and subjectivities compliant. Disciplinary power thereby forecloses 'agency' or 'the event', by producing subjectivities that are habitual, useful and self-regulating. This is Foucault's account of the production of what Arendt calls '*animal laborans*'. Discipline does this as a mode of productive power operating at the micro-level of the body's movements, spatiality and temporal rhythms to realign the body's forces and powers. Foucault summarises this pacifying process as follows:

> Discipline increases the forces of the body (in economic terms of utility) and diminishes these same forces (in political terms of obedience). In short, it dissociates power from the body; on the one hand, it turns it into an 'aptitude', a 'capacity', which

it seeks to increase; on the other hand, it reverses the course of the energy, the power that might result from it, and turns it into a relation of strict subjection. (Foucault 1979: 138)

Subjection and normalisation for Foucault, then, turn not so much on rendering the self passive, in the sense of negating what political theorists might understand as 'free will', but on the political harnessing the body's 'powers' and energy to form 'aptitudes' and habits that conform to prevailing social and economic ends. This is not a case of reducing the active body to mere 'biological life' or 'life process' driven by necessity or need. For Foucault, there is not a substrate of pure biology or nature, driven by necessity, that the person, stripped of the capacity to act with others, would be reduced to. Disciplinary power is productive and manipulative rather than prohibitive and repressive. Interestingly, in *The Origins of Totalitarianism* Arendt comes close to formulating this idea that political power works directly on the body (rather than on consciousness, thought or judgement) when she describes the extreme techniques for reducing interns of concentration camps to 'bare life' with the aim 'not to kill the body' but to 'manipulate' it 'in such a way as to make it destroy' what makes us human, that is, spontaneity or natality (OT: 453). But, as we will discuss in sections II and III, for Arendt this is an example of the operation of power as 'force of movement', which goes much further than normalisation by disciplining the body: it produces living corpses. Arguably, though, what Arendt exposes in her account is the essence of how natality may be eliminated through work on the body. Foucault just refines this idea in terms of the micro-operation of normalising power on the body so that it is applicable to the everyday non-totalitarian processes of normalisation. Nevertheless, Foucault's account also provides an explanation for how a population could be 'coordinated' to go along with the rise of totalitarian biopolitics and its hatred of difference.

The second kind of political power over 'life' that Foucault addresses is *biopower*, which, together with normalising techniques of discipline and surveillance, place human 'life' at the centre of politics in liberal democracies. Foucault's accounts of biopolitics (which he describes at one point as a 'governmentality' that meshes the 'state' with 'the population' – Foucault 2007: 116) more obviously resemble Arendt's account of the operation of normalising political power in the social precursors of totalitarianism insofar as the initial aim of biopower is not to train the individual body, but the 'regularisation' and correction of the person's biological identity in relation to the biological 'life' of the population. Foucault's detailed explanation of the emergence in the nineteenth century of a nexus between political power, categories of identity, biology and health is sufficiently similar, conceptually, to Arendt's accounts of the rise of the social that a summary of the main points will suffice for our purposes of comparison. In *The History of Sexuality, Volume I* (1980a), before his brief discussion of biopower, Foucault elaborates the self-identifying (subjectifying) techniques of power, such as 'confession', that pervade the medical and social sciences that emerged in the nineteenth century. These techniques of power divide populations into normal and abnormal in terms of an identity tied to some aspect of the person's organic, visible and/or behavioural being (sex, madness, race, sexuality, health and so on) and are techniques through which people come to identify themselves in terms of the prevailing norms of identity only to be targeted for 'correction' if they are considered 'abnormal'. One key difference between Foucault's and Arendt's accounts (although of little philosophical consequence) is that

Foucault's primary example of the normalisation of identity in *The History of Sexuality, Volume I* is sexuality, whereas Arendt's focus in *The Origins of Totalitarianism* is racial identity, or rather Jewish identity, and other categories of identity that came to be deemed deviant, alien or criminal in Nazi Germany. We note, though, that Foucault certainly mentions race and gender as key targets of biopower in that text (Foucault 1980a: 136–7). Second, a more substantial difference is that Foucault claims that, by the end of the nineteenth century, bio*politics* pervaded the medical and social sciences and all spheres of human life and is not *essentially* a threat to democratic plurality, whereas Arendt, in *The Human Condition* at least, laments the reverse, what she considers to be a comprehensive invasion of the political *by* the biopolitics of 'life processes'.

With regard to his account of *biopower*, Foucault indirectly clarifies two aspects of Arendt's account, in *The Human Condition*, of how management of 'life processes' consumes the politics of modernity. First, he develops the idea, particularly in *Society Must Be Defended*, that the target of biopower is beyond the individual body–identity it seems to aim at (whether in terms of sexuality, race or health). The actual target of biopower is the biological processes of the 'species body' – with the aim of improvement of the 'life' of the human species – and so it operates through political concerns about the health or the well-being of the 'population' (Foucault 2003: 253). This is a more developed account of what Arendt had observed in *The Human Condition* about the normalising effect of the turn to population statistics and behaviourism in the social sciences. As we will see in section II, in *The Origins of Totalitarianism* Arendt also argues that political power gradually came to target biological processes beyond individual identity, but in the form of the 'masses', a concept which is subtly different to that of population. Interestingly, Foucault locates the target of biopower on the border between the socio-political (*bios*) and the natural (*zoe*), in that he describes 'population' as a 'man-as-species' but also a 'social' body (Foucault 2003: 343). This means that, for him, biopolitics aims at management of the 'population' as a set of '*natural* processes' (Foucault 2007: 351; emphasis added) that are enmeshed with *social* norms. This management proceeds by tracking and correcting birth and death rates, trends in health and illness, ageing and reproduction, but also economic phenomena that are 'social' but that have come to be understood in terms of processes that are considered 'natural', for example wealth accumulation (Foucault 2007: 350–2). With regard to the latter point, given that both Arendt and Foucault critically analyse the intertwining of the rise of biopolitics and the (neo-)liberal free-market economy, they would not be surprised by a current boom in 'egg freezing' (or oocyte cryopreservation) at any cost ($11,000 in 2017) in private fertility clinics in the US, where the preservation, 'banking' and enhancement of the life (but only the 'life' of the wealthy) is not only viewed as 'natural' but also a legitimate and highly lucrative business that stock market analysts on Wall Street view as 'ripe for a merger and acquisition cycle'.[5] Foucault's main point is that via public health and hygiene policies, public and private management of human reproduction, food and drugs, contagious disease control, and so on, biopower aims to enhance or decrease (that is, 'regularise') these biological or 'natural' processes across the population (Foucault 2003: 243–5). Foucault argues, again similarly to Arendt, that the management of these processes through techniques of power represents 'nothing less than the entry of life into history, that is, the entry [. . .] of the *life of the human species* into the order of knowledge and power, into the sphere of political techniques' (Foucault 1980a: 141–2, emphasis added). By the end of the nineteenth century, it was 'life more than the law that became the issue of political struggles', even if this was misleadingly formulated in terms of individual 'rights', the right to 'life, to one's body, to health, to happiness, to the satisfaction of needs' (Foucault 1980a: 145).

Crucially, for Foucault, biopower is just as effective as discipline at foreclosing the 'event' (natality and plurality in Arendt's terminology) in human relations within liberal democracies. Foucault directly echoes Arendt's concerns about how categorisation by 'biological identity' can lead to discrimination against difference from an implicit norm when he describes how biopower, through practices that attend to population health and welfare, aims at curtailing 'unpredictable', 'random events' and at 'achieving overall equilibrium' in a population, with the promise of protecting 'the security of the whole from internal dangers' (Foucault 2003: 249). It is in this 'regularisation of life' by biopower that discrimination is at play. Judgements about 'normal' and 'abnormal' and about which biological and random events, and which kinds of life present a 'danger' to the population get aligned with discriminatory norms of race, sex, sexual reproduction, family, sexuality, body size, national identity and so on. While Foucault's main published account (originally in 1976) of the operation of biopower focuses on discourses of sexuality, in his 1975 lecture course (published eventually as *Society Must Be Defended*) he shows how biopolitics depends centrally on racism (Foucault 2003: 254).[6] At one level this means that, in the effort to achieve 'equilibrium' in biological processes across a population, the state ends up aiming to optimise 'a state of life' which, when combined with the ideal of uniformity across a population, starts to look like aiming

NORMALISING BIOPOLITICS AND TOTALITARIANISM

for racial purity (Foucault 2003: 246). Whatever the categories at play, Foucault notes that this operation of biopower relies on people self-identifying within its terms (of race, sexuality, religion, health, fertility and so on), a practice Arendt identifies in the precursors of totalitarianism to do with identity and that Foucault explains in terms of subjectifying practices of surveillance and 'confession'.

A second feature of biopolitics that Foucault highlights and clarifies, besides the idea that its target are the 'aleatory and unpredictable' biological processes of a human species, is that biopower is a modern version of the state assuming the *right of power over life and death*. That biopolitics is fundamentally about a non-sovereign, but state-centred, right of power over life and death is important for understanding the key contribution Arendt has made to understanding how normalising but non-totalitarian biopolitics can crystallise into totalitarian genocide. While sovereign power (which, according to Foucault, dominated industrialised nations up until the nineteenth century) amounts to the 'right of life and death [which] is actually the right [of the sovereign] to kill' (Foucault 2003: 240), biopower is the right to life and death transferred to the state, where 'power's objective is essentially to *make live* [and . . .] *let die*' (Foucault 2003: 254, emphasis added). Or, as he explains in *The History of Sexuality, Volume I*, by the nineteenth century the 'ancient right to *take* life or *let* live was replaced by the power to *foster* life or *disallow* it to the point of death' (Foucault 1980a: 138). There are two main points Foucault is making in this contrast between sovereign power and biopower. First, sovereign power is the *explicit*, external, top-down exercise of the power of the sovereign (or ruling class) to kill members of the populace as required to protect the ruler's or state sovereignty (as in Hobbes's political theory, for instance).

In contrast, biopower, like discipline, is a less visible and more subtle form of state control of life and death that is characteristic of liberal democracy. Biopower proliferates precisely because it manifests not as an exercise of political power but as fostering life through concern for the health, well-being and the quality of 'life' of people. The second key difference between sovereign power and biopower lies in the nature of the 'life' that is at stake in each. Under sovereign power, the right to life, or the 'life' to be preserved, is that of the sovereign/ruler or the sovereignty of the nation state. The ruler has the right to put to death any member of the populace as necessary to preserve the ruler's own life, either indirectly through war (where the lives of the people are sacrificed for the sake of preserving the life of the leader) or directly, in retribution for threatening the sovereign's rule. In contrast, under the exercise of biopower in liberal democracies, the ruling class no longer has the right to kill citizens (the practice of capital punishment in the US is highly anomalous in this regard) because the 'life' at stake in democratic polities is not that of the sovereign but the 'life' of the population.

Foucault's point is that while biopower is a less visible operation of political power than the sovereign right to kill, it constitutes, alongside disciplinary power, a more thorough-going form of *state-centred political power over human life*, which has thereby become 'managed' at every level in ways envisaged by Arendt. Moreover, even though power is organised in liberal democracies around the political investment and regulation of human *life* rather than around the threat of death, death still serves a political function. From the perspective of a citizen, death is the 'limit' of state power, 'the moment that escapes' power (hence the growing political interest in, and state and church opposition to, suicide and euthanasia beginning in the

nineteenth century) (Foucault 1980a: 138–9). From the perspective of the state, the right to kill has been supplanted by the
right to 'disallow' or 'let die' any life that is considered unviable
or a threat to the life of the general population (which is how
war is now justified). It is around the newer political function
of death that, according to Foucault, more obvious forms of
discrimination can occur in liberal democratic polities. Indeed,
Foucault goes so far as saying that, if genocide can be viewed as
a 'dream of modern powers' apparent from the early twentieth
century, 'this is not because of a recent return of the ancient
right to kill; it is because power is situated and exercised at the
level of life, the species, the race, and the large-scale phenomena
of the population' (Foucault 1980a: 137).

In a direct echo of the conclusion to Arendt's analysis of the
social precursors to totalitarian biopolitics, Foucault discusses
how the power to decide what life should be fostered and
what should be left to die is where racism enters biopolitics.
Indeed, Foucault defines racism as the primary 'way of introducing a break into the domain of life that is under power's
control: the break between what must live and what must die'
(Foucault 2003: 254). Subdividing the human species into
different races (as a form of innate identity) and the emergence
of a 'hierarchy of races' have become an especially dominant
form of political control of life in democratic polities (Foucault
2003: 255). Foucault describes how biopolitics can work against
particular races or groups *within* a population that, for biological
or 'scientific' reasons, are viewed as a threat to the optimum
life of the population. While the genocide unleashed by the
Nazi regime is the extreme example, arguably many contemporary public health campaigns (like the 'Northern Territory
Intervention' into Indigenous communities in 2007 in Australia,

or forced sterilisation of native American women in the 1970s and 1980s in the US, which we return to in Chapter 3) are examples in democratic regimes of Indigenous people's rights being suspended under the rationale of improving the health of their children (the Australian example) or 'optimising' (that is, reducing) the size of the Indigenous population (the US example). Ladelle McWhorter (2009) deftly reworks Foucault's approach to biopolitics to extend this idea of biopolitical racism to the endless range of 'biological identities' implied in Arendt's analysis. In her compelling genealogy of 'scientific racism' in the US, especially since the Second World War, McWhorter demonstrates how racist, heterosexist, sexist, and able-ist discourses intertwine to 'normalize individuals and regulate populations' in a way that facilitates the 'elimination' from the population of *anyone*, though especially, but not exclusively, 'black people', who become viewed as biologically 'abnormal' or 'deviant' (McWhorter 2009: 14, 90, 239). Foucault also ties this racism to the way war is waged and justified since the nineteenth century: the state's right to put one's own citizenry at risk of death through war is rationalised in biolopolitical terms of protecting the life of 'our' population from an 'inferior race' *external* to it (Foucault 2003: 255). However, what is missing from Foucault's analysis of biopolitics, as we show in Chapter 3, is the relationship between biopolitical 'racism', in the broader sense, operating in these examples and the biopolitical suppression of women's reproductive self-determination in what Arendt refers to as the first order of the birth of new beginnings.

Foucault's work on disciplinary power and biopower allows us to clarify Arendt's account of the totalitarian elements in normalising biopolitics characteristic of the rise of the social. And his accounts of disciplinary power and biopower have certainly revolutionised the way we understand the operation of regimes of subjection and discrimination in contemporary liberal democracies and in population health. But he fares less well in dealing with the extreme endpoint of biopolitics, that is, totalitarian genocide. In his brief discussion of Nazism, Foucault again echoes Arendt in suggesting that both disciplinary power and biopower 'permeated, underpinned, Nazi society' and that '[c]ontrolling the random element inherent in bio-logical processes was one of the regime's immediate objectives' (Foucault 2003: 259). But his explanation of how all-pervasive biopolitics could tip into totalitarian genocide, where all Nazis were gradually granted, and willingly took up, the right to kill, is too swift and ultimately unsatisfactory: he suggests that in this case the state-centred biopolitical right to 'let die' somehow mutated into 'must die' and finally back into the 'old sovereign right to take life' or to kill (Foucault 2003: 259). According to Foucault, in the case of Nazi society 'murderous power and sovereign power are unleashed throughout the entire social body' with the objective not so much of the 'destruction of other races' as achieving absolute obedience and confirming the superiority of its own race by exposing the entire population to death (Foucault 2003: 259–60).

As we will argue in section II, Arendt's discussion of totali-tarian organisation and terror and, in particular, her definition of 'unprecedented' totalitarian power in terms of the 'force of movement' provide a different, and we think more compelling, account of *how* biopolitical normalisation and state-sanctioned 'hatred of difference' of all kinds can turn into 'total domination' without recourse to dictatorial government or sovereign power. Unlike Foucault, Arendt's genealogy of totalitarianism provides a detailed diagnosis of specific techniques of organisation, a kind of biopower in the form of the 'force of movement' and, eventually, 'experiments' in 'total domination' in the concentration camps. In so doing she accounts both for the historical biopolitical precedents of totalitarianism, some of which are discussed in this section, and for the crystallisation of those elements into the 'event' of totalitarianism, her analysis of the 'most gruesome face' of which, as Dorota Glowacka points out, 'predates seminal reflections' by other scholars of the Holocaust 'by almost two decades' (Glowacka 2013: 41).

II. The Genocidal Biopolitics of Totalitarian Movement

As we have shown in section I, even though Arendt does not use the term 'biopolitics', she makes normalising biopolitics, anti-Semitism and hatred of difference in general the centre of her analysis of the social preconditions of totalitarianism. In this section we focus on the biopolitical and genocidal character of totalitarianism itself, where the state's power to 'foster life' and 'let die' turns into a biopolitics of living death. As Arendt puts it, in totalitarianism 'the most intimate details of [. . .] life and death depend upon political decisions' (OT: 409). Such an investment of power in all aspects of life and death is an extreme form of biopolitics, where human existence is reduced to biological life and where natality is eliminated entirely. For Arendt, the eradication of natality, which is synonymous with the destruction of the human as such, is possible only under the conditions of *total domination*, by which she means a *specific heightened manifestation of biopower*, as indicated in her penultimate claim:

> Total domination, which strives to organize the infinite plurality and differentiation of human beings as if all of humanity were

just one individual, is possible only if each and every person can be reduced to a never-changing identity of reactions, so that each of these bundles of reactions can be exchanged at random for any other. (OT: 438)

Our analysis of Arendt's account of totalitarian biopolitics specifically takes issue with Agamben's interpretation of Arendt. While Agamben is one of the few philosophers who acknowledge Arendt as the first thinker of biopolitics, he limits her contributions to the analysis of 'the social' in *The Human Condition* and claims that her earlier interpretation of totalitarianism lacks a biopolitical perspective (Agamben 1998: 120). Thus, in order to understand the relationship between biopolitics and totalitarianism, Agamben proposes to negotiate between Foucault's biopolitics, which ignores the Nazi death camps, and Arendt's analysis of totalitarianism, which (according to Agamben) ignores biopolitics. And he proposes his own analysis of sovereignty and 'bare life' as a means of such mediation. By contrast, we examine how Arendt opens a new approach to biopolitics that accounts for totalitarianism and its culmination in the death camps, without relying on the logic of sovereignty, upon which Agamben's work depends, and which, as mentioned above, slips back into Foucault's account of the genocidal extreme of biopolitics.[7]

Instead of relying on a notion of sovereignty, Arendt explains the transformation of normalising biopolitics (of the kind discussed in section I) into totalitarian genocide by analysing how the totalitarian elements of its precursors – the history of anti-Semitism, the biopolitical normalisation of social identity, the human remnants of imperialism and colonialism – are brought together by the dynamic and never-ending 'force of movement' that aims for total domination (OT: 417–19). Arendt describes this 'absolute primacy of the movement' as 'an entirely new and unprecedented concept of power' (OT: 412, 417). In her genealogy of totalitarianism, Arendt diagnoses the emergence of this self-accelerating movement of domination, characterised by 'expansion for expansion's sake' (OT: 131), not in the older formation of sovereignty but in the rise of imperialism in the nineteenth century. As discussed in Chapter 1 (in an analysis of Hobbes's philosophy of death, violence and expansion), imperialism, while economic in its origins, becomes political when the export of the surplus of capital is accompanied by the export of both superfluous labour and governmental power in order to colonise new territories (OT: 150). However, in totalitarianism, the acceleration of domination is purged of all economic, national or class interests (OT: 410–19). By separating itself from the political and economic character of imperialism, the totalitarian 'force of movement' nonetheless preserves one of its features – the never-ending expansion for expansion's sake.

In Arendt's analysis, we argue, the totalitarian 'force of movement' is generated by the biopolitical technologies of total domination: the 'ruthless' techniques of mass organisation (OT: 410), terror, the extermination of the 'objective enemies' and, ultimately, the destruction of the human in the concentration and death camps. These technologies 'use socialism and racism by emptying them of their utilitarian content, the interests of a class or nation' (OT: 348). Instead, they aim to 'liberate' and 'accelerate' the movement of nature or history from all institutional constraints, positive laws, utilitarian calculations and, in the last resort, from the impediment of human actions of any kind by extreme political/genocidal means (OT: 466). Even the biopolitical 'regularisation' of the life process of the population, analysed by Foucault, is no longer sufficient to remove the unpredictable consequences of human actions. Consequently, the main objective of totalitarian acceleration of the force of movement is the destruction of natality as such: that is, the eradication of the spontaneity, action, difference (OT: 405) and 'uniqueness' of all persons (OT: 454), so that they can be turned into interchangeable, superfluous 'specimens'.

Arendt distinguishes the two totalitarian regimes of the twentieth century – Nazism and Stalinism – in terms of different kinds of 'laws' of the movement: either natural, based on biological racism (Nazism), or historical determinism, based on a notion of 'dying classes' (Stalinism). While she accounts for the specificity of Nazism and Stalinism, she ultimately concludes that the biopolitical/genocidal movement of total domination makes the distinction between history and nature, or *bios* and *zoe*, irrelevant. This is because totalitarianism aims to radically alter both nature and history and make them indistinguishable: both nature and history are viewed as ruled by the 'objective laws' of linear movements, which genocidal biopolitics aims to accelerate. As a result, in totalitarian regimes history becomes naturalised and nature – politicised. As both Foucault and Arendt point out, even class in the Stalinist regime starts to function in a manner similar to biological racism once the 'purity' of proletarian origins is emphasised and the remnants of other classes are seen as 'the dying', that is, condemned to death by history itself. However, in order to accelerate natural or historical development, totalitarian biopolitics aims to have all 'life' and 'death' totally determined by the 'objective laws' of these movements.

As these preliminary remarks indicate, Arendt is the first thinker to argue that totalitarian biopolitical techniques are dynamic rather than static and therefore cannot be understood in terms of any stable structures of power centred on the state or a ruler (no matter how despotic totalitarian regimes appear to be). Different from tyranny, sovereignty, dictatorship, imperialism or any other previous political forms of domination, the site of this operation of power is the biopolitical/genocidal acceleration of the 'force of movement'[8] liberated from human and institutional constraints and embodied in every stage and every element of the totalitarian regime: from its initial techniques of mass organisation to the function of totalitarian terror; from totalitarian ideology to the 'experimental' production of the new 'species' in the concentration and death camps. What follows is an examination of two aspects of such dynamic technologies of totalitarian biopower: (1) techniques of integrating the masses into mobile totalitarian organisations during a regime's struggle for power; and (2) how terror functions as the very 'essence' of genocidal biopolitics once totalitarianism takes hold.

The deadly dynamism of totalitarian biopolitics is already evident in the techniques of organising the masses. In the early stages of totalitarian regimes these techniques mobilise anti-Semitism, racial supremacy or Stalinist classless society as 'organizational devices' (OT: 378) in order to institute the new 'scientific' principle of collectivity based either on biological race purity or on natural/historical class purity. As Arendt puts it, totalitarianism 'succeed[s] in organizing masses – not classes, like the old interest parties of the Continental nation-states; not citizens with opinions about, and interests in, the handling of public affairs, like the parties of Anglo-Saxon countries' (OT: 308). In order to account for the specificity of these genocidal/biopolitical organisational techniques, first we have to distinguish between different forms of collectivity in Western modernity, in particular between citizenship, population and the modern masses, because it is the masses rather than citizens, or populations, who are susceptible to totalitarian organisation. What is at stake in these distinctions are the crucial implications, often ignored in biopolitical theories, of Arendt's analysis: namely, the claim that the disintegration of political relations, human plurality and the democratic institutions that protect this plurality facilitates fascism and totalitarianism. And conversely, political plurality, relational agency and community, which we discuss in Chapter 1, are important sources of resistance to totalitarian biopolitics.

The notion of 'the masses', so frequently discussed at the beginning of the twentieth century, differs in important ways from Foucault's idea of 'population'. As we have discussed in section I, as a target of biopower, population is 'social' and biological. 'Population' consists in the 'society' of 'life processes' and normalised identities of Arendt's analyses, which Foucault describes as 'the horizon of social naturalness' or the 'human species' (Foucault 2007: 350). This means, as Foucault argues in his lecture course *Security, Territory, Population*, that population is explicitly distinguished from any collective political organisation or community. Biopolitics, as we have seen, operates on a different level: the state's role with regard to the population, understood as a conglomeration of 'natural processes', is to 'manage and no longer to control through rules and regulations' (Foucault 2007: 353). To her own analyses of the 'management' of these 'life processes', Arendt adds another precursor to totalitarianism: the emergence of the modern *masses*. The masses are neither a social body of a population nor a political organisation of citizens, nor an economic class structure, but the dispersed remnants of the disintegration of communal and political bonds, destroyed by 'the upheavals of unemployment, inflation, war', or statelessness.[9] This disintegration of political membership and community, or what we might call in terms of *The Human*

Condition the destruction of human plurality, can be either the effect of political economy – for example, the disintegration of the nation states and the loss of citizenship in the age of Western imperialism – or the effect of deliberate political violence – for example, the destruction of Lenin's system of the councils by the Stalinist regime (OT: 321–2) – or, to note a contemporary example, the destruction of political opposition in Syria by the Assad regime. In the aftermath of such disintegration, the masses represent isolated individuals 'in their essential homelessness' (OT: 352), who exist outside of all political, economic and social relationships (OT: 311, 317).

The only positive characteristic of the masses is their numerical magnitude. Like a perversion of the mathematical sublime, characterised according to Kant by the numerical magnitude that overwhelms our powers of representation, the masses consist of an unprecedented number of superfluous people. By 'superfluous' Arendt means something specific: the atomised individuals who make up the masses are so alienated and lacking even self-interest and self-preservation that they are replaceable and ultimately expendable (OT: 444, 455). Their world is so devoid of 'common sense', that is, a shared sense of 'reality', that they crave order, 'consistency' and simplicity in order to escape their current predicament (OT: 352). Such masses are ripe for totalitarian organisation and propaganda because they welcome any promise of consistency, certainty and a new reality. The nexus of biopolitics, racism and totalitarian organisational technologies enters politics to fill this vacuum left by the disintegration of political structures and relations, and introduces new means of mass organisation on the basis of life itself.

Combining Foucault's and Arendt's genealogies, then, we can say that, by the beginning of the twentieth century, 'the masses' alongside 'populations' are the two targets of biopolitical racism. Neither populations nor the masses can be explained in terms of national citizenship and state sovereignty. If the population is a target and effect of biopower 'regularising' biological processes in non-totalitarian regimes and normalising identities in societies displaying totalitarian tendencies (including German society in the early 1930s), the masses – the by-product of political and socio-economic disintegration – are the direct targets of the new techniques of totalitarian organisation. As Arendt puts it, the masses provide 'inexhaustible material to feed the power-accumulating and man-destroying machinery of total domination' (OT: 311).

Another important point of Arendt's argument is that the totalitarian organisation of the masses requires specific biopolitical techniques of power: first, novel organisational devices; and second, the operation of terror, which aims to eliminate randomness and unpredictability on both the collective and the individual levels. Totalitarian techniques of organisation aim to reintegrate dispersed superfluous individuals into a uniform, dynamic mass movement on the global scale and to fabricate a 'fictitious world' according to the lies of propaganda (OT: 420, 436, 438). We stress Arendt's emphasis on the organisational technologies because, for her, anti-Semitic propaganda and the claim of Aryan supremacy in Nazi Germany were not merely a means of engineering a collective identity, as Nancy and Lacoue-Labarthe claim in their erroneous interpretation of Arendt in their essay 'The Nazi myth' (Lacoue-Labarthe and Nancy 1990), but also the biopolitical techniques of dynamic mass organisation. As Arendt argues in her 1946 essay 'The image of hell' (EU: 197–205), without these 'techniques and technicians', 'without the means of fabricating a false reality according to a lying ideology', Nazi anti-Semitic propaganda would not have been able to destroy common sense (EU: 199, 202). That is why Arendt concludes that the 'forms of totalitarian organization [. . .] are designed to translate the propaganda lies of the movement, woven around a central fiction – the conspiracy of the Jews, or the Trotskyites, or 300 families, etc. – into a functioning reality, to build up, even under non-totalitarian circumstances, a society whose members act and react according to the rules of a fictitious world' (OT: 364).

The first and primary biopolitical principle underlying all such totalitarian organisation is a notion of *racial identity* and racial supremacy, mobilised as the 'biological', scientific law of both collective belonging and individual self-definition. This was exemplified in Nazi Germany, where the regime capitalised on the normalising process of biopolitical identification analysed in section I: each individual was required to search their family genealogy and prove the family's Aryan racial purity in order to belong to the movement. However, the genocidal consequence of the dynamic character of the movement required that the identity criteria for belonging became increasingly arbitrary and changeable. Indeed, in Nazi Germany, says Arendt, 'we find the notion of a racial "selection which can never stand still" [to quote Himmler's SS manual] thus requiring a constant radicalisation of the standards by which the selection, i.e., the extermination of the unfit, is carried out' (OT: 391). In the end it is not even the superiority of the German race that matters but the master Aryan race which is yet to be produced and to which only the SS belong (OT: 412).

The second organisational technique is the frequently discussed *'leader principle'* of the totalitarian movement. By rejecting notions of sovereign power, dictatorship or personality cult in order to explain the emergence of totalitarianism from a fledgling democracy, Arendt thoroughly reinterprets the leader principle in terms of the specific organisation of power. The centrality of the totalitarian leader is produced by the secret labyrinth of power rather than by the authoritarian structure of the hierarchical pyramid, with a clear chain of command stemming from the top, which, according to Arendt, may explain tyranny and dictatorships but cannot account for totalitarianism (OT: 405). Arendt also frequently describes the organisation that supports totalitarian leadership as having 'the structure of the onion' (BPF: 99 and OT: 413, 430) in order to distinguish totalitarian organisation of the masses from the authoritarian government characteristic of tyranny. Located in the empty centre of the onion-like structure, rather than outside or above, the totalitarian leader is surrounded by the multiple layers of membership, characterised by the different degrees of initiation into the secret knowledge of, and participation in, the criminal policies and plans for extermination (OT: 381). As Arendt points out, '[a]ll the extraordinarily manifold parts of the' totalitarian organisation and movement 'are related in such a way that each [layer] forms the façade' that 'plays the role of normal outside world for one layer and the role of radical extremism for another' (BPF: 99). Not only does this structure normalise an increasingly genocidal violence and hide it from the non-totalitarian world, but the deliberate confusion about the chain of command of intermediary power structures supports the centrality of the leader principle, because without clear hierarchical levels of mediation between the ruler and the masses everyone seems to be confronted with the will of the leader directly: the 'will of the Führer [which is] embodied everywhere and at all times' (OT: 405). Since the leader's will is thereby mysteriously everywhere (OT: 373) and assumes responsibility for all events, it maintains the submission of the masses while removing their responsibility: 'nobody ever experiences a situation in which he has to be responsible for his own actions or can explain the reasons for them' (OT: 375).[10] Hence, the leader principle is not based on dictatorship, sovereign power or even a charismatic personality but, as the party elites knew only too well, is a 'simple consequence' of this 'terrible efficiency of totalitarian organization' (OT: 387, 419).

A third technique of mass organisation, which generates the *self-accelerating momentum* of the totalitarian movement, is its expansion on the global scale beyond the limits of the state. All the technologies of power aim to sustain the dynamic character of the movement and avoid any capture within institutional structures of the state:[11] the 'totalitarian ruler must, at any price, prevent normalization from reaching the point where a new way of life could develop' (OT: 391). The international scope of modern anti-Semitism was a key element of this global expansion and was one of the reasons, in addition to the Nazi notion of racial supremacy, why it was 'the nucleus around which the fascist movement crystallized all over the world' (EU: 141). World war for the sake of racist supremacy or Soviet 'communism' is the more obvious means of such acceleration, but equally important is secrecy. To keep the dynamic momentum of power beyond the limitations of the state and to preclude any stability of political or administrative structures, totalitarianism deploys secrecy in order to confuse the masses about where the power of decision resides. Hence, as Arendt points out, many of its organisational techniques are borrowed from secret societies. For example, the confusing administrative labyrinth increases the effectiveness of the secret police and enhances the organisational efficiency of the movement because it enables arbitrary and rapid changes of policy and swift relocations of power. Consequently, if, in Arendt's analysis, biopolitics in non-totalitarian regimes replaces the public/private division with the rise of the social, in totalitarianism such division, and especially the possibility of public appearance of political agents, is destroyed by secrecy.

While the dynamic character of totalitarianism aims to prevent the stabilisation of political and administrative arrangements, it also increasingly normalises genocidal violence, virulent anti-Semitism, racism of all kinds and terror across the masses that are integrated into the population. Such normalisation of violence in totalitarian biopolitics builds upon but ultimately exceeds the three trends attending the rise of the social discussed in section I: the deformation of the political doctrine of equality and diversity into differentiation between the normal and abnormal; the emergence of a notion of immutable identity tied to a biological or organic trait; and the criminalisation of some identities, rather than acts. If biopower in non-totalitarian societies exhibits totalitarian tendencies in dividing 'life' into the normal and abnormal, virtue and vice, with the aim of regularising or eliminating unpredictability and abnormality, totalitarian biopower aims in part to normalise the criminal and murderous policies of the movement in order to prepare the ground for genocide and the Final Solution. As Agamben rightly points out, biopolitics in totalitarianism turns into thanatopolitics, in which mass murder and extermination become a new norm.[12]

If the first distinction between biopolitics in totalitarian and non-totalitarian regimes consists in secrecy and 'terrible efficiency' in organising the masses into a dynamic, self-accelerating movement, the second difference lies in the specificity of totalitarian terror, which leads to genocide and ultimately to the destruction of the human condition of natality as such. Whether tyrannical, despotic or revolutionary, terror is usually understood as 'unlawful' violence against political enemies in situations where military means are either lacking or impossible: thus political opponents use terror against what they perceive to be oppressive regimes, or despotic states use terror to subjugate hostile, suspect or undesirable groups (see, for example, Honderich 1995: 900). But, both Nazi and Stalinist regimes continued to deploy this kind of brutal terror after they had gained power and crushed all possibility of political resistance – which according to Arendt occurred 'about 1935 in Germany and approximately 1930 in Soviet Russia' (OT: 422). In doing so they unleashed a type of total terror previously unknown in human history, aimed at total control over the life and death of human existence.

In her 1953 radio address 'Mankind and terror' (EU: 297–306), and in the concluding chapter of *The Origins of Totalitarianism*, Arendt characterises the unprecedented violence of totalitarian terror in terms of its four key features. First, totalitarian terror does not aim for the subjugation of the regime's enemies; on the contrary, as total terror is unleashed after these regimes gain power and popular support, it targets a staggering number of entirely innocent people (EU: 299) – in Nazi Germany European Jewry and those who were considered 'unfit to live' and in Stalinist Russia whoever was classified as a member of one of the 'dying classes'. The second characteristic of totalitarian terror is that it remains entirely 'outside the category of means and ends' (EU: 303) – that is, from the point of view of military strategy and instrumental thinking, total terror is 'useless', since it targets its victims irrespective of their actions. Third, total terror, like the movement itself, is endless, since it does not stop with the victory of the regime but rather

146

begins with such victory: '[t]here is no end to the terror, and it is a matter of principle with such regimes that there can be no peace' (EU: 299). Terror stops only with the end of the regime. And finally, totalitarian terror cannot be explained by irrational hatred, sadism or unlawful violence: its terrifying novelty consists in its logicality and in its claim to execute the 'objective' laws determined by the 'forces of nature or history' (OT: 466).

As Dana Villa (1999: 16) notes, according to Arendt total terror, which is no longer instrumental, is the very 'essence' of totalitarianism (OT: 464), where the 'essence of government' is motion (OT: 466). Within the frame of biopolitical theory, we can define this 'essence' as the ongoing conversion of biopolitics into thanatopolitics, which targets biological life in its 'historical' (that is, human) dimension. What for Arendt makes totalitarian biopolitics indistinguishable from thanatopolitics is the fact that totalitarian genocide and the extermination of millions of innocent victims are inseparable from the total destruction of human agency, freedom and the human condition of natality. As Arendt puts it, terror aims to release the forces of history and nature from all the 'impediments' of human actions: '[t]otal terror, the essence of totalitarian government, exists neither for nor against men. It is supposed to provide the forces of nature or history with an incomparable instrument to accelerate their movement' (OT: 466). And whoever nature or history decides is unfit to live or belongs to a 'dying class' will be eliminated in the process. Since terror is supposed to accelerate and make more efficient genocidal 'forces' of natural or historical 'movement' (OT: 468–74), its operation is endless.

Because total terror accelerates the movement of both history and nature, it eliminates the disjunctive temporality (or the gap between the no longer and the not yet) characteristic of the event of natality. Total terror makes history indistinguish-able from the biopolitically engineered force of nature and, vice versa, transforms nature into historical development, acceler-ated by political means. Ultimately, it is totalitarian terror that erases the oppositions between nature and history, *zoe* and *bios*.[13] Thus, despite crucial ideological differences between the Nazi and Stalinist regimes, Arendt argues that in totalitarianism 'the movement of history and the movement of nature are one and the same' (OT: 463). The genocidal biopolitics of totalitarian-ism thus reverses the project of Western modernity aiming to dominate and transform nature into the product and the self-image of *Homo faber*. Instead, total domination aims to destroy both political and economic agency in order change humanity into a 'naturalised species', merely behaving according to the autonomous laws of natural history.

In order to make the biopolitical movement of history more efficient and autonomous, terror removes from its path the obstacles – Jews, 'inferior' races, 'deviants', the already 'dying classes' – which would have been eventually destroyed by the laws of historical/natural development, or so totalitarian logic suggests. Since terror executes the verdict of naturalised history, the multitudes of its innocent victims are labelled the 'objective' (rather than political or social) enemies of historical movement (OT: 424). In contradistinction to political enemies, who are targeted on the basis of their actions and convictions, the selection of 'objective' enemies does not depend on human motives, actions or political orientations but, rather, is supposedly dictated by historical or natural necessity. It is the genocidal logic of historical or natural development that declares particu-lar categories of innocent people – 'Jews, Eastern subhumans', the 'incurably sick', 'dying classes' or other undesirables (OT:

350) – as obstacles to its linear progression: 'practically speaking, this means that terror executes on the spot the death sentences which nature is supposed to have pronounced on races or individuals who are 'unfit to live', or history on 'dying classes', without waiting for the slower and less efficient processes of nature or history themselves' (OT: 466).

Insofar as they are supposedly condemned by the objective laws of history/nature, the notion of 'objective enemies' radicalises the social classification of the 'inferior types' carrying criminal or contaminating tendencies (discussed in section I) (OT: 422–5). In the context of totalitarianism, such classification appears too static, not capable of increasing the speed of violence and not 'objective' enough – that is, it is based on social norms and the categories of the social sciences rather than on supposedly autonomous historical laws. 'Objective enemies' do not merely represent a threat to society but, in the last instance, are obstacles to the movement of nature/history. That is why in totalitarianism the distinction between those who are viable and those who are unfit to live is constantly changing, and new categories of objective enemies have to be produced – otherwise, history or nature itself could come to an end (OT: 464). Since terror speeds up the movement of history, 'the people who are the executioners today can easily be transformed into the victims of tomorrow' (EU: 303) and the masses themselves, even party elites, can be targeted as objective enemies. Ultimately, anyone who retains a capacity to think and change their mind is a potential obstacle to totalitarian movement and thus a possible victim of terror.

The categorisation of innocent victims as 'objective enemies' reveals another unprecedented feature of totalitarian terror, namely its *logicality*. Rather than being a manifestation of irrational violence, hatred or sadism, total terror, Arendt argues, aims to produce a strict correspondence between the logical rules of argumentation, such as the law of non-contradiction, and the 'objective' laws of historical development. Once the 'logical necessity' is transferred from scientific thought to the domain of history, it becomes a form of rigid compulsion, since it abolishes the need to act or think differently.[14] Following the rules of logic, the entire biopolitical movement of history and nature is supposed to be governed by deduction from the single central premise of totalitarian ideology: racial supremacy, dying classes. Totalitarianism 'treats the course of events as though it followed the same "law" as the logical exposition of its "idea"' (OT: 469), although not the idea in the sense of the Platonic eternal form or the Kantian transcendental idea, which the totalitarian principle of history distorts. While totalitarian ideology formulates the '*logic* of an idea' (OT: 469, emphasis added), terror implements this logic in reality. Ultimately, for Arendt, the logicality of terror destroys the very possibility of a new beginning characteristic of natality: 'As terror is needed lest with the birth of each human being a new beginning arise [. . .] in the world, so the self-coercive force of logicality is mobilized lest anybody ever start thinking' (OT: 473). And conversely, as Arendt puts it, '[o]ver the beginning, no logic [. . .] can have any power' (OT: 473).

Because neither life nor history – and especially not actions – are predictable or 'logical', terror operates at once on the level of ideological pseudo-scientific explanations of history and on the level of reality, ensuring their strict correspondence. On the level of historical explanation, the logicality of totalitarian thinking achieves the 'emancipation of thought from experience' (OT: 471) by remaining self-referential and circular in its deductions; by closing itself to alternative explanations; by remaining doggedly consistent so that one explanation becomes a factual premise for other claims. Yet, totalitarianism does not stop at providing pseudo-scientific ideological explanations but deploys terror in order to manufacture history and nature to fit these explanations: '[t]he movement of history and the logical process [. . .] are supposed to correspond to each other, so that whatever happens, happens according to the logic of one "idea"' (OT: 469). Terror fabricates the frightening identification of history with logic by eliminating all the events and obstacles that might contradict it. Since the Nazi 'scientific' verdict was that Jews were 'unfit to live', the Final Solution was implemented. Since the Nazis claimed that Poles had no intelligence, Polish intellectuals had to be exterminated in order to remove this 'logical' contradiction. Following Arendt's analysis, we disagree therefore with Roberto Esposito's criticism that the logicality of violence is a wrong philosophical interpretation of totalitarianism (Esposito 2013: 103–7). What Esposito fails to take into account is the fact that, for Arendt, total terror functions not only on the level of historical explanation but also, as the technology of genocidal biopolitics, it operates on level of historical and biopolitical life.

The logicality of totalitarian terror transforms the claim that 'everything is possible' (total domination) into the assertion that 'everything is necessary'. In the context of totalitarianism, everything is possible means that there are neither objective obstacles nor human resistance to total domination. This means that objective laws of history/nature can be fully actualised, while the futural potentiality of action (discussed in Chapter 1) can be utterly eliminated. Generated by totalitarian organisation and terror, such total domination is nonetheless not arbitrary because ultimately it claims to be based on logical necessity.

According to modal logic, something is necessary when nothing is impossible. Totalitarianism transforms this negative logical formulation of necessity (nothing impossible) into a positive reality of power: 'everything is possible' means everything is necessary, and vice versa. In order to underscore this transformation of possibility into logical and historical necessity, Arendt claims that the essence of totalitarianism cannot be described by the claim that 'everything is permitted'. This formula ('everything is permitted') still implies a reference to morality, whereas totalitarianism replaces moral law and political actions with the logical compulsion of necessity.

Since the murderous violence of total terror aims to implement logical necessity, totalitarianism also eliminates the difference between lawlessness (the leader's arbitrary violence) and the scientific laws of history. This is the case because, despite the centrality of the leader principle, terror does not execute arbitrary personal decisions, but claims that these decisions manifest historical objective necessity (OT: 470). Consequently, according to Arendt, totalitarianism is not a tyranny or despotic state (based on lawlessness or the arbitrary will of a tyrannical ruler) but an entirely new form of government, which resolves the contradiction between the lawlessness of tyranny and lawful government. Although totalitarianism suspends or totally ignores constitutional law and human rights, it does so not for the sake of the regime's arbitrary violence (which would be lawlessness) but for the sake of the 'higher' law of nature and historical movement (which therefore represents a new type of lawfulness). This 'higher' law – the elimination of everything that is considered harmful and 'unfit to live' (OT: 471) or that obstructs the movement of history – ceases to be a stabilising institutional context for the dynamic and innovative power of human speech and action. On the contrary, by eliminating any possibility of any new beginning and action, totalitarian law itself becomes the only 'legitimate' force of movement – the linear, causal force of biological and historical determinism.

However, in order to manufacture life according to the logic of totalitarianism, the biopolitical transformation of human nature is required. Especially, what needs to be utterly destroyed is the basic human condition of natality in all its manifestations. In order to destroy natality, the unprecedented genocidal logic of total terror has to engineer a *new species*, behaving or, more precisely, reacting according to the immanent logic of historical/natural necessity: 'Precisely because man's resources are so great, he can be fully dominated only when he becomes a specimen of the animal-species man' (OT: 457). Aside from her novel account of how normalising biopolitics in a democracy can morph into totalitarianism without the explicit exercise of sovereign power or dictatorial force, what sets Arendt's diagnosis of totalitarian biopower apart from Foucault, Esposito and Agamben[15] is her novel account of the biopolitical *experiment* of the totalitarian regime, aiming to fabricate what does not yet exist: a new human/animal 'species' reducible only to 'bundle[s] of reactions' interchangeable with any other animal (OT: 438, 456). Such a monstrous experiment not only introduces the genocidal division between the superior races and those who 'are unfit to live' but ultimately, by eliminating all 'individuals for the sake of the species' (OT: 465), destroys natality as such.

Before moving to Arendt's analysis of such a deadly biopolitical experiment in the concentration and death camps, a brief note follows on the difference between Foucault's and Arendt's use of the term 'species' in these texts. For Foucault 'species' refers to the biological life of a 'population', which is the target of biopower in both totalitarian and non-totalitarian regimes. Also, for Foucault totalitarianism is the result of the fusion of normalising aspects of disciplinary power and biopower and biopolitical racism with the 'old sovereign right to take life' or to kill (Foucault 2003: 259), which *divides the human species into those who must live and those who must die.* Arendt, on the other hand, uses the term 'species' to refer to the new 'human species' the Nazi regime tried to manufacture in the concentration and death camps, a possibility conceivable only under totalitarian conditions of 'total domination', as she understands this term. Consequently, in Arendt's analysis the genocidal deployment of anti-Semitism, biological racism or the notion of already 'dying classes' is far more pernicious than 'introducing a break into the domain of life [. . .] between what must live and what must die' (as Foucault defines biopower in totalitarianism – Foucault 2003: 254), because it destroys the natality and plurality characteristic of the human condition. Totalitarian biopolitics no longer in-dividualises but, on every level of its operation – organisational technologies, terror, concentration camps – is entirely totalis-ing and lethally productive. Its inversion into thanatopolitics dispenses with the compulsion to 'make live' by making both executioners and the victims of terror utterly superfluous.

III. Sovereignty, Bare Life, the Camps

As we have seen, the aim of racial terror is total domination and fabrication of what does not yet exist: the new animal/human 'species' of life that exhibits no spontaneity, plurality or dif-ferentiation (OT: 438) and that is reducible to a 'bundle[s] of reactions' interchangeable with any other animal (OT: 438,

456). In this section we argue that Arendt's analysis of the totalitarian biopolitics of this new 'species' makes her the first thinker
of what Agamben calls 'bare life'. To be sure, Arendt does not
use this specific formulation, but deploys three related terms: the
production of the new species incapable of resistance in Nazi and
Stalinist concentration camps; 'living corpses' as the final stage
of dehumanisation in the camps (OT: 447, 451); and the pre-
totalitarian precursor of this dehumanisation, namely, 'abstract
nakedness' (which we will call 'naked existence'), characterising
the plight of stateless people and refugees (OT: 297). However,
although Arendt's notions of naked life, 'human species' and
the living corpse resonate with Agamben's concept of bare life,
we nonetheless stress two crucial differences of their respective
accounts. The first decisive difference is that, for Agamben, bare
life is the target of sovereign violence in the entire history of
Western politics, whereas, for Arendt, statelessness and living
corpses in concentration camps are unprecedented biopolitical
phenomena, which cannot be explained in terms of sovereignty.
The second difference is that Arendt makes the distinction
between the extreme vulnerability of the naked existence
of the refugees and the production of the 'living dead' in the
concentration camps, whereas Agamben describes both of
these catastrophes in terms of bare life. What is at stake in the
distinction between different forms of bare life – in Arendt's
case, the difference between statelessness and the inmates of the
concentration camps – is not only the specificity of the totalitarian camps, but also the eradication of spontaneity and all aspects
of human 'agency', including that of resistance.

Before engaging Arendt's argument in greater detail, let
us begin with Agamben's biopolitics of bare life. As Ziarek
(2008) discusses in more detail elsewhere, Agamben adds to the

Aristotelian distinction between biological existence (*zoe*) and the political life of speech and action (*bios*) a new term, 'bare life'.[16] Neither a natural life nor a politically constituted life, bare life is an effect of extreme political destitution: it refers to damaged bodies stripped of their political/cultural significance and exposed to murderous violence, which does not count as crime. This extreme vulnerability and destitution of bare life point to another dimension of biopolitics: different from the disciplinary normalisation of bodies, the normalisation of identities in the rise of the social, the management of the population or totalitarian organisation of the masses, the fabrication of bare life is based on the total destruction of the diverse socio-political power relations, norms and modalities of living, or, in Arendt's terms, of both 'what-ness' and 'who-ness' (*bios*). As Agamben puts it, the political character of such existence consists only in its exclusion from the political. For Agamben, bare life is therefore a constitutive exception, the exclusion of which constitutes the political realm.

Where Agamben and Arendt differ is, first of all, in their explanations of the violence that produces bare life. For Agamben the expulsion and the production of bare life is the essential aspect of sovereignty, whereas for Arendt it is an effect of statelessness (and thus the loss of national sovereignty), on the one hand, and the consequence of the crystallisation of totalitarian elements apparent in the precursors of totalitarianism into fully fledged 'totalitarian domination', on the other. In the history of Western political thought, the power of sovereignty is characterised in two inter-related ways: the power to kill or the monopoly on violence (as in Hobbes's political philosophy and as analysed by Foucault and Arendt), and the decision on the state of exception, for example on the state of emergency (stressed, for example, by

Schmitt and Agamben). For Schmitt and Agamben, the supreme sovereign will is authorised by the law to exceed or suspend the law in situations of emergency. The monopoly on violence (on decisions about who must live and who must die) and the capacity to suspend the law in the state of emergency manifest the power of sovereign decision. For Agamben, these character-istics of sovereignty are intertwined with the production of bare life. By suspending the constitution or eliminating human rights in the state of emergency, the sovereign decision in modern democracies has the power to reduce the life of citizens to bare life, stripped of political attributes. And conversely, because bare life is a target of the sovereign monopoly on violence, the killing of such life does not constitute murder or homicide.

Since bare life is interconnected with the sovereign decision on the state of emergency and the use of violence, it reveals for Agamben the hidden biopolitical structure of sovereignty, which, he claims, in contrast to Foucault and Arendt, is apparent from antiquity to present (Agamben 1998: 71–91). What is different in totalitarianism, according to Agamben, is that the sovereign decision on the state of exception is no longer in response to any factual danger, but declares a permanent state of emergency (Agamben 1998: 168–9). Moreover, since sovereign power in totalitarianism derives its legitimacy directly from the life of the people, each sovereign decision on emergency declares at the same time what constitutes viable forms of col-lective life – for example, the German people – and on what life is no longer worthy of living – for example, Jewish life. (On this point about legitimacy, Agamben concurs with Arendt's claim that in totalitarianism the Führer is not a dictator because in his person the law and life supposedly coincide.) The permanent state of emergency (which becomes a new norm) and the decision on what kinds of lives are unworthy of living account for the extension of sovereignty from politics into medicine and science. According to Agamben, such an expansion of sovereign power establishes for the first time the absolute biopolitical space in the concentration and death camps (Agamben 1998: 123). Hence, this new meaning of sovereignty constitutes for Agamben the new meaning of biopolitics, summarised by Arendt's claim that in totalitarianism everything is possible. It is in the camps that a temporary state of emergency is transformed into a permanent territorial arrangement. (For Agamben, the camp is the new political element added to the territory, law and birth, characterising nation states.) And the exceptional status of bare life becomes a new thanatopolitical norm of modernity in that, for Agamben, despite their horrific novelty, the camps reveal the hidden biopolitical paradigm of modernity (Agamben 1998: 124).

Alexander Weheliye (2014) is right to criticise Agamben's generalisation of bare life and the camp into the hidden thanatopolitical 'nomos' of modernity and liberal democracies. As he points out, such generalisation is oblivious to different historical forms of brutal biopolitical racisms, including Germany's 'colonial camps' in south-west Africa (where eighty per cent of the Herero population were annihilated in 1904), genocides of Indigenous peoples everywhere, the 'Middle Passage' (the stage of the slave trade where millions of Africans were shipped to the New World) and racial slavery of all kinds; Agamben thus fails to analyse the 'constitutive relationality' of concentration camps 'in the modern world' (Weheliye 2014: 36). There are two important points to make in this context: first, Arendt is one of the early and rare critics who insist on the crucial relation between colonialism, imperialism, anti-Semitism, racism and the

Scramble for Africa in her genealogy of totalitarianism, even if her analysis does not go far enough in this direction; and second, Arendt refuses to generalise Nazi death camps or totalitarianism itself into a hidden matrix of modernity – on the contrary, she focuses on their historical specificity while warning about the danger of the repetition of the roots of totalitarianism – which she listed in her 1945 essay 'The seeds of a Fascist International' (EU: 140–50) as 'Anti-Semitism, Racism, Imperialism' (EU: 150) – in the new historical circumstances.

Moreover, and crucially, Arendt's analysis of totalitarian bio-politics differs from Agamben's theory because it departs from the logic of sovereignty. For her, totalitarianism represents a historically unprecedented form of biopolitical government that emerged from democracy and was based on a new kind of power, the force of movement, supposedly driven by the dynamic law either of nature or of history. Government accelerating either 'natural' or 'historical' development cannot be described in terms of either lawless tyranny or a state of emergency created by a sovereign decision. More specifically, what supersedes state sovereignty are the two features of totalitarian movement analysed in section II: first, the momentum of endless expansion on a world scale generated by new organisational techniques; and second, the exercise of terror, which puts 'life' in the hands of the logical necessity of nature or history. At first sight, totali-tarian terror might seem similar to sovereign power, because it also suspends constitutional law, eliminates human rights and exercises the absolute power over life and death. However, as we have shown, because totalitarianism supposedly realises the alignment of the will (decision) of the leader with the logical necessity of historical/natural development, a sovereign decision in the true sense of the word is no longer necessary. We could argue, therefore, that in Arendt's theory of totalitarianism the sovereign decision is replaced by the impersonal biopolitical logicality of historical (uniform classless society) or natural (racist supremacy) development.

Arendt's analysis of statelessness ('abstract nakedness') and total domination in the concentration camps allows us to make two additional arguments for the biopolitics of bare life not being reducible to sovereignty. First, the pre-totalitarian emergence of stateless people and refugees shows that their 'naked existence' is an effect of the loss of national sovereignty rather than the target of sovereign violence. Second, the totalitarian 'experiment' of total domination in the concentration camps supersedes sovereignty insofar as it aims to fabricate a new species that behaves according to totalitarian logic and is thus incapable of either obedience or resistance.

Although Agamben does not credit Arendt, arguably his theory of 'bare life' develops the main implications of Arendt's analysis of the 'abstract nakedness' of human life (OT: 297) characterising stateless people and refugees migrating across Europe in the early twentieth century.[17] Usually, the critical commentaries on Arendt's discussion of statelessness focus on her analysis of the deadly paradox of universal human rights, that is, despite their supposed universality, human rights are not enforceable apart from nation states.[18] Thus in political situations where these universal rights are most needed for those who have lost their citizenship, they offer no protection whatsoever (OT: 292). While the 'right to have rights' based on natality is an essential part of Arendt's analysis of statelessness, the limitations of human rights do not sufficiently address the biopolitical framework of her analysis, which Agamben stresses in his own work on bare life. For Arendt, the 'calamity' of statelessness

160

not only entails the loss of political status and legal protection, but, first and foremost, the destruction of political community, human plurality and the common world. The loss of the common world and political community (the central meaning of natality understood as being with others) entails the loss of the politically significant framework in which human actions and speech matter. It is this deprivation of the public significance of action (but yet the destruction of agency itself) and speech that reduces human beings to the 'abstract nakedness' of human existence (OT: 297). Such a naked existence is dispossessed of the political modes of living, of cultural, publically shared attributes of identity – that is, of 'whatness' or *bios*. Arendt compares statelessness to the ancient problem of slavery, but argues that the 'dehumanisation' of refugees and stateless people is even more complete than in the 'crime against humanity' of slavery insofar as slavery, motivated by economic interests, did not entail complete superfluousness of the human (in the sense of a natal being), even though that 'humanity' is commodified and subjected accordingly.

As Arendt concludes, there is 'nothing sacred in the abstract nakedness of being human' (OT: 299); on the contrary, such abstract nakedness is intertwined with extreme vulnerability and exposure to the 'greatest danger'; that is, it leads to extermination and the experiment of total domination in the concentration camps. 'The survivors of the extermination camps, the inmates of concentration and internment camps [. . .] could see [. . .] that the abstract nakedness of being nothing but human was their greatest danger' (OT: 300). As she argues, '[e]ven the Nazis started their extermination of Jews by first depriving them of all legal status [. . .] and cutting them off from the world of the living by herding them into ghettos and concentration camps

[. . .]. The point is that a condition of complete rightlessness was created before the right to live was challenged' (OT: 296) and before the possibilities of all agency were destroyed.

Although previous forms of historical violence, genocide, racial terror and exploitation often eliminated political opposition and temporarily suppressed the agency of the subjugated people, the potentialities of struggle – and thus natality in Arendt's terms – survived as aspirations and hopes for freedom. Indeed, in the leftist and decolonial traditions, from Marx to Fanon, the most oppressed peoples – those who have nothing to lose but 'chains themselves' – are often regarded as the bearers of the possibility of action and the struggle for freedom. What for Arendt is monstrous about 'total domination' is that it aims not only to destroy political opposition, but also to eliminate entirely the human capacities of acting, responding to others and spontaneity in all aspects of a human's life. According to Arendt, this destruction of all possibilities of agency and natality can be achieved only when both the sympathisers of the movement and its victims are transformed into exchangeable 'specimens' of a 'new' human species (OT: 438), characterised only by predictable biological responses to external stimuli. Arendt's insistence on the unique character of total domination and biopolitical engineering of 'living corpses' has therefore a specific meaning and, as suggested above, does not preclude what Weheliye describes as a 'relational historical analysis' of different forms of genocide, racial terror and brutal biopolitics of racism. On the contrary, Arendt's genealogy of totalitarianism in a certain way precedes Weheliye's argument that 'concentration camps shared an intimate history with different forms of colonialism and genocide before being transformed into the death camps of Nazi Germany' (Weheliye 2014: 35). Nonetheless, Arendt is arguably

162

guilty of the charge Weheliye directs toward other biopolitical theorists for failing to 'sufficiently address how deeply anchored racialization is in the somatic field of the human' (Weheliye 2014: 4).

According to Arendt, the biopolitical experiment of total domination was carried out for the first time under the limited and 'scientifically' controlled conditions of the Nazi concentration camps, where biopower, converted to the force of movement, was deployed in experiments on human bodies:

> The camps are meant not only to exterminate people and degrade human beings, but also serve the ghastly experiment of eliminating, under scientifically controlled conditions, spontaneity itself as an expression of human behavior and of transforming the human personality into a mere thing, into something that even animals are not. (OT: 438)

In order to eliminate natality, spontaneity and the possibility of action and, hence, resistance,[19] the biopolitics of 'total domination' has not only to reduce political life to naked existence, characteristic of refugees, but also to 'fabricate something that does not exist, namely, a kind of human species resembling other animal species' (OT: 438). Every aspect of the camp administration, from the inhuman conditions of mass transport to nameless and mass exterminations, aims to eliminate uniqueness from individuals and thus to convert human beings into a 'bundle of reactions' devoid of personality that is a part of a larger uniform being (OT: 441). As Arendt argues, a person 'can be fully dominated' only when that person 'becomes a specimen of the animal-species man' (OT: 457).

The fabrication of this new 'species' characterised only by identical biological reactions to external stimuli 'so that each of these bundles of reactions can be exchanged at random for any other' (OT: 438) is tantamount to the biopolitical production of biological determinism. Such biopolitics of the species not only destroys human uniqueness and plurality, but is in fact inseparable from a new type of genocide – the mass production of 'living corpses' suspended between life and death (OT: 447). Total domination, according to Arendt, is possible only when human beings, as bearers of natality, are 'killed' as such prior to the extermination of their physical bodies: 'the society of the dying established in the camps is the only form of society in which it is possible to dominate man entirely' (OT: 456). Recall Foucault's claim about the role of death in the biopolitical power over life and death: from the perspective of a citizen, death is the 'limit' of state power, 'the moment that escapes' power (Foucault 1980a: 138–9). Arendt's suggestion that the accelerating genocidal character of totalitarianism culminates in the annihilation of all aspects of natality (in the production of 'living corpses') prior to mass extermination means that totalitarian biopower also eliminates this limit of state-centred biopolitical power so there is no possibility of escape, even in death. For this reason Arendt claims that the 'real horror of the concentration [. . .] camps', their 'radical evil', lies in evoking the 'possibility to give permanence to the process of dying itself and to enforce a condition in which both death and life are obstructed equally effectively' (OT: 443). Such mass killing of the human prior to physical extermination and the transformation of people into 'superfluous human material' incapable of agency and spontaneity (OT: 443, 475) are what was, according to Arendt, unprecedented about the total domination that is totalitarianism. The new 'radical evil' of the camps (OT: 443, 459) is beyond understanding and beyond all the existing political vocabularies (including that of sovereignty). Only the 'fearful imagination' (OT: 441) of those who did not suffer themselves but who are affected by the testimonies of the survivors of the Holocaust and the Nazi and the Soviet camps can attempt try to approach these horrors (OT: 444).[20]

According to Arendt, the destruction of natality in the death camps is characterised by three precisely calculated stages of the annihilation of the human prior to physical genocide. The first step aims to destroy the juridical person; the second one aims to kill the moral person; and the third one exterminates human uniqueness and all spontaneity, even the spontaneity of life itself. Although Arendt does not return to juridical and moral personhood when she explicitly theorises the condition of natality in *The Human Condition*, the implications of *The Origins of Totalitarianism* are that the moral, juridical and bodily frameworks are an essential part of the human condition of natality, because these frameworks safeguard the possibility of a new beginning and agency.

The concentration camps destroy first of all the juridical person. The juridical framework is demolished because, according to Arendt, it enables the judgement of actions, for example the correlation between guilt, deeds and punishment. The arbitrary selection of inmates – criminals who had served their sentence, the members of political resistance and the over-whelming majority of innocent people who had never done anything but merely belonged to the undesirable groups – Jewish people, disabled persons, homosexuals – utterly destroys any meaning of action, judgement or punishment. Ultimately, the killing of the juridical person aims to destroy the very capacity for action of any kind, political or 'criminal' (OT: 447), because the arbitrary persecution in the camps makes the consequences of actions irrelevant. The destruction of the juridical erases even the difference between the opposition to and the support of totalitarianism, because, as Arendt argues, the free support of totalitarianism is also an obstacle to total domination.

The second step toward the destruction of natality intends to annihilate the moral person by making solidarity among the inmates 'martyrdom' (OT: 451) and moral choices between good and evil impossible (OT: 452). The camps attempt to destroy moral decisions about the meaning of one's own death – for example, choosing to die to save others – and ethical responsibility by forcing victims to make impossible moral choices. Arendt cites as an example the Greek mother forced to select which one of her children should be killed. In the context of the camps the moral choices between good and evil become irrelevant, as the victims are forced to choose 'no longer between good and evil, but between murder and murder' (OT: 452). The most pernicious aspect of the camps in this respect was the calculated implication of the victims in the crimes of the perpetrators by forcing the inmates to share the administration of the camps, for instance as members of the Capos or Sonderkommandos.

The last stage of total domination destroys natality by annihilating singularity ('who') and any 'spontaneity' of the inmates. The complete elimination of the possibility of agency is, for Arendt, synonymous with the obliteration of human uniqueness. In this last stage, the terror of biopolitical experiments focuses on the calculated infliction of pain and the gradual destruction of human bodies: totalitarianism strives 'to manipulate the human body – with its infinite possibilities of suffering – in such a way as to make it destroy the human person as inexorably as do certain mental diseases of organic origin' (OT: 453). Although she does not develop this point, Arendt comes close to formulating the idea that genocidal biopolitical power also tortures bodies in addition to destroying the juridical context of action and moral personhood. For Arendt, the terrifying emblems of such a destruction of the human are victims led to death without any resistance.[21] By killing the human through the manipulation of the body and enhancement of suffering, total domination also eliminates unpredictable spontaneity in all its manifestations, including the spontaneity of 'life itself, in the sense of simply keeping alive' (OT: 438). Not limited to human actions and responses, spontaneity has to be eliminated even from organic life, because all aspects of spontaneity are intertwined with unpredictability, or what Arendt calls in her later work the possibility of the impossible.

The destruction of natal being and the fabrication of the new species in its place make the biopolitical and genocidal character of total domination indistinguishable, as it entails the destruction of human life and death, natality and mortality. For Arendt, human beings whose capacities for resistance and spontaneity are replaced by predictable reactions to external stimuli are 'living corpses', suspended in limbo, neither alive nor dead (OT: 444), as if they were never born. Only the medieval images of hell, stripped of all theological associations with the last judgement and divine mercy, could barely approach the conditions of the endless torment inflicted on earth, in the interval between 'after life' but before physical death. But even such images fail to account for the destruction of individual death and 'the mass production of corpses' (OT: 441).

The horrors of the concentration and death camps confront us with the contradiction between their incomprehensible monstrosity, which exceeds understanding and common sense, on the one hand, and the logical, systematic machinery of total domination, on the other. This contradiction speaks to the ethical difficulty of any writing about the extermination camps and the Holocaust, because, although one can account for the calculated machinery of destruction, one fails to approach the torments of the victims. Thus, the analysis of the camps always seems superficial and powerless. Nonetheless, the reconstruction of the machinery of total domination is important for the way it calls for new political judgements and vigilance with respect to contemporary political events.

The enduring legacy of Arendt's genealogy of the historical precursors and essential elements of totalitarian biopolitics is not only as testimony to the radical evil of total domination lest it is erased from historical memory, nor just as a wellspring for biopolitical theory, acknowledged or not. Crucial for Arendt, and for us, is that her analyses provide the basis for judging contemporary political events in three ways. First, no matter from what side of the political spectrum one derives one's views, the 'insight into the nature of total domination' provided by the camps introduces into political deliberations 'the politically most important yardstick for judging events in our time, namely: whether they serve totalitarian domination or not' (OT: 442).[22]

Second, we can tell what may serve totalitarian domination by recalling the precursors and elements that crystallised into the event of totalitarianism. As mentioned above, after the defeat of Nazism in 1945 Arendt summarised the 'root causes' of totalitarianism as anti-Semitism, racism and imperialism (EU: 150). In her 1951 critique of Senator McCarthy's denunciations of (ex) communists within the US entertainment industry and public administration (in 'The eggs speak up' – EU: 270–84), she goes further in elaborating a number of apparently 'lesser evils' than totalitarianism that feed into it (EU: 271) and that may resonate more directly with events in the early twenty-first century. These include 'homelessness, rootlessness, and the disintegration of political bodies' and the normalisation or ruin of other kinds of community normally engendered by the mutual disclosure of natality (EU: 271). And, crucially, Arendt condemns McCarthy's (and the FBI's) decade-long internal anti-communist crusade (as a substitute for acting against the Stalinist totalitarian regime, which she does herself) as akin to the kind of biopolitical racism discussed in section I: communists were not only an early target of the Nazi biopolitical normalising of identity, but, as Arendt argues in this essay, the 'technical' and 'destructive' thinking underlying McCarthyism – that is, 'you can't make an omelette without breaking eggs' (EU: 283) – is precisely the biopolitical rationality that supports normalising and 'regularising' the population and opens the way for 'regularisation' to turn into 'fabrication' (*Homo faber*) of a 'species'. These analyses are prescient in the context of contemporary politics, characterised by the rise of the right-wing populist movements in mainland Europe, the UK and the US, the military destruction of worlds in Syria and Yemen, the global refugee crises, rampant Islamophobia, renewed proliferation of sexual and domestic slavery and ongoing racism of all kinds.

Third, judgement of political events using the yardstick of whether they serve the totalitarian erasure of natality is tantamount to having one's conscience pricked to act 'against conditions under which people no longer wish to live' (OT: 442). This kind of judgement underscores Arendt's politics of natality aimed against those supposed 'lesser evils' that may very well 'crystallize into that one supreme and radical evil' of totalitarianism (EU: 271). We examine and expand Arendt's politics of natality and action in the following three chapters.

Notes

1   In her 'Reply to Eric Voegelin' (EU: 401–8), first published in 1953, Arendt denies an 'essential sameness' 'between totalitarianism and some other trends in Occidental political or intellectual history' and she denies that 'liberalism, positivism, and pragmatism' can be considered essentially totalitarian, even if they contain 'elements [that] also lend themselves to totalitarian thinking' (EU: 405).

2   We therefore also reject Roberto Esposito's claim that Arendt locates the origin of totalitarianism in 'an originary loss' of the Greek understanding of the political, a loss 'which condemns all subsequent history to the depoliticization that is destined to flow into the antipolitical drift of totalitarian domination' (Esposito 2013: 103). This is one possible critical interpretation of her genealogy of the politics of modernity in *The Human Condition* where Arendt decries the 'victory of *animal laborans*' over her vision of the political based on the disclosure of natality through speech and action (a criticism we address in Chapter 3). But with regard to *The Origins of Totalitarianism*, Esposito's criticism is certainly misplaced and it ignores Arendt's account of her genealogical method, which is irreducible to what Esposito sees as a 'traditional philosophy of history' that assumes continuous development (Esposito 2013: 103).

3   Arendt also analyses this phenomenon of the 'exception Jew' in her biography of Rahel Varnhagen (RV). Pitkin (1995) provides a helpful analysis of this phenomenon of 'from pariah to parvenu' in terms of one aspect of the rise of the social.

4   'The subject and power' was first published in 1982, after Foucault's analyses of the normalising processes related to both disciplinary power in *Discipline and Punish* and biopower and confession in *The History of Sexuality, Volume I*. Hence, it provides an excellent summary of Foucault's fully developed approach to various kinds of normalising and regularising power. In that paper he refers to these collectively as 'pastoral power', in acknowledgement of the Christian origins of the rhetoric of care and the subjectifying practice of 'confession' that are so central to modern forms of power, especially biopower, that pervade practices of care for the health and welfare of the population. Foucault provides a more extensive account

of 'pastoral power' in the lecture course, published as *Security, Territory, Population* (2007).

5 As reported by Jessica Glenza, 'How egg freezing became a hot commodity on Wall Street', *The Guardian Weekly*, 12 January 2018, p. 14.

6 Since Foucault's lecture courses on biopolitics have been published (starting in 2003), Foucauldian and biopolitical theorists interested in race and racism, such as Ladelle McWhorter (2009) and Alexander Weheliye (2014), have found Foucault's biopolitical theory of much value. Weheliye does find fault with what he claims is a distinction Foucault makes in *Society Must Be Defended* between 'biological racism', characteristic of biopolitics, and earlier forms of 'ethnic racism', and argues that all modern racism is 'biological' and hence biopolitical (Weheliye 2014: 59–60).

7 While Foucault rejects the logic of sovereign power in most of his analyses of biopolitics, he does explain extreme versions of racist biopolitics, such as Nazism as a regime 'which has generalized biopower in an absolute sense, but which has also generalized the sovereign right to kill' (Foucault 2003: 260). Agamben explains this coincidence of biopower and sovereignty in terms of the production of 'bare life'.

8 Dana Villa also stresses the dynamic and accelerating 'law of motion' of totalitarian terror, which makes totalitarianism different from static despotism (Villa 1999: 14–17). Foucault also discusses the governmentality of totalitarianism in terms of the 'inflationary', 'continuous and unified' 'power of expansion', although without due acknowledgement of Arendt (Foucault 2008: 186–8).

9 For a lucid account of Arendt's notion of the masses see Margaret Canovan (2000: 31–3).

10 We discuss the problem of responsibility in Chapter 4. For now we note that Arendt begins to develop her views on responsibility in the Third Reich in her discussion of the Nazis' perversion of conscience in Chapter 8 of *Eichmann in Jerusalem*, 'Duties of a law-abiding citizen' (EJ: 135–50). She notes the pernicious distortion of the Kantian categorical imperative among the executioners of the Final Solution: "Act in such a way that the Führer, if he knew your action, would approve it" (EJ: 136). As she concludes, 'the law of Hitler's land demanded that the voice of conscience tell everybody: "Thou shall kill"' (EJ: 150). Even though murder was 'against desires and inclinations of most people', Nazis like Eichmann 'had learned how to resist temptation' not to murder.

11 For an analysis of the distinctive features of Arendt's theory of totalitarianism as the dynamic destructive movement of total domination, see Canovan

(2000). Canovan argues elsewhere, along with other commentators, that Arendt's reflection on totalitarianism influenced her entire political theory (Canovan 1992: 17–60). Like Canovan, Villa also stresses the difference of Arendt's theory from the classic interpretations of totalitarianism as a static despotic structure (Villa 1999: 11–35). However, neither commentator links this dynamic destructive character of totalitarianism to biopolitics.

12 Also enabling this turn to thanatopolitics is, according to Arendt, the absolute division, borrowed from secret societies, between us (the movement) and them (the world conspiracy against 'us') (OT: 380). Totalitarianism thus subsumes all differences, including the traditional distinction between friend and enemy (which, in principle, enables toleration) (OT: 443), into the new principle of 'all' versus 'nothing', which should never have a place in politics: 'all' means the victory of the movement; 'nothing' means the destruction of the human condition of natality, which is co-extensive with the destruction of humanity as such.

13 As Arendt argues, the distinction between nature and history had already been problematised by the work of Marx and Darwin in the nineteenth century. The advent of biopolitics and the rise of the social in nineteenth century further undermined the antithesis of history and nature not only in 'theory' but also in terms of the operation of power.

14 As Arendt points out, this manufactured logical consistency of fictitious reality and the scientific prediction of the future compensate for the loss of belonging to the common world and for the loss of *sensus communis* (in the Kantian sense of the term).

15 Esposito claims that Nazism is based on 'an absolutely natural given' (Esposito 2013: 106). By contrast, Agamben stresses 'the production of facts' by the totalitarian regime, but associates it not with the biopolitical experiment of the 'new species' but with the power of the sovereign decision, which no longer responds to the factual situation of danger, but creates that situation. That is why Agamben claims that the sovereign decision is indistinguishable from the production of facts (Agamben 1998: 171).

16 Agamben's reframing of biopolitics in terms of 'bare life' has provoked much debate about the notion. For example, see the essays collected in *Politics, Metaphysics, and Death: Essays on Agamben's Homo Sacer* (Norris 2005) and *The Agamben Effect* (Ross 2008).

17 For further analysis of Jewish refugees, see Arendt's essay, 'We refugees' (Arendt 1994) and Agamben's response to it, which is also entitled 'We refugees' (Agamben 1995).

18 Conversely, Peg Birmingham (2006) provides an excellent analysis of the complexities of human rights in Arendt's work. She develops Arendt's claim that 'the right to have rights or the right of every individual to belong to humanity, should be guaranteed by humanity itself' (OT: 298) in an analysis of how natality provides this basis of human rights, which aims to redress the shortcomings of traditional rights discourse.

19 In his book *Hannah Arendt and the Limits of Total Domination*, Michal Aharony (2017) challenges Arendt's thesis by citing as evidence of resistance the experiences and oral testimonies of well-known and non-canonical writers who survived the Auschwitz and Buchenwald concentration camps. The fact that, thankfully, the Nazi regime did not successfully implement total domination in all cases does not invalidate Arendt's analysis of their murderous technologies and monstrous attempts to do so.

20 Although Arendt does not develop an account of imagination in *The Origins of Totalitarianism*, she makes it clear in her subsequent work (LM, LKPP) that imagination is a condition of memory, a point taken up in the analysis of narrative and action in Chapter 5. Consequently, 'fearful imagination' is intertwined with a predicament of memory, which has to remember despite its impulse to flee such horrors.

21 Arendt's readings and the selection of quotations from the first accounts from the concentration camps stress this point. She especially refers to David Rousset's *L'univers Concentrationnaire* and *Les Jours de Notre Mort*, both published 1947.

22 Arendt's formula of political judgement here is remarkably similar to Adorno's formulation of a new categorical imperative − 'to arrange [. . .] thoughts and [. . .] actions so that Auschwitz will not repeat itself' (Adorno 1997b: 365).

3

Natality, Abortion and the Biopolitics of Reproduction

I. Introduction: Biopolitics as 'Making Live'

The analysis in Chapter 2, firstly, reframes Arendt's accounts of the 'rise of the social' and the 'social' precursors of totalitarianism as significant for a diagnosis of similar trends in contemporary biopolitics and as pre-empting Foucault's definition of biopolitics, understood as state control of the power both to 'make live' and to 'let die' through the regularisation of the biological life of the population. Second, also as a warning against trends in contemporary politics, the analysis focuses on how biopolitics, by suppressing the event of natality, can, in the extreme, transform one pole of biopolitics, the state control of the power to 'let die', into totalitarianism and a politics of 'making die' or of (living) death, without recourse to the state exercise of sovereign power. Arendt's analysis also shows that the biopolitical 'experiment' of total domination destroys both the conceptual significance of, and the political institutions based on, the distinctions between private and public, nature and history. Hence, totalitarianism also erases the difference, as defined in classical thought, between *zoe* (natural or biological life) and *bios* (political life) in a specific way. In subjecting human existence to the 'laws of movement', totalitarianism destroys both the stabilising and the novel aspects of people acting within political community; it destroys any expression of uniqueness and the means of disclosing natality to and by others; human existence is reduced to a (determined) product of the movement of nature or history (EU 340–1); and *bios*, is transformed, not into *zoe* or natural life per se, but rather into what Arendt calls 'abstract nakedness' (OT: 297–300) before further reduction into 'living corpses' (OT: 451) without the capacity to act at all.

In this chapter we address the other pole of biopolitics – the biopolitics of 'making live' – through analyses of what Arendt refers to as the birth of the new beginning, including that 'inherent' in human birth. Our specific focus is on the most ignored implications of Arendt's philosophy of natality for feminist accounts of the biopolitics of reproduction and birth control, including how a biopolitics of 'making live' (for example, through prohibition of abortion) can also undermine 'political community' (the space of 'appearance' through the mutual disclosure of natality) and, hence, action and 'agency' in Arendt's sense. While Arendt did not address the biopolitics of reproduction directly and would not consider it a political issue, she puts the question of human birth at the centre of politics, in the first instance through her definitions in *The Human Condition* of natality and the political. As discussed in the Introduction, Arendt considers 'natality', understood in the most basic sense as the 'new beginning inherent in birth', or the idea that we 'are not born in order to die but in order to begin', to be the 'central category of political [. . .] thought' (HC: 9, 246–7).[1] While Arendt's explicit definitions of the event of natality tend to distinguish the first order of birth from the 'second birth', that into the political order of speech and action (HC: 176), we argue, along with several commentators on Arendt who also engage with the relationship between the two orders of birth, that they are inseparably intertwined without assuming that is essentially problematic.[2] Indeed, we go further, to argue that the event of natality that is integral to political action and inter-relational agency *is dependent upon* ensuring that women's inter-relational agency with regard to the first order of birth is acknowledged and preserved. It is toward this end that the analysis of the biopolitics of reproduction (and, specifically, the biopolitics of 'making live' through, for example, abortion law) in this chapter is aimed, beginning with some critical interventions into Arendt's approach.

Even though Arendt separates the two orders of birth, it is also apparent that she assumes, in two ways relevant here, that natality in the sense of the first order of birth is inescapably a political notion. First, socalled physical birth is always already implicated in the common world we share, in the operations of power, technology, medicine, law and economy. Arendt herself says that birth, like death, is not a 'simple natural occurrence' – human birth and death presuppose a fabricated, significant and human world, 'whose relative durability and permanence makes appearance and disappearance possible' (HC: 96–7). The second (and related) way that Arendt co-implicates the two orders of the birth of the new is by implicitly assuming that the disclosure of natality in the political order (the witnessing of others and their actions *as* beginning the new) relies on the event of the exposure of the newborn to the world carrying that same significance for those already inhabiting the human world, namely the appearance of a new beginner enacting new beginnings. As Arendt says: the 'new beginning inherent in birth can make itself felt in the world only because the newcomer possesses the capacity of beginning something new, that is, of acting', where 'action' is understood in Arendt's special sense as the appearance of a beginner enacting a new beginning (HC: 9). This formulation allows us to redefine the first order of birth in terms of the event of our primary exposure or 'appearance' to others as a 'beginner' and as 'unique distinctness', which prefigures the political as the inter-relational disclosure through speech and action of beginners beginning something new (and vice versa), not only for the newborns and the political actors we become, but also for a political community that welcomes natal beings and their actions.[3] This is what makes natality, for Arendt, the 'central category of political [. . .] thought' (HC: 9).

However, despite putting human birth at the centre of politics in these ways, Arendt's latter formula for the co-implication of the two orders of natality bypasses the central issue for a feminist politics of reproduction, where, we argue, the focus is on the conditions that must be in place for the relationship between these two orders of natality to operate as Arendt suggests. While granting the newborn the status of a beginner who 'appears' to, and is welcomed by, others as a fledgling agent, the formula says nothing about the agency and disclosure of uniqueness of the woman giving birth (which is precisely the expression of natality that we argue is targeted by biopolitics of 'making live'). Are not her actions that are 'behind' the birth of the newborn also welcomed as expressions of natality and does not she, as the birth-mother, appear to others as a 'who', as a unique distinctness enacting, through giving birth, the 'capacity of beginning something new'? Arendt does not provide direct answers to these questions. The most likely reason for this silence in *The Human Condition* and for Arendt not including women's reproductivity anywhere in discussions of the political is that she views it as continuous with 'private', 'social', biological and bodily matters, which, as we discussed in Chapter 1, she associates with biopolitical determination of life (that is, acting from 'necessity') and the subsuming of the political under the normalising, biopolitical, bureaucratic order of the social (for example, HC: 45–7; OR: 58–9/54–5). This impression that maternity is devoid of action and agency in Arendt's sense (either by definition or as an effect of the biopolitical normalisation and regularisation of life) is accentuated by the little she says about women's reproductivity in *The Human Condition* in her genealogies of the concrete conditions of modernity across three spheres of 'life' (HC: 28–49, 79–109). There she describes philosophical views of women's reproductivity as either continuous with the cyclic, repetitive realm of biological or natural life (*zoe*) (HC: 46, 96) confined to the (traditionally subjected realm of the) household (HC: 30–1) and/or, following 'Locke and all his successors', as equivalent to a labouring body ('*animal laborans*') driven by or modelled in 'the image of the life process itself' (HC: 105). While it is unlikely that Arendt accepts any of these conventional views, her silence on the matter implies that women's reproductive labour lacks the temporality that, as discussed in Chapter 1 and expanded below, is characteristic of natality and agency, irrespective of whether women are disclosed as agents, or beginners of the new, through other (political) activities. This impression has also led to misinterpretations of Arendt's two orders of birth as echoing classical liberal (and contract) political theory, which since Locke has described the difference between the private and public spheres in superficially similar terms of first and second births.

Mary G. Dietz has provided an enduring and convincing critique of this sort of interpretation, especially of commentators who claim that in *The Human Condition* Arendt retains not only the hierarchical distinction between the public and private spheres but also the traditional 'gendering' of these spheres (male/female) and the related dichotomies between active political life (*bios* or *vita activa*) on the one hand and body/labour/biological life (*animal laborans*) on the other (Dietz 1995: 23–6). As Dietz argues, this simplistic interpretation 'effectively erases Arendt's commitment to a *tripartite* notion of activities (labor: work: action) with its corresponding basic conditions (life: worldliness: plurality)' (Dietz 1995: 24, emphasis added; HC: 7–8). Nevertheless Dietz concedes that Arendt's accounts do tend to 'gender' *animal laborans* (the labouring body, including reproductive labour) as 'feminine' and *Homo faber* (work or the realm of 'means-end fabrication') as 'masculine'. But, says Dietz, Arendt is describing historical preconditions of modernity that are contestable and Arendt's radical (and implicitly feminist) move is to 'displace' this gendering by a gender-neutral 'politics of "unique distinctiveness" and action' (Dietz 1995: 20, 29). Anne O'Byrne, on the other hand, questions whether Arendt's account of the political and action in *The Human Condition* is posed as this kind of *solution* to what Arendt concludes is the 'victory of *animal laborans*' (HC: 320–4) accompanied by a reduction of 'creativity' to 'fertility' or, rather, as an account of what has been lost (the event of natality) to the human condition generally through this 'victory' (O'Byrne 2010: 98–9).

While agreeing that Arendt's notion of political action is gender-neutral, we argue that a feminist politics of reproduction and, more broadly, Arendt's notions of political action and plurality *depend on ensuring* that the reduction of women's reproductive labour to *animal laborans* (by definition or by the biopolitical regulation of life and death) is *not presented as a fait accompli*. While bypassing rich feminist scholarship on both reproduction and Arendt, Miguel Vatter goes partway toward countering any impression that (totalitarian) biopolitics has or could succeed in destroying natality within human reproduction (for example, through eugenics and terror) by reclaiming Arendt's descriptions of biological fertility as a process of singularisation of life: 'natural fertility of biological life [. . . is] never opposed to natality in Arendt because this fertility makes "automatic" singularization of life' (Vatter 2014: 150). Even though Vatter attaches this interpretation of natality to freedom by presenting biological fertility as a kind of freedom (Vatter 2014: 151), this does little to augment women's reproductive agency. Instead, the idea that this 'singularization of life' is 'automatic' seems too close to the notion of creationism in political theology that we critique in section II, precisely for negating women's re-productive agency. Without focus on the issue of reproduction, O'Byrne (2010), in contrast to Vatter, counters the assumption that *animal laborans* has taken hold of any aspect of modernity by reconfiguring Arendt's notion of (inter-relational) action as a mode of 'being in time' (which she calls 'syncopated temporality') that O'Byrne argues is characteristic of action *in any realm of modern life*. We offer in this chapter (and throughout the book) other notions of bodily being and alternative interpretations of Arendt's notions of natality and the political that similarly avoid disqualifying activities, including giving birth or deciding not to, from the status of 'action', in the sense of the action of a beginner enacting the beginning of something new.

Even though Arendt's worry that certain sorts of negative biopolitics suppress natality may explain her insistence on quar-antining political life from attention to biological, bodily and 'social' matters, it is doubtful such quarantining is possible or desirable. Even in the most enlightened democracies, biopolitics already encroaches upon all sorts of socio-biological processes, including the first order of the birth of the new beginning, and even though biopolitics is deeply implicated in categorising different bodies and activities as either agentic (and fully human) or not (for example, merely labouring), it also involves some benefits (biopolitics entails, for example, state funding of health and welfare measures as part of state regulation of life and death). If biopolitics has taken hold in contemporary democracies such that the domestic sphere, the family, sexuality and women's re-productivity lie at the centre of modern politics, then it would seem to be more astute to enhance critical scrutiny of biopolitics (along the lines of the contestation of meaning/sense that is at the centre of Arendt's notion of the political) while enabling the benefits, rather than disavowing its grip on modern life. Moreover, given our arguments in Chapter 1 that the mutual disclosure of natality always contains some reference to con-ventional interpretations of the 'what-ness' of others, even as those conventions are transformed in the process, then arguably it is also impossible to liberate the political from tendencies to categorise bodies (for example, in terms of race, gender, age, health and so on). Instead, political scrutiny of biopolitics must entail challenging any discriminatory aspects that arise from the tendency to dismiss some bodies, including the maternal body, as merely labouring and non-agentic.

Foregrounding this link between the natality 'behind' human birth and political natality is not to 'gender' the concept of natality in a way that *privileges* 'women's experience of giving birth and mothering', which is a particular 'gynocentric' feminist reading of Arendt that Dietz also rightly criticises (Dietz 1995: 28). Nor is it an uncritical embrace of fertility as the 'singulariz-ation of life' devoid of any critical analysis of the biopolitical regulation of women's reproductivity, including the politics of abortion.[4] Rather, the task of this chapter is to expose and critique the way biopolitics already targets women's reproductivity and other aspects of the event of natality in the domestic and other spheres not usually considered to be 'political' at the same time as disqualifying a plurality of 'labouring' bodies from counting as agents and actors in Arendt's sense. Critiquing rather than avoiding this political reality, we believe, is a prerequisite to achieving equality of unique distinctness and 'freedom', as the in-between communal welcoming and disclosure of natality, which Arendt sought through her action-based notion of politics. This requires rethinking the labouring body as also political and therefore agentic, inter-relational, and a beginner of the new, which is tantamount to insisting on public/political acknowledgement of women who are engaged in reproductive activities as fully fledged political actors. Before our critical analyses of contemporary biopolitics of women's reproductivity in terms of state-centred (bio)power to 'make live', we provide a brief overview of how biopolitical theorists have approached the topic.

That women's reproductivity lies at the centre of biopolitics is acknowledged, albeit obliquely, in Foucault's foundational definition of biopolitics where, we recall, 'biopolitics' is understood as the 'regularisation' of the biological life of a population where the state holds not only the power to 'let die' but also the power to foster life and '*make live*' (Foucault 2003: 254). Holding the right to 'make live' is fundamentally about controlling the first order of biological birth, although not just this. The state exercise of the power to 'make live' (and 'let die') saturates institutional regulation of all forms of population health and welfare and the normalising techniques of power with which it is entwined extend into the sphere of private medicine and non-government welfare services. Indeed, Susanne Lettow (2015) has extended Foucault's account of biopolitics of the population to argue that the biopolitical regulation of reproduction has not only been central to the aim of 'improving' the population since the emergence of biopolitics itself, but also has been 'pivotal to the formulation of the genealogical concept[s] of race' and heteronormativity (Lettow 2015: 268). We explain that point in terms of the impossibility of separating the two poles of biopolitics – 'letting die' and 'making live'. As we saw in Chapter 2, even in the Nazi death camps the production of 'living corpses' involved the intertwining of the biopolitics of life and death that, in Arendt's account, stripped people of their humanity and forced them into a passive state of suspension between 'life' and 'death'. At the other pole of biopolitics, the form of 'making live' that is more common in liberal democracies and that puts women's reproductivity, sexuality and the home at the centre of biopolitics, is *forced birth* implicated in the regulation of contraception, abortion, adoption, new reproductive technologies and so on. But as we will see in section IV of this chapter, even this kind of 'making live' is linked to (a less public) programme of 'letting die' that is differentiated from 'making live' along racial lines. Racism and colonialism still pervade contemporary biopolitics of reproduction in liberal democracies so that the biopolitical imperative to 'make live' applies more to the reproductivity of women of the ('white') governing race and is offset by 'let die' being applied to the reproduction of subjugated races within a nation. Indeed, as discussed in Chapter 2, Foucault defines the racism of biopolitics as 'a way of introducing a break into the domain of life that is under power's control: the break between what must live and what must die' (Foucault 2003: 254).

183

While feminist theorists have long recognised that women's reproductivity is a favoured target of disciplinary power and biopower, (male) biopolitical theorists who are defined as such have been slow to recognise this or the central problem of *forced birth*.[5] Roberto Esposito (2008) is a rare exception. He has acknowledged the coincidence of modern biopolitics and women's reproductivity by noting the escalation in one kind of 'forced birth': the practice of 'mass ethnic rapes', which not only exemplifies a modern form of eugenics whereby life 'emerges from death, from violence, and from the terror of women', but also demonstrates a 'drastic perversion of the event that brings essence to self', which we define as the event of natality disclosed to and by others (Esposito 2008: 6–7). Robin May Schott (2010) has analysed in more detail the biopolitics of war rape from an Arendtian perspective. She is critical of Agamben[6] on the topic and rightly takes into account the impact on the 'subjectivity' of the women of this practice (Schott 2010: 61). She argues that war rape 'radically transform[s]' the 'fundamental meaning of birth' by turning birth into 'a *weapon of death*' (Schott 2010: 63) and 'natality' (which, she says, as a principle of inter-relationality, 'implies dependency') into a 'source of violation and abandon-ment' (Schott 2010: 63–4). Without denying the importance of Schott's analysis, we shift the focus in the first instance away from women's *experience* of natality to put the spotlight on the external operation of the kind of biopolitical governmentality that treats women's bodies, not as the appearance of natality that we are, but as non-agentic vessels for both ethnic cleansing and the birth of other natal beings.

Going beyond Esposito's brief mention of forced birth, we argue in this chapter that any form of forced birth is a kind of 'making live' that amounts to a *perversion of the event of natality* that is the principle of democratic plurality. Instead of focusing on deadly and violent modes of 'making live', such as ethnic war rape, our analysis highlights the 'making live' and 'letting die' involved in the general biopolitics of birth in liberal democracies. We make this our focus in order to address a neglect among those considered to be the leading (male) contemporary biopolitical theorists of arguably the most explicit form of state control over the right to 'make live' in liberal democracies: legislation surrounding abortion and contraception and, more generally, state management of women's reproductivity. This also allows us to apply Arendt's notion of natality to the kind of biopolitics targeting the first level of human birth that is typical of liberal democracies in the early twenty-first century.

State-centred power over life via management of women's reproductivity is not just one among many examples of modern biopolitics in liberal democracies; we claim that women's reproductivity is *the central target* of biopolitics. Ruth Millar similarly argues that, if we assume that the primary mode of government of the nation state is biopolitical, then 'the fundamental [. . .] right has been the right to make live and let die – if we place sexual and reproductive legislation at the center of citizenship formation, and understand political activity as biological passivity – then we need to rethink' our understanding of the liberal nation state and the male as ideal citizen and see 'women as the norm' and women's reproductive bodies as the centre of the modern biopolitical state (Millar 2007: 149). This is by no means a privilege: occupying the centre of the biopolitical state puts women in the zone of 'indistinction' between *zoe* and *bios*, which, at least in Agamben's analysis, makes women particularly vulnerable to being reduced to 'bare life' (or to the 'labouring body', to take a step back from bare life and to use Arendt's terminology). Or, as

Allaine Cerwonka and Anna Loutfi suggest, acknowledging this centrality 'might usefully serve as a tool for analyzing the "relentless *inclusion*" of women in the biopolitical state' (Cerwonka and Loutfi 2011: 5). Given this relentless inclusion, feminist theorists have rightly chastised Foucault and Agamben for ignoring the extraordinary control that the liberal democratic state seems to exercise over women's reproductivity, especially, although by no means exclusively, through abortion law.

Foucault's apparent neglect of the issue is forgiven because at least he highlights the broader place in politics of women's sexuality and reproductivity by equating these with one of four key 'domains' for the deployment of sexuality and the medicalisation of human life in modernity (Foucault 1980a: 104). And he does mention abortion as an exemplary site of contestation between the institutional normalisation of bodies through disciplinary power and the resulting 'counter-attack' of 'resistance' by the same bodies (Foucault 1980b: 56). However, as noted in Chapter 1, we find Foucault's understanding of 'resistance' to be underdeveloped, if not inadequate, for accounting for political agency. Instead, in sections III and IV of this chapter, we rely on Arendt's accounts of action and 'alliance' to explain feminist 'counter-attacks' against the biopolitics of 'making live'. While Foucault does not elaborate with regard to women's reproductivity as a key domain of biopolitics, Agamben remains silent on the topic, apart from tying physical birth to biopolitics via discussion of its inscription in the nation state. Following a muted acknowledgement of the connection Arendt makes between the nation state and human rights in 'The decline of the nation-state and the end of the rights of man' (OT: 226–302), Agamben offers an alternative thesis about the connection that foregrounds biological birth. Since the French

Declaration of the Rights of Man in 1789, he argues, it has been 'simple birth' (which he equates with 'bare life'), rather than the 'free and conscious political subject', that has been 'invested with the principle of sovereignty' in the 'passage from subject to citizen' (Agamben 1998: 128). In this way 'birth' has become equivalent to 'nation' as one (fragile) basis upon which 'man' is afforded rights. Agamben is of course wary of this biopolitical unification of the 'principle of nativity' and national sovereignty (Agamben 1998: 128, 132, 175). Significantly, though, as a consequence of ignoring Arendt's idea that the meaning of the event of human birth plays a central role in shoring up the political event of natality, Agamben makes no mention of what should be obvious: that *women and maternity must be key targets of biopolitical erasure of political natality* (agency) in order for this reduction of 'birth' to 'bare life' to 'nation' to occur. This curious oversight may be explained by Catherine Mills's wider suggestion that a fundamental problem with Agamben's conception of women becomes apparent in the few places he touches on gender: as in most Western philosophical traditions, he seems to take for granted that women have a 'closer relation to the physiological or biological' than men (Mills 2008: 115). This, says Mills, allows Agamben to dismiss gender (race, class and so on) as 'ontic' and irrelevant to political ontology and, as a consequence, he 'risks abstracting too far from any recognition of the unequal distribution of the burdens of vulnerability and violence across social, economic and (geo)political spheres' (Mills 2008: 136).

Penelope Deutscher provides another particularly interesting diagnosis of Agamben's 'nonengagement with the place of women in the biopoliticization of life' (Deutscher 2007: 57). She points out, for instance, that viewing women's reproductivity as central to biopolitics would contradict one of Agamben's primary theses: that, *contra* Foucault, biopolitics, or the political capture of biological life, is a long-standing phenomenon and not new to modernity (whereas state control over abortion is decidedly modern) (Deutscher 2007: 57). Moreover, while a case could be made that foetal life may be considered a form of 'bare life', or 'threshold' political life, in the sense that it is not fully human life yet is the subject of intense political conflict, the foetus does not actually fit Agamben's definition of bare life as human political life that has been *subsequently* 'stripped of that status or subjected to a threshold status' (Deutscher 2007: 58). Of more interest to our analysis is Deutscher's ensuing antidote to Agamben's neglect of the topic, where she uses his notion of the 'state of exception' to demonstrate the centrality of women's reproductivity to modern biopolitics. She argues that just as, for Agamben, the state of exception is a key technique of government for establishing national sovereignty and the legal order, 'the repeated creation of abortion as a state of permanent exceptionality [for example, anti-abortion law creates an exception to the rule of self-sovereignty supposedly afforded all citizens] has been one of the essential workings of twentieth- and early-twenty-first-century biopolitics concerning women's reproductivity' (Deutscher 2007: 65).

We are similarly convinced of the centrality of the relation between biopolitics and women's reproductive bodies, partly because this intersection marks the site of some of the more surprisingly volatile conflicts over the meaning of democracy in contemporary political life, two of which we examine below. But we move beyond Deutscher's informative extensions of Agamben's and Foucault's analyses to show how the significance of these conflicts lies in the way they bring together the literal and political senses of the event of natality – women's capacity to give birth to new human life and political agency in Arendt's sense of the 'appearance' of the birth of the new though inter-relational speech and action. In analysing the connection between women's reproductivity and political agency we also continue to challenge the distinction between 'labouring bodies' located within family, intimate or work contexts and *bios* (political actors performing and welcoming natality in public life). We thereby explain the relationship between the foreclosure of natality through biopolitical management of women's reproductivity and the foreclosure of natality in spheres of activity that are more obviously political. In conferring political status upon women's actions to do with giving birth (and choosing not to) amid inter-relations in 'private' domains, we do not accept that this is tantamount to accentuating the outcome that Arendt's philosophy is pitted against: the foreclosure of natality and therefore of action and freedom through biopolitics. On the contrary, we argue that if a key principle of democracy is maintaining political agency and freedom through the inter-relational disclosure of unique distinctness and plurality, then democracy entails *extending that principle to all spheres of activity, including women's reproductivity*.

In this chapter we argue that, while natality is not equivalent to maternity, the preservation of the world for its expression is severely jeopardised, to the extent that maternity is *determined* by government regulation of abortion and contraception or by religion and theology. In other words, control of the power to 'make live' by the state or the church not only denies women's political agency (in Arendt's sense, which we elaborate below), but also it damages the disclosure and welcome of the new beginning and human plurality that is the *raison d'être* of democracy. Central to that argument is, first, the conviction that, by reducing human life to organic life, which is assumed to begin at conception, 'pro-life' arguments and anti-abortion legislation effectively destroy the notion of human birth as a unique event marking a new beginning. Second, they entrench perceptions of women and maternity as *animal laborans* or biological life devoid of 'action', or agency in Arendt's sense. This in turn sets up 'debates' about abortion and contraception in terms of an unresolvable battle of rights between two forms of 'life': the foetus's individual right to life and a woman's individual right to do with her body what she will (as has been the case in the Republic of Ireland since 1983 via the Eighth Amendment of the Constitution of Ireland, until the referendum of 2018 which voted in favour of a replacement provision). Conversely, as we will see in the remainder of this chapter, Arendt's notions of agency and freedom (in terms of the disclosure of natality to and by others) displace the issue away from arguments based on dubious and uncontested assumptions about 'life itself' to considerations of ways of enhancing the inter-relational freedom and plurality of the world we 'share'. In this context access to birth control and abortion releases women from biopolitical necessity and confirms their status as human agents, beginners, participating in the mutual disclosure of natality through action.

For the remainder of this chapter we will focus on three issues in contemporary politics that facilitate our analyses of three aspects of the relation between natality, biopolitics and women's reproductive self-determination, even though Arendt herself does not directly analyse these relations. First, through the example of a volatile debate in the US in 2012 over whether health insurance should be required to cover terminations, we examine the often ignored role of political theology in the biopolitics of reproduction. We focus on this case rather than on the blatant attempts of the Trump administration in 2017 to impose a pro-life agenda in the US because the earlier case demonstrates the often overlooked biopolitical entanglements of reproduction, access to healthcare and what Carl Schmitt, in 1922, had referred to as 'political theology' (Schmitt 1985), that is, the persistence of religious concepts in the secular notions of political sovereignty. The US example helps explain the relation between state sovereignty, women's reproductivity and the Christian church. The second issue pertains to another short-lived, volatile and also surprising debate, this time in the Australian parliament in December 2005 over the licensing of RU486, the so-called 'home abortion pill'.[7] We take this event as an illustration of how state control over access to abortion can provoke political action as a counterforce to the spread of biopolitics, not action as 'resistance', but as a fully fledged mobilisation of what Arendt means by 'acting in concert', that is inter-relational political agency and freedom. The third issue engages not a particular event or debate but the racism that pervades the abortion debate and the biopolitics of reproduction in general in a way that traverses the first two examples. We examine the biopolitics of Indigenous women's reproductivity in Australia and the US to show how both the pro-choice and pro-life sides of the debate bypass consideration of the racial division operating in biopolitical determinations of what must live and what must die. Aside from acknowledging the genocide that has operated in both countries by placing Indigenous re-production on the side of 'let die' or 'must die', the analysis also includes discussion of the notion of 'reproductive justice' that some women of colour in the US have put forward as a form of collective agency that may begin to reverse the racism that pervades the biopolitics of reproduction.

191

All three issues indicate that the maternal body that gives birth is a labouring body that traverses *zoe* and *bios* and is no less agentic for that. The analyses also demonstrate the reality of the ongoing intersection between the two orders of birth of the new beginning (the 'private' and the public or political) and why legislative control and the biopolitical normalisation and management of women's reproductivity remains hotly contested. What is actually contested in these disputes is what activities, processes and bodies are 'exposed' or 'appear' as expressions of natality and who or what has power over the primary signifiers of natality: whether control should be in the hands of women, the state or the gods, or if, in Arendt's analysis, the signification and disclosure of natality are given by the witness of other humans who welcome it as such. This makes the maternal body one important domain for the disclosure of natality and hence a site for the ongoing contestation of political agency and freedom as understood by Arendt. As we go on to argue in more detail, maternity is both the target of biopolitical regulation and an expression of natality and hence agency. And that is because the primary signification of natality through the first order of human birth is neither natural nor God-given: it is a significance that is given through the unpredictable 'in-between' of human interaction (political agency in Arendt's sense). Hence, this is where, in times of political insecurity, government and church in some democracies will attempt to regulate the unpredictable consequences of the birth of the new beginning. Conversely, self-determination regarding giving birth and activities related to human reproduction more generally often become the first battleground for countering the spread of unjust state-centred biopower.

II. Natality and Political Theology:
The US 'Birth Control Mandate' of 2012

In February and March 2012, the Republican Party presidential campaign veered away from its disciplined focus on promising to fix the economic crisis and engaged instead in what media called 'the war on women', the resurgence and intensification of which we saw in the transition to the Trump presidency in 2017. The 'war' in 2012 was initiated by conservative responses to President Obama signing the 'birth control mandate', requiring all health insurance providers, including religious institutions, to cover birth control. The Democrats and most women, including ninety-eight per cent of American Catholics, viewed the mandate to be about women's health, reproductive rights and access to medical coverage.[8] The Republicans and many church leaders responded that such a requirement violates the freedom of religion. For instance, Cardinal Dolan, the president of American Catholic Bishops, claimed that the mandate threatened religious freedom and the capacity of the Catholic Church to protect the most vulnerable populations – 'victims of human trafficking, immigrants and refugees' – without having to refer them 'for abortions, sterilizations or contraception'. As this quote suggests, the churches were implying that providing the opportunity for abortion or contraception amounts to subjecting people, who have already been stripped of all human rights and reduced to what Arendt calls 'abstract nakedness' (or 'bare life', to use Agamben's term), to further violation.

This case indicates the complexity of the birth control issue in contemporary American politics: it is a knot that ties together religion with democratic freedoms, the rhetoric of war, the protection of the dispossessed, health, economic interests and biopolitics. Consequently, the debate in the 2012 presidential race about birth control and the agents entitled to exercise such control – churches, citizens, free market or the state – muddled the distinctions between religion and the state, citizenship and reproduction, political and the private, natural (*zoe*) and political (*bios*) life. And in 2015, as the Republican Party began the selection of its presidential candidate for the 2016 election, the anti-abortion rhetoric seemed even more radically conservative. Not one of the Republican candidates supported women's right to choose whether or not to continue a pregnancy and the leading candidate, Donald Trump, who had previously supported 'women's right to choose', went so far as to say in an interview with Chris Matthews at MSNBC that women who have an abortion should be 'punished'.[9]

This example of the political contest over abortion demonstrates not only the ever-present threat to erode women's reproductive self-determination but also the convergence of biopolitics with political theology, which closes down possibilities for political action and hence political agency in general. The term 'political theology' comes from Carl Schmitt's short treatise under this same title first published in 1922 in which he argues that '[a]ll significant concepts of the modern theory of the state are secularized theological concepts' (Schmitt 1985: 36). Schmitt does not deny the process of secularisation and the formal separation of state and church, but claims that such separation does not entail a complete break from theology. Rather, theology continues its existence in modern politics by other means, namely by inhabiting and shaping the conceptual and rhetorical apparatus of the state. It is this conceptual dependence of secular politics upon the structure of theological thought that is called by Schmitt 'political theology'.[10]

The main figure in Schmitt's political theology is the analogy between the transcendence of God in religion and the transcendence of the sovereign power in politics: 'The transgression of the laws of nature [. . .] brought about by direct intervention' of God is like 'the sovereign's direct intervention in a valid legal order' (Schmitt 1985: 36–7). Another way Schmitt describes the sovereign's power to intervene and suspend the law is by comparing it to the theological notion of 'the miracle' (Schmitt 1985: 36). Just as divine intervention in the form of a miracle suspends the supposed natural order (the miracle introduces a gap between past and future, as Arendt puts it for reasons discussed in Chapter 1), so too the sovereign (or the agency of the state) can suspend the legal order and disrupt the continuity of historical time. For Schmitt, such a suspension of the valid legal system constitutes the sovereign decision on the state of exception. As he famously puts it, the 'sovereign is he who decides on the exception' (Schmitt 1985: 5). The force of the exception is the unspecified threat to the order of the state (exemplified by the case of civil war) and the decision on what is to be covered by the state of exception (for example, a state of emergency) reveals the quintessential power of sovereignty.

Although Schmitt himself does not address biopower directly, the convergence between political theology and biopolitics is implied in Agamben's interpretation of his work. The biopolitical dimension of the sovereign decision on the state of exception, according to Agamben, is disclosed by the banishment of 'bare life', that is, human life stripped of political significance and exposed to death (Agamben 1998: 71–91). In other words, sovereign power enacts the state of exception by targeting bare life and thereby constituting it as such. Agamben, however, tends to overlook Schmitt's insights about the theological underpinning of the state of exception and sovereignty. And when he addresses political theology directly, he argues that the inscription of birth in the secular nation state replaces transcendental underpinnings of the 'divinely authorized' sovereignty. Because birth replaces the relation between the sovereign and divine power, it is not surprising that the term 'nation' is etymologically derived 'from *nascere* (to be born)' (Agamben 1998: 128). Contrary to Agamben's position, we argue that the central role of birth in the definition of secular nationality does not weaken the interrelations between biopolitics and political theology but quite the opposite – intensifies them – and makes women's reproductive decisions the central target of both sovereign and religious powers. As the US example shows, the point here is that the biopolitics of reproduction not only involves state power to make live (as well as let die) but it also reveals the *theological investment in this operation of power*.

In what sense can Arendt's thought of natality allow us to intervene into the biopolitical and the theological regulation of birth? Although Arendt has been regarded as a staunch secularist opposed to Schmitt's theology, she too borrows certain concepts from Augustine's theology, most notably his account of the creation of the human in terms of the temporality of the new beginning (natality) and of change.[11] Augustine claims that the mysterious reason for divine creation of the human is to introduce novelty (that is, the new beginning), because, from the perspective of eternity, there is no change or novelty. Arendt quotes Augustine as follows: 'Since created things have come into existence, they change and alter. Their coming into existence was the first change, from non–being into being, and the law of change will from then on preside over their destinies' (LSA: 52). The following quotation from Augustine's *The City of God* is the recurrent refrain in Arendt's own political thought: 'Augustine writes that "this beginning did in no way ever exist before. In order that there be such a beginning, man was created before whom nobody was"' (LSA: 55). For Arendt, as discussed in Chapter 1 with regard to natality and temporality, this means that the creation of 'man' introduces a new dimension of time, because it interrupts the circular movement of the universe and introduces a possibility of radical novelty:

> The beginning that was created with man prevented time and the created universe as a whole from turning eternally in cycles about itself in a purposeless way and without anything new ever happening. Hence, it was for the sake of *novitas*, in a sense, that man was created. Since man can know [. . .] his 'beginning' [. . .] he is able to act as a beginner and enact the story of mankind. (LSA: 55)

We argue that Arendt's notion of natality is a strategic political use of Augustine's theology, evident in her frequent references to his work. This secular notion of the beginning is mobilised against Schmitt's subordination of the 'exception' to the power of sovereignty, on the one hand, and against secular versions of determinism, on the other hand. For Arendt, the main issue is whether the force of exception – its unpredictable disruption of the constituted legal order, of natural causality and of biopolitical regularisation of life – can be radicalised as the source of inter-relational agency in secular politics. Her idea of *natality is arguably the state of exception separated from the sovereign decision* and reinterpreted instead as a new beginning in political life enacted by the disclosure of natality 'between' political agents. In other words, Arendt proposes a strikingly different paradigm of exception as the new beginning in politics. What we wish to emphasise is that the condition of this new beginning in politics (created through speech and action) is human birth, which signifies for humans the most radical change of coming into being.

For birth to be understood as a new beginning, however, it has to be removed from the domain of biological necessity, historical determinism and sovereign power, and reinterpreted instead within the parameters of maternal desire and agency. Only then can the event of birth be a creative inter-relation, since the source of the newborn's existence and the disclosure of natality remain outside, in others who witness and welcome the event. We concur with Arendt (and oppose the church's assumptions underpinning the US example) that this 'outside' is not the domain of God, but that of the maternal body and historical community. That is why we also disagree with those interpreters who either see in natality a new expression of weak messianism (Gottlieb 2003: 139–40; Sjöholm 2015: 92) or claim that natality is 'rooted in divine creation of human beings' (Vatter 2014: 154–5).

Since Arendt calls this beginning the politics of natality, she performs a radical displacement of divine creation not only to the sphere of political action but also to the domain of the maternal body, agency and desire. Such a double displacement of the beginning undermines the quasi-theological legitimation of sovereignty, while radicalising Schmitt's critique of natural causality and historical determinism.[12] This perhaps explains, and certainly contests, the church's persistent interventions in the issue of abortion and women's decisions regarding reproduction.

As Arendt is well aware, one cannot mobilise political theology and its account of the new beginning against natural causality without a thorough critique of the often invisible uses of political theology in the secular formulation of historical determinism. Such determinism suggests a view of history from the perspective of eternity, as if it were possible to step outside of time. Against a theologico-historical conception of eternity, Arendt's notion of temporality stresses instead a possibility of historical transformations, which suspend not only the established patterns of power/knowledge but also perhaps the cyclic time of nature. As she writes, the 'new always happens against the overwhelming odds of statistical laws and their probability [. . .]; the new therefore always appears in the guise of a miracle' (HC: 178). Only when birth remains beyond any schema of biological or historical determinism, and outside the purview of both state and theological legitimations of sovereignty, can it appear in the guise of a miracle. Then the connections between a new beginning, human inter-relations and natality may get mobilised for political action, as is the case in our second example of political conflict over the power to 'make live', the RU486 event.

III. Natality and Political Agency: The Australian Case of RU486

A public debate erupted in Australia in late 2005 when, in an unprecedented move, four women senators from across the political party spectrum sponsored a private member's bill to repeal the federal Minister for Health's jurisdiction over the licensing of RU486 (the so-called 'home abortion pill').[13] On the surface of things, the senators were protesting about how the then conservative Australian government (the so-called Howard government) was continuing to block the licensing of the drug despite Australia's relatively liberal approach to surgical abortion,

which has become available gradually throughout Australia since
the 1970s.[14] The debate exposed how the Howard government,
in one of its first legislative acts after assuming power in 1996,
had (quietly) placed abortive agents such as RU486 under its
own jurisdiction (instead of the independent body, the Thera-
peutics Goods Administration, which regulates all other drugs).
With the benefit of hindsight, by 2005 this legislative move in
1996 looked like a blatant escalation of state power over the
right to 'make live' and 'let die', even though it raised barely
any protest at the time. Even though protest at this situation in
2005 was well overdue, it was surprising that jurisdiction over
the licensing of RU486 *in particular* became the focal point then
of contestation of government authority over 'life'. There were
a number of other aspects of the Australian government's wider
legislative agenda in the mid-2000s that were more obviously
contrary to the ideals of democratic plurality and were more
publicly contested – harsh refugee policies, participation in the
war in Iraq (2003), draconian anti-terrorism legislation (2003
and 2005), including anti-sedition legislation that threatened
to curtail criticism of government, legislation de-unionising
the labour market (2005) and tightening the marriage act to
define marriage explicitly in terms of heterosexuality (2004).
Yet only RU486 succeeded in mobilising a wave of defiance
of prime ministerial authority sufficiently strong to push the
debate in parliament to a rare 'conscience vote' (a 'free vote' that
suspends the usual allegiance to one's political party required in
the Westminster system) and, even more rare, a vote that the
Prime Minister (Howard) and Minister for Health (Abbott) lost.
Perhaps heartened by the success of this expression of dissent,
others within the government (and the Labor opposition)
began to challenge other aspects of the Howard government's

conservative legislative agenda, eventually leading to a change of government in 2007.

What does this 'RU486 event' reveal about the relation between the biopolitics of women's reproductivity, political agency, law and state-centred biopolitical regularisation of the 'life' of a population? Why did prime ministerial control over the licensing (and hence availability) of a home abortion pill become such a focus of dissent against biopolitical govern-mentality, sufficient to effectively rejuvenate the fundamentals of democracy? As we go on to argue, the action to wrestle control of RU486 away from the centre of government demonstrates Arendt's notion of agency in all its complexity: agency that is necessarily performed in the space of 'potentiality' of human *interaction* (in the in-between space of freedom as Arendt puts it); agency as a counterforce against the spread of state control of birth (the right to 'make live') and death ('let die'); and political agency that emerges in-between unlikely political allies because a threat to women's decisions to *give* birth freely amounts to a threat to the way that the signification of natality is grounded, not in force, but in the mutual disclosure of the new beginning as the power of 'potentiality in being together'.

Answering these questions requires an initial reminder of the relationship between Arendt's notion of political agency (as the inter-relational performance of natality) and the first order of human birth. For Arendt, the defining feature of the 'human condition' (what defines our 'humanness') is being a beginner enacting the 'initiative [. . .] element of action': 'the new beginning inherent in birth can make itself felt in the world only because the newcomer possesses the capacity of beginning something anew, that is, of acting' (HC: 9). While agency is characterised by the 'capacity' to begin something unprecedented, for reasons explained in Chapter 1, Arendt cannot mean 'capacity' in the usual sense of a skill already acquired (for example, the power of reason or physical ability) that is said to enable the person to be the master of their actions, thoughts and/or destiny. Instead, this 'capacity' stems, in part, from the 'fact of birth', which for Arendt is the event of unforeseeable novelty that occurs without the newborn's control or witness: 'to be capable of action [. . .] is possible only because each man is unique, so that with each birth something uniquely new comes into the world' (HC: 178). This means to be a beginner, a unique human agent, is to be regarded, witnessed and welcomed *as such* by others. Hence, the beginning announced by the birth of the newborn is already the event of human plurality (being-singular-plural, in Nancy's terms): its meaning is exposed and disclosed *to and by others* and the event puts us in relation with each other as *acting toward* others while remaining distinct (singular, unique).

This makes agency inter-relational, performative and worldly in two ways. First, with regard to the person's relation to their own birth: since we are not the authors of our birth, the relation to this beginning estranges us from ourselves so that we remain an enigma to ourselves; we continue to rely on the witness of others to have a sense of '*who* we are' (HC: 11), which sets us on the 'quest for worldliness [that] changes who' we are, as Peg Birmingham explains (2006: 78–9). As '*who* we are' is inter-relational and worldly, 'who' we are remains indeterminable (which we discuss further in Chapter 5).

Second, of more direct relevance to the analysis of the biopolitics of birth in this chapter, insofar as human agency is inter-relational and performative, our *status as human agents* (as unique beginners who enact new beginnings) relies on being disclosed and welcomed by others as 'unique distinctness', no more or less. Moreover, not only does being a beginner require ongoing witness and disclosure by others, but also so do the person's actions: a person is disclosed as a beginner if their actions are also viewed as agentic, as beginning something new, as making a difference to the world. It is at this level of human agency that the biopolitics of reproduction (and biopolitics per se) has its initial impact insofar as it erases or does not acknowledge the maternal body and the acts of this body as a unique beginner beginning something new.

We go beyond Arendt, then, in arguing that these connections between the political realm of inter-relational agency and human birth are maintained only if women's reproductive self-determination is also maintained. This is not a question about whether Arendt or democratic politics overlook women's agency per se. There is no doubt that women are included in Arendt's notion of the political (as the realm of 'appearance' of beginners beginning the new), and in contemporary liberal democracies (in principle at least), as fully fledged agents who are exposed, appear to, and are disclosed by, others as beginners beginning something new. Rather, the issue is about the socio-political *disappearance of this agency* when the biopolitical focus is, specifically, on sexuality, reproduction, maternity and giving birth; the issue for a politics of women's self-determination is about the non-appearance of the agency 'behind' the appearance of the newborn as a beginner. Our claim is that the way government regulation and biopolitical regularisation of women's reproductivity efface women's agency is by not regarding the capacity to give birth (potentially or actually) as a 'capacity of beginning something anew' and that this disavowal undermines the way the first order of physical birth supports the inter-relational disclosure of natality in more publicly political arenas. The claim is also that both this effacement of women's reproductive agency and the attendant challenge to democratic plurality are why women's reproductive self-determination so often becomes a site of intense political struggle. The centrality of the appearance of women's reproductive agency to the maintenance of the inter-relational disclosure of the natality (which Arendt equates with the political) also perhaps explains why those four senators chose the availability of the 'home abortion pill' as the centrepiece of their battle to salvage political agency and democratic plurality generally from threats on multiple other fronts. But making this claim of a connection between political agency and reproductive self-determination involves also reconsidering the concept of temporality in Arendt's work, since it is the question of time (specifically, the idea that natality 'signifies' a gap between past and future) that supposedly distinguishes the orders of physical birth and political birth of the new beginning and contests the related contrast between biological determinism and political freedom, understood as inter-relational agency.

In *The Human Condition* especially, Arendt indicates that the difference between *zoe* and *animal laborans*, on the one hand, and *bios* and *vita activa* on the other, is not just about the type of birth – that is, physical versus political birth of the new beginning – but also about temporality with regard to the distinction between biological determinism and political agency. In classical thought, *zoe* refers to that aspect of human existence as biological or natural life, the temporality of which is viewed conventionally as cyclic because of its apparently passive reproduction (HC: 96–7) and the temporality of *animal laborans* (the labouring body) is linear insofar as it is understood in terms of 'life process' or as the 'labouring body' ministering to 'the necessities of life' (HC: 79–80, 98–100). Consequently, as *zoe* (natural or biological life) is considered to be a thoroughly determined mode of 'life' and as *animal laborans* too is driven by necessity rather than (political) concerns for stability in the common world, those aspects or modes of embodied existence are traditionally excluded from politics and contained in the private realm on that basis (HC: 46–7). It is not clear whether Arendt agrees with any of these positions with regard to human reproduction but she does not explicitly refute the notion that *zoe* and *animal laborans* are devoid of the kind of agency that could be viewed as political. We discussed in Chapter 1 Arendt's ambivalence about the place of the body in politics and it suffices to note here that she leaves undisputed the notion that maternity is assumed to be an activity of a labouring body rather than involving actions of an inter-relational agent.

Significantly, though, Arendt does qualify her position on the classical distinction between *zoe* and *bios*, nature and culture, by suggesting that it is *from the perspective of the public world of natality*, the world of inter-relational actors who are 'unique, unexchangeable, and unrepeatable', that 'life itself' seems like 'changeless eternal recurrence' (HC: 97). This qualification is significant in underscoring the argument here that if women's reproductivity is to be genuinely regarded as the domain of fully fledged human agents, this requires public acknowledgment via collaborative political action on the part of agents in public life, including within government. That is, *reproductive agency must make an 'appearance' as such* to the public political world of inter-relational unique actors. Explaining this claim requires a reminder about what Arendt does with the conventional notion of *bios* with regard to temporality. While it is doubtful that Arendt thinks the distinction between *zoe* and *animal laborans* on the one hand, and *bios* on the other is absolute, she is clear that *bios* has a different temporality to both. *Bios* refers to human being as political 'agent' caught up in 'historical and biographical' time between birth and death – a lived temporality that she tends to describe in *The Human Condition* as linear – but that presupposes a human socio-political world of speech and action from which *bios* emerges but through which it is also revised and contested (HC: 96–7). The point here is that *bios*, while conditioned by the common world in which we dwell, unlike *zoe*, is not determined. As we discussed in Chapter 1, Arendt refines her account of the temporality of natality in works after *The Human Condition* by indicating that natality refers to the *opening of a gap in any potential continuity between past and future.*[15] Reading this idea of temporality back into her account of the political in *The Human Condition* we can say that, for Arendt, it is because of its temporality that *bios* is the exclusive realm of political agency, although not in the conventional sense of individual exercise of free will or individual sovereignty. For her, political agency consists in a beginner beginning something anew, including new chapters of historical and biographical time, through speech and action disclosed as unique to and by others. As discussed in Chapter 1, agency for Arendt is per-formative and centrally dependent on engagement with and witness of others, by virtue of which our dynamic 'identities' *and* the common world we share are transformed. Even when Arendt discusses the event of natality in terms of judgement and thinking, rather than action in the usual sense, she seems to conclude that it is a person's 'insertion' into the world, where 'insertion' implies appearance and revelation of a new beginning to and by others, that 'deflects' cyclic time or introduces a 'dif-ference between past and future' into 'everlasting change' (LM I: 207–8). Hence, a precondition of preventing the erasure of natality and, hence, closure of the gap between past and future, and so a precondition of preventing the political from descending into biological or historical determinism, is that beginners of the new, including and most critically the *beginners who give birth to other beginners* of the new, are disclosed to and by others as unique distinctness and agents.

While *bios* lies at the nexus of the conditioned and unconditioned fulcrum of human existence it can be rendered invisible and political agency dampened when history is viewed as the inevitable progression of linear time (for example, when a person or group is viewed as 'the embodiment of law', where law is understood to flow inevitably from either 'Nature or History' – OT: 460–2) or through some forms of normalising biopolitics where biological life becomes a model for political life or public life is infiltrated by technical thinking and the 'science of process' (for example, HC: 322–3). As we have discussed Arendt's accounts of this in Chapters 1 and 2, we leave the details aside for now. The point being emphasised in this chapter is that it is crucial that we do not leave unquestioned patriarchal or religious assumptions that activities to do with human procreation are driven by necessity or acts of God and devoid of agency or that biopolitics has succeeded in reducing those activities to the order of *animal laborans*.

Equally important, our claim is also that biopolitics can erase natality and plurality through the state exercise of the power to 'make live', for example by taking over control and regulation of birth. At one level, 'making live' by prohibiting abortion amounts to, as Barbara Baird argues, 'withholding of the cultural and material means that enable certain performances' such as non-pregnancy; thus, the 'prohibition or even the limitation of abortion by law' significantly determines the pregnant woman's future self (Baird 2006a: 123–5). This also poses a threat to women's agency, understood in Arendt's sense of beginning something anew, because if *birth is coerced* then it is not strictly an expression of natality nor would it be disclosed as such to or by others. Moreover, for the same reason, anti–abortion laws are also a threat to women's equality understood in Arendt's terms (explained more fully in Chapter 1), as equality of 'unique distinctness', or equality of the capacity to *be* the beginning of the new (HC: 176).

This is why women's reproductive self-determination has to be included in any formulation of agency and the politics of natality, even though Arendt herself fails to do so. Bearing in mind that political agency is the inter-relational disclosure of a human being as a unique beginner and a 'who' rather than a 'what', a thing, (HC: 10–11) and that the in-between of this disclosure is also the space of freedom, understood as the 'experience of a new beginning' through interaction with others (OR: 21–2/19), then women's reproductivity must be governed by women's choices, free from coercion by state control of reproduction or other kinds of imperatives to 'make live'. It is precisely this disclosure and witnessing of uniqueness within the web of human relations that disrupts the continuity of time (for example, as 'life process') and opens a gap between past and future. And vice versa: the political, understood as the 'space' of this disclosure provides the conditions for political agency. Witnessing and welcoming the unknowable uniqueness of others, or natality, institutes the self and the worlds we share as futural, undetermined, or as *potentiality* (HC: 199–201). So, not only do anti-abortion laws compromise women's political agency, but also, in doing so, state-centred power over the right to 'make live' thereby undermines the public mutual disclosure of natality and hence power of 'potentiality in being together', which, as discussed in Chapter 1 (section III), is the principle of democratic plurality.

While it is lamentable that Arendt excludes the activities related to the first order of birth from her analyses of political life, she nevertheless provides the means of revealing how and why human birth is both the first expression of natality and among the first targets of biopolitics under conservative government. This means that, just as Arendt suggests that birth and death are already historical and subject to biopolitical normalisation and regularisation, it is necessary to think of biological life not in terms of cyclic repetition or linear process driven by necessity, but as worldly, subject to various forms of power, technology and economy infused with natality. The appearance of natality with bodily acts of all kinds, including through the physical birth of human beings, is an expression of agency insofar as such appearance opens a gap between past and future, suspends any appearance of a temporal continuum, and enables a transformation of meaning and being. Arguably, being born is the 'first' public expression of being a beginner in any individual person's life. Yet for birth to be an expression of natality (and not simply the work of God or nature), two crucial conditions have to be fulfilled. First, regarding the 'action' of birth, the woman's decision to give or not to give birth, while conditioned by countless factors, must be as free as it can possibly be. Among other interested parties, neither the state nor the church has jurisdiction over her decision or over this right to 'make live'. Second, regarding the 'appearance' and disclosure of this 'action' by others, the *diversity* inherent in expressions of natality relies on being witnessed and welcomed as indeterminate uniqueness in the realm of the political. It is this 'public' disclosure of natality (the equality of unique distinctness) and the plurality of human existence that women's struggle for reproductive self-determination implicitly aims to preserve.

Despite the destructive effects of biopower, natality remains a fragile condition of the inter-relational 'capacity' to begin anew, to transform the world we share, to initiate political transformation and to experience mundane freedom. Such agency is neither the property of the isolated subject nor the effect of historical development but is fundamentally relational and contingent, and emerges through acting with others to create a new beginning in history. Arendt often connects this political capacity to enact with others the 'birth' of a new world with 'biological birth', which interrupts the 'circular movements of biological life' (for example, BPF: 42), a formulation of natality that connects it with the creative aspect of collective action, where actors come together for the common cause of freedom, that is, for the sake of maintaining the plurality and equality of uniqueness of all members of a collectivity. This, it would seem, is what those four women senators from different political parties were doing in contesting the government's control of the licensing of RU486, the 'home abortion pill': acting in solidarity temporarily with others who would ordinarily be political opponents, not from the position of common interest, nor out of necessity, but, rather, acting for the sake of freedom. As Arendt writes, though we are mortal, we 'are not born in order to die, but in order to begin' (HC: 246). This is the case because, for Arendt, only action, including giving birth or deciding not to, can interrupt natural and historical necessity and initiate something unpredictable. As Arendt puts it: 'In the language of natural science, [action] is the "infinite improbability which occurs regularly"' (HC: 246). In the language of political theology, it is a 'miracle'.

IV. Racism and the Biopolitics of Birth: Indigenous Women's Reproductivity

While not obvious at the time, the coalition that succeeded in contesting state control of the licensing of RU486 in Australia not only put on display Arendt's concept of political agency as collective interaction pitted against the biopolitical regulation of women's reproductivity, but also it interrupted (albeit temporarily) the insidious intertwining of racism, the biopolitics of maternity and nationalism, given that RU486 potentially delivers access to abortion to all women irrespective of race, ethnicity, religion and socio-economic background. The effectiveness of alliance against the racism inherent in the biopolitics of reproduction is even more apparent in the work of a coalition of women of colour working in the US, which we examine in this section. The connection between biopolitics of birth, racism and nationalism is not obvious, at least not to women of privilege, but it is deeply entrenched in Australia and the US and complex enough to complicate and thwart the pro-choice agenda of (white) liberal feminism. The inter-relation between fertility, biopolitics and different types of racism has also been ignored both by Arendt herself and her critics, despite the fact that Arendt in a different historical context underscores the disastrous politics of racism, imperialism and colonialism as key preconditions of totalitarianism. Consequently, in this section, we move beyond the limitation of Arendt's thinking on race and turn to feminist and women-of-colour theorising the racist politics of reproduction.[16] Focusing specifically on Indigenous women's activism and theories of reproductive agency – theories often ignored in mainstream feminism and biopolitical theory alike – we at the same time develop some important parallels between their work and Arendt's, concerning the key role of the world, alliances and action.

With regard to the Australian context, Barbara Baird (2006b) explains the complex racism of the biopolitics of reproduction that the activism surrounding RU486 interrupted. Baird shows, in her comprehensive historical analysis of the relation between maternity, whiteness and nationalism in Australia, that outbreaks of political concern about maternity in the twentieth century (including moral panics about abortion) have usually coincided with nationalist concerns about reproducing the nation, which have been summarised through the slogan 'populate or perish'.[17] Such concerns were *explicitly* tied to race up until the 1970s. Baird notes various government reports over the first half of the twentieth century that pointed to the need to stimulate the birth rate of the *white* Australian population at the same time as curbing Indigenous reproduction and multiculturalism in general. For instance, running parallel to this political rhetoric of 'populate or perish' in Australia have been incidents of forced sterilisation of Indigenous women and an explicit policy (up to 1972) of removing light-skinned Aboriginal children (now referred to as the 'stolen generations') from their mothers and placing them in the care of white families or institutions. So, even though the imperative to reproduce the nation applied only to white women, Indigenous women have not escaped the biopolitics of birth; on the contrary, it has been applied to Indigenous women more severely through practices that some label genocide.

While devoid of explicit racist language since 1972, the contemporary biopolitics of birth in Australia continues to tie nationhood to race. Baird argues that the political rhetoric surrounding the RU486 event in the mid-2000s continued to entrench this 'race/reproduction bind', a term she borrows from Alys Eve Weinbaum's (2004) parallel analysis of the US and European situations regarding the intersection of the politics of race and maternity (Baird 2006b: 203–6). By this Baird means that the biopolitics of reproduction remains essentially racist. On the one hand, the biopolitical imperative to 'make live' continues to be enacted though Australian government measures to stimulate the birth rate since the mid-1990s, including the intro- duction of a 'baby bonus' in 2001 – a cash payment to mothers upon the birth of each new child (the Treasurer at the time appealed to women to give birth to 'one baby for the mother, one for the father, and one for the nation')[18] – alongside state- sponsored challenges to existing abortion legislation such Health Minister Abbot's 'outburst of anti-abortion sentiment' following the federal election in 2004 and four changes to abortion legisla- tion across several state jurisdictions between 1998 and 2004 (Baird 2006b: 211). On the other hand, accompanying these measures have been indications that the biopolitics of birth in Australia continues to be about reproducing the *white nation*, including signs that Indigenous women in particular are im- plicitly considered to be unfit for motherhood. For instance, up to the Rudd government's 'apology' to the 'stolen genera- tions' of Indigenous Australians in 2007, the federal government continued to resist the recommendations of the 1997 *Report of the National Inquiry into the Separation of Aboriginal and Torres Strait Islander Children from Their Families*. More spectacularly, before losing office in 2007, the Howard government, amid a blaze of publicity, enacted the Northern Territory National Emergency Response (also known as 'the NT Intervention'): a raft of changes to welfare provision, law enforcement, land tenure and health measures in response to allegations of rampant child sexual abuse and parental neglect in Northern Territory Aboriginal communities. While many of these communities do experience serious social and health problems, the demonisation of Indigenous parenting accompanying the NT Intervention was at best an overstatement given that by 2015 no prosecution for child abuse had come from the exercise and given the ongoing failure of governments to improve living conditions and restore dignity and a sense of worth to people in these remote communities. The impact of that demonisation has been to cement the nexus between the biopolitics of race, the biopolitics of maternity and nation-building, so that increased state control over reproduction is aimed at eliminating the unpredictable not only in terms of the *rate* of birth but also in terms of *race* of the nation.

The racist biopolitics of birth is also prevalent in the US, where the genocidal relation between of reproduction, racism and settler colonialism continues to this day. That is why women of colour – African-American, Native-American, Asian-American and Latinas – struggling against the different effects of racist biopolitics of reproduction have consistently opposed the narrow, liberal pro-choice approach dominating white mainstream feminist opposition to state limitations of women's access to legal abortion and birth control. As Jael Silliman contends, 'pro-choice' feminist arguments, which are based on the protection of women's individual decisions against the encroachment of big government into private lives, obscure the racist biopolitics of reproduction and population control: 'This emphasis on individual choice [. . .] discounts the ways in which the state regulates populations, disciplines individual bodies, and exercises control over sexuality, gender, and reproduction' (Silliman 2002: xi). Because of the history of subjection to involuntary sterilisation and long-lasting, illegal and unsafe birth control in the twentieth century, by both the US government and physicians, one of the main issues distinguishing the political struggles of women of colour from the mainstream pro-choice movement is the claim that the access to safe, affordable abortions and birth control is inseparable from the right to have children, to raise them as members of political communities and to create a non-toxic, non-violent world. Consequently, the reclaiming of their reproductive agency by women of colour is inseparable from both political action and the deep concern with the protection of the world against environmental destruction. Despite the lack of direct engagement between women of colour and Arendt, and despite important differences in their diverse positions, we see nonetheless an important parallel in the emphasis on the worldly character of human birth and, therefore, on the worldly character of reproductive agency, often missing in mainstream white feminism.

As Jael Silliman, Marlene Gerber Fried, Loretta Ross and Elena R. Gutiérrez (2016) argue in their the ground-breaking book *Undivided Rights: Women of Color Organize for Reproductive Justice*, women of colour in the US have been for decades engaged in documenting, diagnosing, theorising and engaging in action opposing racist biopolitics of reproduction. The specificity of Native American women's activism lies in the fact that their political actions are inextricably intertwined with the struggle against settler colonialism, cultural and political genocide, and for Native sovereignty,[19] community, land claims and environmental justice. Again, the parallel between these broad coalitions for reproductive rights and Arendt's emphasis on inter-relational agency and political alliances gathering diverse participants for action is rather striking. As discussed in Chapter 1, dynamic, participatory and plural political *alliances* generate power as potentiality of being together. And if such power is preserved in the aftermath of action by continuous commitments and mutual promises, it leads to an enduring transformation of political relations and the world. Since Arendt's articulation of alliance occurs primarily in the context of her theory of revolution (OR: 165–78/156–70), juxtaposing *Undivided Rights* with *On Revolution* has two important implications. First, it allows us to see Indigenous women's struggles for reproductive agency not only in terms of cultural and political survival but also in terms of revolutionary struggles for a just, non-toxic world without racism. Second, this juxtaposition points to the important limitations in Arendt's account of the American and French Revolutions; it reinforces Gines's point about Arendt's' 'egregious omission of the Negro question and slavery in the French context' (Gines 2014: 76, 59–76), and underscores her disregard of gender, the political relevance of slavery and settler colonialism in the American context.

Native American women also struggle against the genocidal uses of biopolitical definitions of racial identity, based on blood quantum, imposed by the US government: 'Generally, one-quarter Indian blood qualifies a person as Indian [. . .] Government interference with the definitions of tribal membership, coupled with population control policies, reduces the number of native people enrolled as members of federally recognized tribes' (Silliman et al. 2016: 114). This biopolitical definition of the federally recognisable Native status not only undermines Native Americans' cultural and political self-definition of communal belonging but also goes hand in hand with the extermination policies of forced sterilisations of Indigenous women in federal Indian Health Service (IHS) clinics, with the loss of Native children either through non-Native adoptions or Christian boarding school systems, and assimilation strategies aiming to destroy Indigenous cultural traditions and languages. Defined by Annette Jaimes as 'statistical extermination',[20] these genocidal policies are part of the larger US political settler colonialism, aiming for continuous expropriation of Native lands because of their natural resources needed for energy production as well as for the ongoing destruction of Native sovereignty (Jaimes 1992: 137; quoted in Silliman et al. 2016: 114).

In the racist biopolitics of settler colonialism, the destruction of women's reproductive capacities is inseparable from the destruction of Native sovereignty, community, culture, language and the world, and the degradation of health and the environment. This genocidal framework of the biopolitical regulation of reproduction collapses the traditional political distinctions between private and public, the biological and the political, *bios* and *zoe*, nature and culture, and confirms Foucault's point that biopower operates such that the distinction between 'make live' and 'let die' is made along racial lines. Only this broad biopolitical/genocidal framework of settler colonialism can explain some of the deadly paradoxes of federal policy and practices of the IHS, which simultaneously violated Native American women's abortion rights, exercised by Native women in their cultures, and perpetrated sterilisation abuses. The refusal of the already extremely limited access to abortion, available only in the case of rape, danger to the mother or incest, in the aftermath of the Hyde amendment limiting federal funding for abortion to these cases (Silliman et al. 2016: 120), allows the IHS to pressure women to undergo permanent sterilisation or dangerous long-lasting contraceptives as birth control methods (Silliman et al. 2016: 119). The object of these policies is the destruction of women's reproductive capacities and agency in order to take control over Native American lands: 'controlling Native women's fertility reduces Native American populations, directly weakening Native American control over their lands' (Silliman et al. 2016: 115). As we see, racism and biopolitical control over reproduction are central operations of settler colonialism, aiming for foreclose what Arendt calls the event of natality in Native American cultures and politics. However, Native American women's activism against involuntary sterilisation and for reproductive rights reclaims natality understood as the disclosure of inter-relational agency, human plurality and the world at the centre of political action, despite the failures of white feminism and white populations to witness their struggles as such. Creating political agency and power through joint action, Native women not only exposed sterilisation abuses and non-compliance with federal abortion policies in the IHS, but since the late 1980s have also created organisations dedicated to training Native women so that they can take charge of their reproductive health, the health of their communities, and become environmental health activists. Indeed, this broad agenda articulating reproductive rights in the context the struggle for decolonisation has been put forth by WARN, Women of All Red Nations, one of the first international Native Women's organisations, established in Rapid city, South Dakota, in 1978 and remaining active today. With membership from over 30 Native nations, WARN, with its links to the American Indian Movement, studied and publicised sterilisation abuses in the 1970s, stopped the mining of uranium and exposed radioactive water pollution on Pine Ridge Reservation, fought the theft of Native lands, and re-articulated feminism in terms of Native American cultures and political struggles (Silliman et al. 2016: 117, 133). In addition to WARN, other organisations and initiatives have included the Native American Women's Health Education Resource Center in South Dakota and the Mother's Milk Project in the Mohawk country of upstate New York (Silliman et al. 2016: 124). Again, by pointing to some parallels with Arendt's thought, we can regard these institutions not only as Native women's organisational achievements but, to evoke Arendt's words, as their 'world-building capacities', as their success of 'constituting stable worldly structure to house, as it were, their combined power of action' (OR: 174/166). By the same token, we are expanding Arendt's notion of revolutionary 'world-building capacities' to include women's struggles for reproductive, inter-relational freedom.

As Winona Laduke, a Native American and environmental activist and political leader, argues, initiatives like the Mother's Milk Project expose another connection between the racist biopolitics of population and the destruction of the environment. In fact, one of the common practices of settler colonialism[21] is 'environmental racism', a term describing the dumping of hazardous materials on or near reservations. As Laduke points out, 'the toxic invasion of Native America' has threatened 317 reservations by toxic waste, targeted reservations 'for 16 proposed nuclear waste dumps' and exposed Western Shoshone land to atomic explosions: 'over the last 45 years, there have been 1000 atomic explosions on Western Shoshone land in Nevada, making the Western Shoshone the most bombed nation on earth' (Laduke 2015: 2–3).

The Mother's Milk Project (MMP), a community-based initiative started by Katsi Cook in 1985, contests such 'environmental racism' directly. In so doing, Cook emphasises the fact that the communal character of political actions is inseparable from the worldly significance of women's reproductive freedom. The MMP arose in response to the PCB toxic contamination of the Saint Lawrence River, food chain and water on Akwesasne land by General Motors, which had been dumping toxic waste on Native lands for twenty-five years. In their research on toxic contamination, MMP, in collaboration with the Tribes Environmental Office, found out that mothers' bodies and breast milk were also contaminated at alarming rates – mothers who ate fish, a traditional diet, from the Saint Lawrence River had 'a 200 percent greater concentration of PCB' than the general population (Silliman et al. 2016: 139; Laduke 2015: 19). The MMP initiative revived traditional midwifery and empowered Mohawk women to become active researchers and political actors in the struggles for both environmental and reproductive justice, and in so doing it became 'a remarkable model of community activism' (Silliman et al. 2016: 143).

As Cook claims, mothers are 'the first environment' linked to the world: 'A woman's body is seen as the first environment and is not separable from the external environment' (Silliman et al. 2016: 129). Consequently, unlike Arendt's neglect of women's bodies and reproductive labour in her theory of natality, Cook stresses the worldly character of women's bodies, which, as the first environment, is a precondition of acting in the world and for the preservation of the world. For Cook and the MMP, the connection between women's bodies and the world is cultural, spiritual and philosophical, that is, based on inter-relational, communal practices, which include practices of giving birth. Environmental racism and devastation destroy this connection. By contrast, 'remembering and restoring the relationship between people and the earth is a crucial part of healing the community from the violations of the industry in their way of life' (Laduke 2015: 20). That is why 'for Native American women, environmental justice and reproductive rights struggles intertwine in the body of each woman' (Silliman et al. 2016: 129).

As Silliman, Gerber Fried, Ross and Gutiérrez argue, women of colour have not only contested racist biopolitics of reproduction but also proposed a broader political theory of reproductive justice.[22] According to Loretta Ross, also the National Coordinator of the SisterSong Women of Color Reproductive Justice Collective, the concept of and the term 'reproductive justice' was used for the first time on the national level at the first national conference of SisterSong in November 2003, and since then it has profoundly influenced the reproductive rights movement:

> Reproductive justice is in essence an intersectional theory emerging from the experiences of women of color whose multiple communities experience a complex set of reproductive oppressions [. . .] Reproductive Justice is a positive approach that links sexuality, health, and human rights to social justice movements by placing abortion and reproductive health issues in the larger context of the well-being and health of women. (Ross 2006: n.p.n.)[23]

This platform has served as the basis of political activism and alliances and for the theoretical reconceptualisation of the political stakes of women's struggles over reproductive rights. Reproductive justice allows, first of all, for broader political coalitions with anti-racist, civil rights, feminist, economic justice and environmental justice movements by locating reproductive politics at the heart of multiple political struggles. It also allows for a fuller diagnosis and critique of the racist biopolitical population control to which women of colour were subjected: 'Women of color have had no trouble distinguishing between population control – externally imposed fertility control policies – and voluntary birth control – women making their own decisions about fertility' (Silliman et al., 2016: 13). Consequently, reproductive justice is both a political theory and action. Such a political notion of reproductive justice not only resonates with Arendt's idea that natality is a central idea of political thought, directly connected with acting in concert, but in fact expands it, by linking women's reproductive agency with political freedom and being in the world (Silliman et al., 2016: viii). As Silliman, Gerber Fried, Ross and Gutiérrez emphasise, the broader political and theoretical framework of reproductive justice, now adopted by the mainstream feminist movements, is eminently political not only because it fights against the wide spectrum of racist biopolitical controls but also, and more importantly, because it demonstrates that 'reproductive rights and freedom are linked to other human rights and social justice issues' (Silliman et al., 2016: viii). As we have seen, in the case of Native American women reproductive justice is based on the interconnections between Native cultures, languages, communities, bodies and the world. And, finally, a reproductive-justice approach positions women of colour not only as the objects of biopolitical regulation and domination but also as theorists and political agents struggling for justice, despite the fact that their contributions have been obscured by the mainstream feminist movement.

In this chapter we have argued that women's reproductive labour lies at the centre of the biopolitics in modern liberal democracies in a way that threatens to erase women's reproductive agency and, in doing so, undermine democratic plurality. We have also revealed the importance of different coalitions for challenging this kind of biopolitics and discussed the inherent racism of the biopolitics of reproduction, particularly in settler nations like Australia and the US. Drawing on Arendt's claim that birth and death are historical and worldly events, and therefore subject to biopolitical regulation, we also reinterpret reproductive labour and the first order of birth in the context of Arendt's theory of natality, understood as the condition of political action, plurality and the expression of uniqueness within political community. Yet for birth to be regarded as a worldly expression of natality, it is crucial that women's reproductive agency, always intertwined with political and worldly concerns, must be welcomed and respected. Such freedom cannot be curtailed either by the biopolitical regularisation of the life and death of the population or by the destruction of the worlds and communities to which these women belong. Second, it is important to recognise that natality, the plurality of human existence and hence the democratic renewal of the 'common' world are also at stake in women's struggles for reproductive self-determination. And finally, we submit that the political and theoretical framework of reproductive justice, proposed by women of colour in the US, is an exemplary articulation of these conditions, as was the alliance that formed around wresting control over the licensing of RU486 away from the centre of government in Australia, albeit at a more modest level.

Notes

1   Indeed, Adriana Cavarero goes so far as to suggest that this basic notion of natality attached to being born as a 'beginner', though underdeveloped in Arendt's thought, is Arendt's most important contribution to twentieth-century thought (Cavarero 2014: 17).

2   Other commentators who, in different ways, agree that the two orders of birth are inseparable include Benhabib (1996: 109–10), Birmingham (2006: 30–3), Cavarero (2014), Guenther (2006: 29–47) and O'Byrne (2010: 90–8). Guenther (whose analysis we return to in Chapter 4) and Cavarero also share our focus in this chapter on the implications of Arendt's discussions of the two orders of natality for a feminist politics of reproduction.

3   To be clear, the focus of the analysis in this chapter of the relation between the two orders of birth/natality is *not* from the perspective of the ontology of the political actor/speaker. Exemplary accounts of this include that by Peg Birmingham (Birmingham 2006: 23–34), who argues (from a Heideggerian perspective and in terms of the temporality of our 'birth' into language) that 'being born' physically is structurally the same as one's birth into language (and into the political): both births are embodied, are about being thrown into a world of others, and so are performative and worldly. Birmingham's account is centred on an interesting explanation of how this relation to one's birth means one's 'identity' (life story) is 'performed in the moment' (the gap between past and future) such that it is constantly transformed. We return in Chapter 5 to discuss, in the context of narrative as action, this issue of how our relation to ourselves and to the political world of others involves a referral to one's own birth and the worldly reiteration of one's story. Rather than viewing the first order of birth from the perspective of the birth of the political agent, the focus here is on how human birth is viewed by the public political world. Our aim is to insert women's reproductive agency into Arendt's formulae of the inter-relation between the two orders of natality in preparation for our critical analysis of the biopolitics of reproduction.

4   Miguel Vatter's disregard of the debates about abortion and biopolitics of reproduction is symptomatic of the many discussions of biopolitics. While he is one of the first thinkers to develop a sustained biopolitical interpretation of natality, in the entire text of part II of *The Republic of the Living*, entitled 'Biopolitics of the family' (Vatter 2014: 99–194), there is no single reference to the biopolitics of reproduction or abortion. The only mention of abortion occurs in an endnote illustrating the confusion between dignity and sacredness of life in the discourse of human rights (Vatter 2014: 223, 355n7).

5   Exceptions to this can be found among a few feminist theorists who analyse the politics of abortion in terms of biopolitics. Catherine Mills provides an interesting biopolitical and ethical analysis of the complex relation between foetal imaging technology and abortion, exposing how the technology intertwines with social norms to shape decisions about 'what counts as a viable or livable life' (Mills 2011: 119). She also shows how the technology has been co-opted by the 'pro-life' side of the abortion debate to enhance the status of the foetus as a vulnerable (human) life. Gila Stopler (2015) provides a comprehensive account of the inequities of abortion law in the US and she mounts a legal argument for the pro-choice case

with brief reference to Foucault's biopolitical theory, although from the perspective of women's individual rights rather than the politics of natality that we discuss here. Erica Millar (2015) provides a compelling account of the racism inherent in the biopolitics of abortion in Australia, which we examine later in this chapter. While more a case of 'fostering life' by selectively encouraging birth rather than 'making live' by enforcing birth, the proliferation and commercialisation of IVF and other reproductive technologies has been critically examined by Walby and Cooper (2008) under the banner of biopolitics.

6 Agamben claims that 'the decisive importance of ethnic rape camps' in the 'former Yugoslavia' is that they mark the point at which 'the principle of birth that assured inscription of life in the order of the nation-state' ceases to operate (Agamben 1998: 176).

7 For a more detailed analysis of the RU486 event in relation to Arendt's politics of natality and Foucault's approach to biopolitical normalisation, see Diprose (2010).

8 See 'Bishops: Obama birth control compromise is dubious' (no author), *USA Today*, 14 March 2012.

9 See the news report by Matt Fegenheimer and Maggie Haberman, 'Donald Trump, abortion foe, eyes "punishment" for women, then recants', *New York Times*, 30 March 2016 <http://www.nytimes.com/2016/03/31/us/politics/donald-trump-abortion.html?_r=0> (last accessed 1 July 2016).

10 A particularly helpful guide to the notion of 'political theology' is provided by Graham Hamill and Julia Reinhard Lupton, who write: 'political theology is not the same as religion [. . .; it] names a form of questioning that arises precisely when religion is no longer the dominant explanatory or life mode' (Hamill and Lupton 2012: 1).

11 Arendt's recurrent return to Augustine has to be accounted for and not simply dismissed, as Paul Kottoman (2012) does, as the recovery of the secular terms from the philosophical theological thinker. Kottoman mentions Arendt's debt to Augustine only in an endnote in which he claims that Arendt is interested in his implicitly secular notion of natality. For an illuminating account of Arendt's uses of Augustine see Birmingham (2006: 75–88).

12 Schmitt's critique of natural and historical causality aims to rescue the domain of sovereign decision while Arendt's critique emphasises the domain of human agency, action and plurality. See Schmitt (1985: 5–15).

13 RU486, or mifepristone, is a synthetic steroid that, in combination with a prostaglandin analogue, provides what is widely considered to be a safe

'doityourself' medical alternative to surgical abortion. It was developed in France in the 1980s, licensed in France in 1988, the UK in 1991 and the US in 2000, and is available in many other countries, including Russia, China, Israel and much of western Europe.

14 Abortion is actually still a criminal offence in most Australian states and territories, although case law has established its legality under certain circumstances and in most jurisdictions. For a summary of the laws covering abortion in Australia, see the feature article by Caroline De Costa and Heather Douglas, 'Explainer: is abortion legal in Australia?', *The Conversation*, 3 September 2015 <http://theconversation.com/explainer-is-abortion-legal-in-australia-48321> (last accessed 23 February 2018).

15 As we have discussed in Chapter 1, Arendt outlines this idea of the event of natality opening a gap between past and future in the preface to the collection *Between Past and Future* (BPF: 10), which is a preliminary summary of her analysis in Chapter 20 of *Life of the Mind, Volume I* (LM I: 202–12).

16 For the most comprehensive critique of Arendt's failed responses to the 'negro question', in particular regarding Afro-American struggles against segregation and for civil rights, see Gines (2014). Although Gines does not address anti-black racism with regard to reproduction, her trenchant analysis is an important diagnosis and corrective of the limitations of using Arendt's political philosophy for that purpose.

17 'Populate or perish' is a slogan coined by Australia's Labor and Immigration Minister Arthur Caldwell in a speech delivered toward the end of the Second World War, where he argued that economic development and military security rested on rapidly increasing the size of the population through immigration (the population was only seven million at the time yet the land mass is about the same size as the continental US). Australian immigration policy at the time was explicitly racist, including its name: it was called the White Australia Policy up to 1965. The slogan 'populate or perish' has been used more generally to refer additionally to policies to increase the *birth rate*. This has also been about increasing the size of the white population. See also Erica Millar's extension of Baird's account in terms of the biopolitics of abortion in Australia, 'a biopolitics that involves three interlocking elements: the disavowal of indigenous sovereignty, the exclusion of non-white others and the promotion of white reproduction' (Millar 2015: 83).

18 The 'baby bonus' was increased from $3,000 to $5,000 before being discontinued in 2015. For an outline and critical analysis of this policy see Ross Guest (2007).

19 The fact that Native American struggles for decolonisation are based on the political claims of Native sovereignty does not mean that tribal sovereignty is conceptually compatible with Western conceptions of sovereignty. As the authors of the *Undivided Rights* (first published in 2004) argue, sovereignty, as defined by leaders of the Iroquois nation in 1977, means self-determination and control over Native lands, law, education, language and culture, production, and reproduction (Silliman et al. 2016: 131).

20 M. Annette Jaimes (Jaimes 1992: 137) quoted in *Undivided Rights* (Silliman et al. 2016: 114).

21 While writing this last section of this chapter in November 2016, another high-profile Native struggle against environmental racism was taking place in the US, namely, the opposition of the Standing Rock Sioux Tribe, with thousands of their national and international supporters, including the United Nations, to the construction of the Dakota Access Pipeline (DAPL), which would carry half a billion barrels of fracked oil a day, threatening the Sioux Tribe's water supply, sacred sites and burial grounds. See <http://indigenousamerican.com/2016/10/29/breaking-the-united-nations-is-headed-to-standing-rock> (last accessed 2 November 2016).

22 We are indebted to Jael Silliman, Marlene Gerber Fried, Loretta Ross and Elena R. Gutiérrez, the authors of *Undivided Rights: Women of Color Organize for Reproductive Justice*, the first collection to have adopted a reproductive justice framework and to have focused exclusively on the contributions of women of colour in the US to political struggles for reproductive justice.

23 For an excellent formulation of reproductive justice, which includes access to abortion, based on precolonial cultural beliefs, see the website of the Native American Women's Health Education Resource Center at <http://www.nativeshop.org/programs/reproductive-justice.html> (last accessed 11 March 2016).

4

Natality, Ethics and Politics: Hospitality, Corporeality, Responsibility

The analysis of the relation between biopolitics and natality in the section IV of Chapter 3 further complicates the relation between, on the one hand, the first order of birth and 'private' (inter-relational) level of the disclosure of natality, and, on the other hand, the 'public' appearance and disclosure of natality. What the analysis there reveals is how the biopolitical regulation of maternity (and the wider government of the birth of the future citizen) is inseparable from the political concern with nationhood and the biopolitics of race. In this chapter we explore the inter-relation of these two orders of natality further, this time in terms of political hospitality and responsibility and the relation between politics and ethics. In turning to the motif of *hospitality*, the analysis takes up not only the way that Arendt considers the event of natality to be the *raison d'être* of politics, but also her configuration of democratic politics in terms of political hospitality. Political hospitality is understood as the disclosure of natality in terms of the *welcome* of the beginner (unique distinctness) and of the new beginning. All spheres of human activity, Arendt says, are 'rooted in natality in so far as they have the task to provide and preserve the world for [. . .] the constant influx of newcomers who are born into the world as strangers' (HC: 9). In a sense, what Arendt calls 'the political' is the publicity of this welcome and disclosure of natality, where each person appears to others as a unique human agent whose words and deeds initiate an unpredictable, but welcome, change to the human world. In this chapter we follow Jean-Luc Nancy's interpretation of this welcome and disclosure of natality (or what he refers to as the 'sharing of singularity' and the affirmation of 'uniqueness') as the *principle* of democracy and democratic plurality rather than a formulation of the political per se.[1] As a *principle* of democratic plurality, the welcome of natality and affirmation of uniqueness is that which must be maintained at all levels of human interaction if we are to prevent the erasure of humanity and of 'reality' through fear of the unknown and the unpredictable as well as through hatred of difference. Moreover, the analyses in this chapter show how failing to uphold this principle at the levels of national and biopolitical government can have a detrimental impact not just in the targets of policies and practices that reject uniqueness and new beginnings but also on the sharing of singularity and the capacity for action throughout the populace.

Also in this chapter we argue, first through Derrida's discussion of hospitality and then Arendt's more thorough account of responsibility, that this principle of the welcome of natality is also an *ethical* principle underlying human inter-relationality in general. At the same time, the analyses give due attention to Arendt's acknowledgement that the 'potentiality of something entirely new and unpredictable' needs to be 'hedged in', not only by what 'memory is for [humanity's] historical existence', but also by 'laws in *constitutional* government' (OT: 465, emphasis added). These are laws that foster the event of natality but also provide the stability of 'a common world, the reality of some continuity which transcends the individual life span of each generation, absorbs all new origins [while being] nourished by them' (OT: 465). Moreover, the analyses reopen the question of the role of the body, affect and temporality, not only in the foreclosure of natality but also in its renewal through political action.

In section I this principle of the welcome, disclosure and sharing of uniqueness is the basis for examining how the laws of hospitality governing the welcome of strangers at the level of the nation (for example, the welcome of refugees, immigrants, asylum seekers) are entwined with the biopolitics of reproduction (the welcome of the newborn), of sexuality and of diversity in the domestic arena and in quotidian inter-relationality. This analysis aims to reveal and explain the connection between the failure of political hospitality and the rejection of the stranger at the level of the nation (for reasons of national security, for instance, and/or securing a unified, mythical national identity) and increased biopolitical regulation of women's reproductivity and moves against plurality and unpredictability within interpersonal relations and the biological life of the population. Both trends aim at eliminating natality, unpredictability and felt instability, to the detriment of democratic plurality, equality of unique distinctness and the ethical treatment of people. Central to this analysis of political hospitality is, first, the claim that the disclosure of natality or the welcome of unique distinctness, whether at the level of the nation or at the domestic or interpersonal level, is always *conditional*. While the communal disclosure of natality through speech and action spawns novelty, potentiality and unpredictability, the simultaneous disclosure and *welcome* of natality is *never unconditional*. Aside from laws that 'hedge in' the boundless consequences of action, as argued in Chapter 1, the event of natality is mediated and foreclosed to the extent that the 'appearance', witness and welcome of the indeterminate 'who' or uniqueness is filtered through identification of others in terms of the worldly meanings of 'what-ness' and the biases that accompany such interpretation of the speech, action and the appearance of others, even if the event of natality also disrupts and transforms that sense of the world. Second, by examining the inter-relation between hospitality at the inter-personal, domestic and national levels, the aim is to reveal ways that this conditionality can be unethical, and how the laws of hospitality at both levels are patriarchal, as well as racist. This points to the *inter-relation of ethics and politics* in one sense: how biopolitics may be unethical insofar as it maintains a hierarchy of 'types' of uniqueness, an inequality of unique distinctness as Arendt would say. This raises the question of what kind of laws of hospitality and responsible government might circumvent such inequality.

In order to explain how these political moves against plurality and unpredictability are connected and to suggest why they have gained popular support recently in some democracies (including Australia, the US and the UK, as well as many Continental European countries), we consider, in section II, how government regulation of labour and the workplace fits into the political picture of the welcome of natality. The analysis shows how the realm of labour (or 'work' and 'fabrication', to use Arendt's terminology) acts as a lynchpin between the home and the nation such that felt instability and insecurity in people's working lives may explain the appeal of (empty) political promises of security, uniformity and stability at the level of the nation. Significantly, in contemporary democracies the trend in government of the workplace and labour relations is not toward stricter government regulation and normalisation but toward *deregulation* of labour and the market, with attendant *intensification of unpredictability*, instability and insecurity in people's working lives. While this trend moves labour and the workplace outside the dominion of biopolitics (as it is usually understood) and beyond Arendt's critical genealogy of the rise of *animal laborans* and the social outlined in *The Human Condition*, the deregulation of labour and the market has been just as effective in eliminating natality from people's working lives. The analysis offers an explanation of the impact of deregulation of labour on the disclosure and welcome of natality, partly with reference to Arendt's various accounts of how both totalitarian-like 'laws of movement' (EU: 340) and neo-liberal notions of 'freedom from politics' (BPF: 149) can reduce human existence to something like 'life process', although with some adjustment to what she means by 'life process'. While this proposal (that working life can thus be reduced to 'life process') will be elaborated in terms of the elimination of disjunctive temporality from human existence and from the fabric of the world of work that people share, the analysis also takes heed of the role of the body in the disclosure and welcome of natality. The claim at the core of this account is that time is experienced and lived by *bodily* beings and that it is at the nexus between time, body and government regulation that both biopolitics and the deregulation of labour impacts on our lives. Understanding this impact requires supplementing Arendt's account of the *animal laborans* in *The Human Condition* with other phenomenological accounts of how labour (and other world-directed) activities temporalise human existence and establish an ambiguous relation between the acting body and the world shared with others through which thinking and judgement arise. This account also involves some revision of Arendt's formulations of the relation between feeling and politics.

Exploration of the role of the body in action and the corporeal impact of biopolitics and severely conditional hospitality facilitates an explanation of Arendt's concept of 'coordination' of a population, the kind of normalisation that renders people, if not fully conditioned or reducible to 'biological life' or 'life process' (which is questionable in non-totalitarian biopolitics), at least compliant and docile. This is the topic of section III. We turn to the motif of *responsibility* to examine how government restriction of plurality at the level of the nation (and through the deregulation of labour) can normalise a population in the sense of dampening 'conscience' (the capacity to judge between right and wrong) and the capacity to contest and act against such trends. The analysis focuses on how this kind of normalisation can lead to loss of 'the common world' (HC: 57–8)[2] and loss of the agentic character of action (for example, HC: 180), but not just with regard to people who are targets of biopolitical regularisation (refugees, potential mothers, 'deviant' sexualities, 'biological identities' deemed aberrant) but also in relation to those among the wider population who are supposedly protected and enabled by that regulation. Exploration of the notion of responsibility also provides an account of how 'conscience' can be reawakened to animate political action, although making the connection between responsibility and the disclosure and welcome of natality requires some further preliminary comments.

Arendt explores the concept of responsibility in several papers written between 1964 and 1968, collected posthumously in *Responsibility and Judgment* (RJ), in response to criticisms of her book *Eichmann in Jerusalem*. In part, this work elaborates in more detail her passing comments in *The Origins of Totalitarianism* about the killing of 'moral person' in Nazi concentration camps, where brutalisation and the suspension of moral categories and 'common sense' led to the destruction of 'conscience' among internees and with this the destruction of the capacity to make moral choices between right and wrong, good and evil (OT: 452). Primarily, though, Arendt's later work on responsibility and moral judgement is concerned with the consequences of the escalation of practices and government policies that generated a hatred of difference and violence in public affairs *outside the camps*, a situation she describes as a collapse of 'established moral standards' in public life that paved the way for the camps (RJ: 52). Arguably, her analysis is relevant for a diagnosis of similar trends in contemporary non-totalitarian politics, such as erecting borders against Muslims, as the Trump administration has done in the US; or putting so-called 'illegal arrivals' into offshore detention camps, as is the case in Australia since 2001 – the 'lesser evils' that Arendt warns could end in further deterioration of democratic plurality (for example, EU: 271). Arendt is not so much concerned with the accountability of leaders of government for policies that reject diversity and foster hatred of difference in public life as she is with the personal responsibility of ordinary citizens (including bureaucrats like Eichmann) who are 'coordinated' by a regime and either go along with those trends or actively support them (RJ: 33–5). But again, she is not out to blame ordinary citizens or hold them legally accountable. Arendt revises the meaning of responsibility away from its 'juridical' sense (of legal accountability and blame) in order to contend with two philosophical problems raised by this issue of the reversal of 'moral standards' in public affairs. First, morality, understood as *fixed principles* for guiding conduct toward others, has no place in politics, which, in Arendt's and others' accounts of democratic politics, is concerned with the *contestation* of principles through *collective* dialogue and action and the maintenance of law, regarded as 'essential to the integrity of our common humanity' (RJ: 22). Hence, Arendt refers to government policies or government-endorsed practices that are an affront to natality and plurality as 'borderline phenomena' between morality and politics (RJ: 104–5). Second, if we are to explain the 'moral disintegration' in politics that is Arendt's focus, then ethical conduct toward others cannot be determined by either the moral norms or the particular laws of the society into which we are born (which is the case with the juridical notion of responsibility). Otherwise, how could such norms be so easily reversed and the reversal embraced or tolerated by a majority of a populace? But nor can 'conscience' be absolutely unencumbered by some normative criteria, otherwise how do some people resist or oppose a reversal of norms whereas others just toe the line? Arendt sets out to explain this possibility without recourse to a notion of absolute freedom or moral relativism. As we will see, conscience, for Arendt, is an experience of natality arising from (a largely Kantian notion of) judgement. However, as Arendt does not really explain how this pricking of conscience might happen for citizens who have been rendered docile by a morally bankrupt regime, it is necessary to supplement her analysis with an account of the corporeal and affective basis of conscience.

So, section III examines, first, how Arendt ties responsibility, not to duty or blame or prevailing moral norms, but to the experience of futurity as *conscience* – the condition of judgement that opens a gap between a past and an undetermined future, the experience of the event of natality. Arendt thereby links responsibility to the maintenance of human plurality (or equality of unique distinctness) that contests and undermines totalitarian 'coordination' or normalising and regularising biopolitics.

Second, the analysis considers further what is largely missing from Arendt's account: the role of corporeal affectivity or sensibility in both the dampening of conscience and its reawakening in responsibility. We provide the phenomenological take on this in section II of this chapter and we draw on Nietzsche for this purpose in section III. While Arendt explicitly credits Nietzsche with the insight that conscience cannot be tied to moral custom (for example, RJ: 103), she rejects a related idea apparent in his work: that the basis of conscience and hence responsibility is a corporeal and affective self-relation. As biopolitics, in foreclosing natality and thus inhibiting action, impacts on bodies, then (acting) bodies are also the sites of recovery from the malaise of 'coordination'.

Finally, the analysis connects Arendt's thoughts on personal responsibility with her work on political community or public inter-action in order to extend responsibility beyond Nietzsche's individualism (and the individualism of classical and neo-liberalism) to include responsibility for others and for the world. This allows reconsideration of the relation between personal responsibility and political responsibility, between ethics and political action. The argument, with and beyond Arendt, is that the dulling of conscience and failure of personal responsibility of a populace in a democratic polity is an effect of *government no longer assuming responsibility for maintaining the conditions necessary for the disclosure and welcome of natality and for human plurality.* Moreover, this failure of political responsibility involves undermining, not so much explicit laws or moral norms, but, with that, the affective corporeal *basis of normativity* (the event of natality) that both liberal democratic politics and ethical conduct would ordinarily share. First, though, we set the scene for that analysis by examining further the relationship between the welcome of natality in the domestic and national arenas: the question of political hospitality.

I. Women's Bodies Between National Hospitality and Domestic Biopolitics

Since Arendt wrote her political philosophy, Jacques Derrida has elaborated her idea of the disclosure and welcome of natality into a political ontology of hospitality, although with reference to the philosophy of Emmanuel Levinas rather than Arendt. Nevertheless, examination of this idea of political hospitality demonstrates how a failure of hospitality at the level of the nation is mirrored in, and impacts on, biopolitical regulation of women's reproductivity, sexuality, activities within the 'home' and quotidian inter-relationality. The analysis also reinforces the need to preserve political agency, in Arendt's sense of the disclosure of natality within human interactions, at *all levels* of human activity, not just the public arena of 'appearance' that Arendt defines as the political.

Through his interrogations of the concepts of hospitality in the philosophy we have inherited, Derrida is in accord with Arendt (although not necessarily with Levinas) with regard to its aporetic structure, but, arguably, he does a little more to expose its patriarchal dimensions. With regard to the aporetic structure of the 'disclosure' and welcome of the new beginning and uniqueness, the claim is that just as there is no absolute separation between the corporeal (or 'biological') and political dimensions of the new beginning, there is no absolute break between the (conditioned) past and (undetermined) future, between determinism and freedom. In his seminars on hospitality, published in *Of Hospitality* (Derrida 2000), and in his engagements with

Levinas (for example, Derrida 1999), Derrida has shown how the play between conditional and unconditional hospitality is the condition of subjectivity, inter-relationality (sociality) and the political. Arendt would agree with Derrida's claim that *unconditional* hospitality, welcoming the absolutely (unknowable) other (or, in Arendt's terms, welcoming or disclosing the event of natality, the 'who', the 'stranger'), constitutes *dwelling* – home, self, nation – *as open to the other* (dwelling as the 'in-between' of potentiality and freedom). Hence, hospitality is not a footnote to human existence: this responsiveness, this welcome of natality, this openness as potentiality *is* subjectivity, agency, being-singular-plural, and so on.[3] Keeping open this space of the unconditional welcome of the new, the affirmation of uniqueness and plurality, without favouring a particular ideal identity for citizenship or a 'truth' of the common, is also the principle of democracy, as Nancy suggests (Nancy 2010: 13–18). But, and Arendt would also agree, Derrida goes on to suggest that, conversely, and paradoxically, 'at the same time' this 'home' in all its guises must take place as a *condition* of hospitality (Derrida 2000: 55); this is the world into which we are thrown. This, then, is the other side of the aporetic structure of hospitality: the welcome of the new, the stranger, is never completely free of *conditions* given by the *laws of hospitality*, by the ethos and interpretations of the culture and language that the host has inherited and through which the person (or nation) affirms uniqueness or assesses, knows and welcomes the beginner and beginning of the new (Derrida 2000: 45). Whether we are referring to the welcome of the newborn, the new beginning through an act, or the refugee, the welcome itself is always conditional, 'hedged in' by laws of hospitality that, ideally, maintain a stable reality that is also nourished by new beginnings.[4]

That the unconditional welcome is always conditioned points to the ethical dimension of hospitality and, therefore, of the political. The more the host enforces traditional laws of hospitality, the more the host adheres to cultural norms and claims to sovereignty in giving refuge to the other, the more injustice is done to the other. Equally, even though inter-relationality at all levels (self, home, nation) requires some stability, predictability and common sense, refusing the new and excluding the stranger in the interests of stability can be just as damaging to sociality and sense as the disruption to sense that the event of natality brings. While some injustice is inevitable in the conditions imposed on the welcome of natality, the ethical question is always where to draw the boundary or, rather, how to maintain flexibility and multidirectional participation in the drawing of boundaries through laws and institutions around the potentiality of dwelling together (for example, HC: 181–2, 190).

While accepting this analysis of the aporetic schema of hospitality, we contend, in the following interrogation of our conventions of hospitality, that underlying the play of unconditional and conditional hospitality across the three classic loci of dwelling (self, home and nation) are not just superficial cultural biases in the interpretation of differences, but deeper sexual, racial, class and religious biases to do with biopolitical containment and regulation of women's reproductivity and sexuality and of unpredictability and 'irregularities' in biological life. These biases become particularly obvious in the politics of many liberal democracies when national security is at issue. While a closure of national hospitality, closure of the welcome of the new, does injustice to others 'outside' the nation (blocking the welcome of refugees and ignoring their plight being the most obvious contemporary example of such injustice), what is less often noted is the impact on women and minority races *within* the polity that exercises severely conditional hospitality. Moreover, extending Derrida's and Arendt's analyses of the futural and undetermined dimensions of hospitality, the additional claim to be explored is that the battle for equality and justice is a battle over *time and the body*: hospitality, as impossible as it is, gives and takes *lived* time, but the more that hospitality at the level of the nation becomes conditional under conservative political forces, the more that the time that it takes is given by, or taken from, women, economically disadvantaged groups and people subordinated on the basis of race, ethnicity or religion. Adding consideration of the relation between time, the body and the welcome of natality within the home and intimate relations helps to explain the impact on women of the foreclosure of hospitality at the national and domestic levels. A third theme of the analysis points to the ways that severely conditional national hospitality undermines the principles of democracy and, conversely, the claim is that working against the injustices exacted through conditional hospitality, and the future of democratic plurality itself, requires time for vigorous contestation of the laws of hospitality, a contestation inspired by the other's uniqueness and implied within the welcome and disclosure of natality.

We have already indicated in Chapter 3 the patriarchal basis of hospitality in terms of anti-abortion laws and the biopolitics of birth in general, although without focusing on the motif of hospitality. Two other examples of the patriarchal dimension of our traditions of hospitality provide the basis for further analysis. First is the shocking example of conditional hospitality with which Derrida ends his two seminars on hospitality, which, until his closing note on 'Difficulties', had focused on the plight of the 'foreigner' caught up in the play of conditional and unconditional hospitality (Derrida 2000: 151–5). Derrida recounts the parallel stories in Genesis (19: 1–9) and Judges (19: 23–30) of the unethical condition of Lot's (or, in Judges, a 'Levite's') conditional hospitality. Having offered hospitality to two angels (or strangers) at the gates of the city of Sodom, Lot, who is a 'foreigner' himself, feels obliged to protect his guests from the Sodomites' customary demand that new arrivals be given over for 'penetration'. This is the example of a severe conditional hospitality: you are welcome (to this nation/city/home) on condition that you submit to the Sodomite's law of sodomy, a violent condition that aims at erasing natality and the possibility of a new beginning that is inherent in the welcome. Lot attempts to protect his guests from these harsh conditions, but only by offering, first his 'virgin daughters' then 'a concubine', to be 'abused' instead. While we do not find out from Genesis what happens to these women, in the narrative in Judges, where a Levite gives hospitality to a 'pilgrim' and his 'concubine' (understood to be his wife) we learn that the men of the city take up the Levite's offer of the 'concubine' as a condition of the hospitality given to her foreigner husband. Her fate is this: after being repeatedly raped through the night by the men of the city, she fell 'dead on the threshold' of the home of her 'husband's host' (Derrida 2000: 155). Her husband, overcome with despair, cuts her body into twelve pieces and distributes it to the Israelite tribes with the request that they ponder and respond to the question whether such injustice had been done to the Israelites since being scattered beyond the land of Egypt.

In evoking this politico-moral tale from core texts of both the Hebrew and Christian traditions, Derrida shows not only how the condition of building any semblance of an impossibly uniform nation state is that the welcome of natality is harshly *conditional* in terms of a range of norms to do with racial and cultural identity, language, sexuality and religion, but also, and most emphatically, that this conditional hospitality is patriarchal. Derrida does not dwell on this final point; he just uses the story to raise the issue of how the conditions of the welcome of natality (or the 'laws of hospitality') give rise to a 'hierarchy of guests and the hostages' (Derrida 2000: 153), and how, when it comes to women and others at the base of this hierarchy, hospitality is put above ethics. In case we are tempted to dismiss this example of the possible consequences of severely conditional hospitality as woefully outdated, it was striking, when re-reading Derrida's analysis of hospitality in preparation for the penultimate draft of this book, how much this story and his closing question resonates with political events of 2016–17 regarding the (mis)handling of the refugee crisis in Europe by most European democratic states, but also by the US and Australian governments. (Australian refugee policies get special mention in this analysis because, while not as widely publicised as those of some European countries and as the anti-immigration stance in the US introduced with the Trump administration in 2017, they are arguably harsher, have been in place for much longer – since 2001 – and exemplify the claims being made here about the damage that severely conditional hospitality can do at all levels of human inter-relationality.[5]) Derrida's final question could be addressed directly to the leaders of those states that are erecting boundaries against the current massive increase in refugee numbers (which increased to 65 million in 2016), as these lawmakers ponder the wide-reaching impact (on democratic plurality and on the spaces of 'dwelling' within the nation) of their severely conditional laws of hospitality:

Are we the heirs to this [racist and patriarchal] tradition of hospitality? Up to what point? Where should we place the invariant, if it is one, across this logic and these narratives? They testify without end in our memory. (Derrida 2000: 155)

Allowing others' uniqueness and their expressions of new beginnings to contest and transform national laws of hospitality requires, in this case, that the refugee is welcomed without conditions that would 'penetrate' their being-singular and erase any distinctness. But equally, laws of hospitality that seek to uphold sovereignty and internal uniformity (of nation or home) put an impossible strain on the possibility of equality of unique distinctness and potentiality of being together *within* the nation. Derrida's closing example, then, reveals that even if the hospitality of the Levite (the 'foreigner' within) is as unconditional as he can manage, given the severity of the laws of hospitality of the polity that he inhabits, he nevertheless still presides over an appalling injustice toward women. Aside from, and arguably supporting, the aporia of conditional and unconditional hospitality in the relation between the host, the guests and the citizens of the city, is the sacrifice of *women's bodies* as well as the loss of inter-relationality and plurality. In these stories from Genesis and Judges, foreigners' bodies do not make sense to the host without 'penetration' by the host, but women's bodies do not make sense at all, either as the origin of sense (the new beginning) or the expression of uniqueness. Women within the home, the family, city or nation are neither guests nor hosts, neither foreigners within nor excluded outsiders. Women's bodies, sexualities and reproductivity *are* (at), and support, the borders of the home, and insofar as the borders of a place of dwelling, whether of the self, the home, the city or the nation, are secured and disrupted by the play between conditional and unconditional hospitality, this play will impact on, and be felt by, the bodies of women. Moreover, the more conditional the welcome of natality and the more the host would secure the borders of what he takes to be his sovereign territory, the more these bodies will be cut to pieces. *This* is the tradition of hospitality that we have inherited. But up to what point do its patriarchal themes 'testify without end in our memory'? And what more can be said of the body as the site of the foreclosure, disclosure and enactment of natality?

Elaborating the role of the body and affectivity in the disclosure and welcome of natality (irrespective of the operation of biopolitics) is enabled by our second additional example of the patriarchal dimensions of our traditional laws of hospitality, which is found in the philosophy of Emmanuel Levinas. Levinas appears here for reasons other than because Derrida credits him rather than Arendt with highlighting the ontology of hospitality at the level of subjectivity and interpersonal relations. Levinas's notion of hospitality is also useful because, in *Totality and Infinity*, in a chapter entitled 'The dwelling' (Levinas 1969: 152–74), he provides an account of how the labouring body and affectivity are involved in opening the temporal dimension of the welcome of natality (the gap between past and future). Moreover, this analysis of labour (which Arendt would call 'work' or the realm of *Homo faber* – fabrication) juxtaposes the workplace and the home in a way that, while reminiscent enough of the sexual division of labour of the 1960s to sound obsolete, does expose (albeit inadvertently) the patriarchal basis of the way the welcome of uniqueness (still) operates across those two loci of dwelling.

For Levinas, as with Derrida and Arendt, 'the dwelling' or 'home' that conditional hospitality presupposes is at once the *place* of one's dwelling (self, home, nation and so on) and the 'event' of natality, or what Levinas might refer to as the *immemorial temporality* of dwelling. That is, dwelling is an ongoing event, apparent in every activity, although exemplified for Levinas by the activity of labour (or 'work' in Arendt's terminology) that lifts the self, home, nation and so on above 'life' and an immediate, affective relation to 'life', which Levinas calls 'enjoyment'. Labour of all kinds (including manual and even repetitive work but also writing, teaching and counting) does this by punctuating time (or the 'timeless') with a difference between past and future. This temporal dimension of human existence and inter-relationality marks the phenomenological understanding of a break with necessity, a break that, as we will show, is especially dependent on the *welcome* of natality (or what Levinas calls alterity or the other).

There are two aspects to how the labouring body temporalises dwelling. First, the labouring body sets up a distance from the world it works on while remaining grounded within the material and common world that is not its fabrication. Hence, there is an 'equivocation of the body', the conditioned freedom of being 'at home with oneself in something other than oneself' (Levinas 1969: 164). And second, as in Arendt's account in *The Life of the Mind* (LM I: 202–13) of how the experience of reflective thinking and judgement institutes a gap between past and future, for Levinas the body that labours effects a 'postponement' of the present and thus 'opens the very dimension of time' (Levinas 1969: 165). This is also where consciousness, 'recollection' and thinking arise: the 'ambiguity of the body is *consciousness*' (Levinas 1969: 165), in that 'to be conscious is precisely to have time', which, as with Arendt's account of the 'path paved by thinking' (LM I: 210), means a past to be remembered and a future anticipated (Levinas 1969: 166). We will return to discuss how this ambiguity of the body at the heart of the temporalisation of dwelling is crucial for understanding the impact of severely conditional national hospitality upon women and others at the bottom of the hierarchy of guests and hosts underlying political hospitality.

First, though, how does the patriarchal basis of our traditions of hospitality figure in Levinas's account of labour? On the up side, Levinas insists that the labourer is not a self-contained individual working for the satisfaction of need, the preservation of their life, or for the sake of their own self, future or freedom. Rather, the precondition of a body ambiguously open to a world (and hence the precondition of self-relation, or 'recollection' and 'subjectivity') is being open to and *for another*. This further precondition to the temporalisation of dwelling such that it is futural and breaks with the past is what gives hospitality its ethical dimension. Levinas usually describes this extra precondition of the break with necessity in terms of the *unconditional* welcome of the alterity characteristic of the 'ethical relation': in order to have a home, world, agency and so on, 'I must know how to give what I possess', including language (speech) and my self-possession (self-relation). That is, dwelling, action and speech are predicated on unconditional hospitality whereby I encounter the 'face of the Other that calls me [and the laws of hospitality that I embody through the common world we share] into question [. . .] by opening my home to him' (Levinas 1969: 171). This hospitality, this welcome of natality, of the absolutely unknowable other, of the alterity or uniqueness that cannot be memorialised or anticipated, gets the temporalisation of time, and its disruption of presence, going.

Arendt, of course, would say that hospitality is never purely unconditional – the disclosure and welcome of natality to and by others is always worldly. Leaving aside the issue of where exactly Levinas stands on this, there are two points to emphasise about his version of hospitality at this point. First, hospitality is not something an agent or a subject *chooses* for the sake of the other; rather, hospitality, as opening to the alterity of the other, *is* human agency (or 'subjectivity' in Levinas's terminology) and the basis of a pluralist sociality ('plurality', in Arendt's terminology) that is open to an undetermined future. So refusing or erasing the other's alterity (denying their uniqueness or in some other way destroying their capacity to express natality) not only denies the other's 'humanity' but it closes down both agency and sociality in general. Second, hospitality, subjectivity, agency is corporeal and affective. Hence refusing or withdrawing hospitality will impact on bodies; the refusal of natality will be felt by the self and by the other; and it may result in an inability to speak, act or think. We will return to discuss the corporeal impact of the refusal of hospitality.

The point to be elaborated now is that this hospitality is not available equally for everyone. In his account of labour/work (and in his account of the sexual relation or 'eros') in *Totality and Infinity* Levinas admits to a patriarchal dimension to hospitality. Before and apart from the play of unconditional and conditional hospitality is an interim and arguably ultimate precondition: hospitality provided by 'Woman' in the home (Levinas 1969: 154–8). 'Feminine hospitality', 'the welcoming one par excellence', is the ultimate condition of labour, 'recollection, the interiority of the Home, and inhabitation' (Levinas 1969: 155, 157). While Levinas does not put it this way, what he is admitting here is that, through 'feminine hospitality', women (and domestic labourers) give time to others in the home and in intimate relations so that others have time for consciousness, labour and the hospitality of the ethical relation. Significantly, just as in Derrida's example, 'Woman' is *not a subject* of this dwelling (she is not the one who welcomes the other in a way that opens subjectivity, action and speech). Nor is 'Woman' the other who is welcomed (she is not the other of the ethical relation, the stranger who is welcomed). Levinas says explicitly that the 'Woman' of the 'intimate relation' for whom the self labours is a 'discrete absence'; that is, the feminine welcome that is a condition of subjectivity and all kinds of dwelling is *not* 'the face' (alterity) of the ethical relation that questions a subject's self-possession (Levinas 1969: 157); she is not a beginner, to return to Arendt's terminology. But Levinas does not say why.

There is one ontological reason of relevance to this analysis for why Levinas insists (wrongly) that this 'feminine' hospitality is a 'silent absence' rather than the actions of a beginner to be welcomed.[6] For dwelling to take hold such that the (labouring) body makes an 'appearance' to others as a beginner of the new while belonging to a world in an enduring but indeterminate way, it cannot be entirely under erasure from contestation by those beginners of the new who extend the welcome. But if that is so, then, equally, the 'feminine' welcome cannot be purely unconditional, as this would require the absolute passivity and hence the erasure of natality from the lives of these women. Feminist theorists have put a similar point in a more politically astute way: a capitalist economy presupposes, without acknowledgement, that the ambiguous autonomy of the one who labours in the world of work or acts in public is dependent upon some stability and support provided by care for and conditioning of the body in the home. Arendt also acknowledges this traditional role of women whose 'life was "laborious", devoted to bodily functions' (HC: 72). But there is no reason why women or anyone need sacrifice their own agency and unique distinctness in welcoming the expressions of natality of others; nor should it be assumed that the labouring body's comportment toward a world is undone into unruly passion or pure 'enjoyment' away from work (or away from public activities). While Levinas argues that the welcome of unconditional hospitality cannot be reciprocated without annulling separation and hence singularity, the subject of that welcome must also be welcomed by someone else if that person is not to disappear entirely into what Arendt refers to as the 'timeless present' (LM I: 207). Levinas usually addresses this question about how equality and justice are achieved in an ethics of non-reciprocal hospitality by suggesting that unconditional hospitality, while not reciprocal between two people, is 'spread around' via the (sexually neutral) third party for whom the other that a person faces is responsible and who is welcoming of that person (for example, Levinas 1969: 212–14). However, when it comes to labour and 'eros', this 'someone else' who supports the subjectivity of labour and of hospitality is not a sexually neutral third party. Rather, for Levinas (and for much political philosophy) it is 'Woman', and she is not herself explicitly given the security of hospitality by someone else. Therein lies the patriarchal dimension of our tradition of hospitality.

More needs to be said to explain the conditions under which the inequities of our traditions of hospitality are reinforced and why it is that, even though those who give time to others as a precondition to hospitality do not have to be actual women (as Levinas also insists), this is usually the case, even in societies where women have achieved equality before the law. More also needs to be said about the impact of these inequities on women and other disadvantaged groups.

II. Natality, Labouring Bodies and the Deregulation of Labour Time

In Chapters 2 and 3 we have examined Arendt's main theses about the conditions under which the welcome of natality is foreclosed in the realm of the political (conditions she refers to as the 'rise of the social', the preconditions to totalitarianism and totalitarianism itself, and that we have expanded to include the biopolitical regulation of human procreation). In general, these analyses show that various attempts to foreclose expressions of natality in order to maintain continuity between past and future tend to dominate government policy and political imagination when the 'boundlessness' and 'unpredictability' characteristic of the disjunctive temporality of natality are felt as insecurity and uncertainty (HC: 190–1). What we are suggesting in this chapter is that there is a specific link between the shutting down of political hospitality (the welcome of natality) at the level of national borders and moves against democratic plurality within the nation and that this impacts on the temporality of labouring bodies within. In particular, democratic plurality is under threat, in part, by the operation of *two forces* that intersect across the *lived time of women* and others at the base of the hierarchy of hospitality discussed in section I. First, there has been an intensification of biopolitics where national security has become increasingly dependent upon the biopolitical government of 'biological life' in the home, which, in turn, relies on the assumption of stability provided by women (and domestic labourers) giving time to others there. The second force in operation has been a rapid deregulation of *labour time*, which more often than not has the effect of increasing a sense of insecurity about the future and, at least in Levinas's account of the temporalisation of dwelling by the labouring body, it may cause spatio-temporal disorientation and fragmentation of being into the 'timeless present'.

There is much empirical evidence to support the first claim. Aside from the US situation cited in the opening paragraph of the Introduction to this book, the political conditions in many contemporary democracies indicate a remarkable coincidence between a combined insecurity about national identity and national sovereignty (manifest in implementing anti-terrorism legislation that undermines democratic freedoms and in closing borders to refugees, for example) and intensification of bio-political regulation of women's reproductivity, sexuality and 'family values' in the home. Poland, in May 2016, for example, in response to the Syrian refugee crisis, closed its borders to all refugees because of 'safety' and 'security' fears. In September of the same year the ruling conservative Law and Justice (PiS) Party attempted to tighten Polish anti-abortion laws (already among the harshest in Europe), proposing to ban it outright except where the pregnant woman's life is at risk.[7]

While less obvious, over the last two decades there has also been a strong correlation in Australia between moves to strengthen policing of national borders against asylum seekers (and certain categories of refugee and immigrant) and intensification of bio-politics in the home of the newborn and over 'private life' in ways that aim at securing uniformity of personal identity and Australian 'values' (whatever that means) such that they reflect those of the nation (and vice versa). During the decade of con-servative Howard government (1996–2007) leading up to the RU486 event of 2005–6 discussed in Chapter 3, when political hospitality became severely conditional, a number of govern-ment policies and public relations exercises intensified that link between those two orders of natality, the home and the nation. When the federal government first closed Australia's national borders to refugees (from Afghanistan and the Middle East) arriving by boat (via Indonesia) in August 2001 it justified this harsh policy by an implicit appeal to Australian 'family values' in the so-called 'children overboard' affair,[8] thus linking political hospitality to the security of the (white, middle-class, Christian) home. At the same time, Prime Minister Howard linked the harsh refugee policy to national sovereignty by launching his party's election campaign ahead of its third term in government with the (winning) slogan of conditional national hospitality: 'We decide who comes to this country, and the circumstances under which they come'. The home was linked to the Iraq war of 2003 and to the government's domestic 'war against terror' in February 2003 with a television campaign and fridge magnet that designated the home the first place from which one should be 'alert, but not alarmed' about the dangers of strangers.[9] Alongside these policies were biopolitical moves against plurality in private affairs and in the homes of the newborn, moves that appeared to be aimed at aligning the home with the nation. These included: the Prime Minister's (unsuccessful) attempt in August 2000 to intervene in federal anti-discrimination legislation (the Sex Discrimination Act 1984) to allow states to exclude lesbians and single women from accessing IVF facilities; passing the Marriage Amendment Act 2004 to explicitly exclude same-sex relations from the definition of marriage; introduction of the 'baby bonus' in 2001, which, as explained in Chapter 3, was part of an explicit exercise in (white) nation-building (the Treasurer at the time appealed to women to give birth to 'one baby for the mother, one for the father, and one for the nation').

The threats to the disclosure of natality and hence to democratic plurality have improved little since the Howard government lost office in 2007. Draconian anti-terror measures have continued to be introduced in Australia since 2005, through various pieces of legislation, and while the Howard government's conservative social policies have been robustly contested since 2007, there has been no substantial change. The notable exception to this is the success of the campaign contesting Howard's Marriage Amendment Act 2004, which ended in a plebiscite supporting the legalisation of same-sex marriage throughout Australia on 7 December 2017. Of particular relevance to this analysis is that the 'no' campaign was destructively fought around the usual assumptions that same-sex relationships are 'unnatural' but also around explicit claims that same-sex marriage is a threat to religious freedom and to the welfare of children. This campaign and the result raise too many interesting implications for feminist politics of reproduction and a politics of action to deal with adequately here, not least of which is the paradoxical situation where feminists who traditionally opposed marriage as a patriarchal institution found themselves voting 'yes' for a biopolitical measure that turns a love relation into a blood relation and thereby establishes the right to grieve and bury those people we love. As for the other threats to the mutual disclosure of natality underlying democratic plurality, the treatment of asylum seekers who attempt to arrive by boat has become harsher with the reopening in 2012 of offshore detention centres on Nauru and Manus Island, where thousands of people have been imprisoned in appalling conditions since. Sadly, this biopolitical exercise in erasing natality has been so 'successful' in 'stopping the boats' that the Australian government boasts that other countries, including the UK, wish to emulate the policy and it has entrenched the kind of biopolitical technical thinking that Arendt despised: 'you can't make an omelette without breaking eggs' (EU: 283). With regard to the other pole of biopolitics, state power over the right to 'make live', in May 2017 the latest attempt by the Greens to repeal the 100-year-old anti-abortion law in the Australian state of New South Wales failed to get majority support in parliament.

In general, through domestic social policies infected with biopolitical racism, the aim has been to secure the borders of the home in Australia in a way necessary for conditional hospitality and, through a kind of isomorphism, the aim of the policies controlling asylum seekers is apparently to secure the borders of the nation against the perceived threat of strangers. Assessing the impact on those charged with the task of keeping the home in order and training future citizens to mirror the conduct of a mythical, notional identity requires further analysis of the effect of the deregulation labour upon the event of natality and on democratic plurality.

The second force impacting on democratic plurality, and on the disclosure and welcome of natality that supports it, is less obvious: the relatively rapid *deregulation of labour time*, with the effect that even those women who have been privileged enough to be paid to contest the laws and norms that govern us no longer have time to give – either to others in the home or to reflective thinking and contesting the laws of hospitality that govern us. Arguably, the impact is also on the wider workforce and may partly explain the popularity of the 'security' measures mentioned above. The deregulation of labour time involves a gradual erosion of the difference between leisure time, home time and work time through technological developments that take work and other 'public' activities into the 'private' domain (academics and administrators need only think of how the advent of email has eroded these boundaries) and a global move toward deregulation of market economies that has led to casualisation of labour and increased underemployment. In Australia this trend has been reinforced by legislation implemented by the conservative government in 2005 (the Workplace Relations Amendment (Work Choices) Act 2005) that radically undermined 'collective bargaining' for workplace conditions in favour of individual work contracts. While the Labor government rescinded the legislation in 2008, its negative impact on working life and labour time has not been reversed and has been enhanced by an increase in job *insecurity* (a phenomenon shared by the UK and other neo-liberal economies) and 'job status' insecurity resulting from the rise of the 'gig economy' and the freelance economy, the 'polarization and variability of hours' worked, and an escalation of wage inequality and the use of short-term employment contracts (including the wide use of 'zero-hour contracts' in the UK).[10] The situation in the US has been exacerbated by the 'subprime mortgage crisis' associated with the global financial crisis of 2007–8 and subsequent increases in underemployment, job insecurity and homelessness and a deepening of divisions between the haves and have-nots along fault-lines of age, class and race. At the same time, for those in regular employment there has been increased micro-management of labour time through a form of biopolitics involving the imposition of performance indicators and systems for measuring productivity against linear time. Work time gets channelled into 'busy time' (a feature of modern bureaucracies) and this is extended into spare time.[11]

The impact of this deregulation of labour on citizens' capacity for political action can be partly explained by both a milder version of Arendt's account (discussed in Chapter 2) of 'totalitarian lawfulness', which actually suspends laws that provide stability *and* novelty in favour of 'laws of movement' (EU: 340), *and* her argument that freedom in the neo-liberal state is understood (problematically) as 'freedom *from* politics' (BPF: 149), which leaves working and economic life entirely alone to 'follow its own inherent necessity' (BPF: 150). Even though the deregulation of labour time would not reduce human existence to 'bare life' or to 'biological life' governed by necessity in the manner Arendt describes, this dispersal of labour time does threaten to destroy the disjunctive temporality characteristic of the experience and expression of natality. An alternative way of explaining how this could happen might be to accept some account of how the labouring body ordinarily temporalises human existence (such as that provided by Levinas, outlined in section I). On the basis of this account, the deregulation of labour and labour time erodes democratic plurality by undermining the way the labouring body temporalises dwelling. While not producing the 'conditioned and behaving animal' Arendt describes under the label of *animal laborans*, the dispersal of labour time nevertheless impacts on bodies, by diminishing the time necessary for consciousness and thinking, and certainly the time for political action. And it undermines the precondition of labour and action – the welcome of alterity or disclosure of natality – that, for Arendt, Nancy and Derrida, is a condition of the contestation of the traditions we have inherited and, hence, of 'democracy to come'.[12] This suggests that Arendt's formula of *animal laborans* as a body reduced to 'life process' is not so much Marx's idea, as formulated by Arendt, that 'labor is the human way to experience the sheer bliss of being alive' (HC: 106), nor a consequence of normalisation by a faceless bureaucracy that produces 'conditioned and behaving animal', or the result of manual or repetitive labour or labouring to satisfy need, but the effect of the deregulation of labour time that fragments the temporal rhythms of dwelling.

The claim in this chapter is also that in the current era, where the insecurity engendered by dispersal of labour time sits alongside a reassertion of the patriarchal themes of our traditions of hospitality, only some of us are expected to take responsibility for this busy time, thus freeing up time for others for the public encounters and contestation of traditional norms from which the new emerges. Either women (or lowly paid domestic labourers who are usually 'guest workers', non-residents or new immigrants) are expected to give lived time to housework in the home or within the business of bureaucracy,[13] or hospitality, as openness to the uniqueness and new beginnings of others, is dampened for all of us by the infinite spread of busy time.

How patriarchal themes can take hold of political hospitality, especially at times of heightened labour and national insecurity, can be explained by adding consideration of the biopolitics of women's reproductivity and sexuality to Levinas's account of the labouring body and Arendt's account of the disclosure and welcome of natality as a principle of democracy. As discussed in Chapter 3, the disclosure of natality to and by others that Arendt claims gives human existence its defining character is a second-order signification of the fact of first-order birth of a new beginning. But, while acknowledging that women give birth in the first order of natality, none of the theorists discussed in this chapter acknowledges that women *give time* to that birth. Nor does Arendt (nor most models of the political) acknowledge that time has been given by someone to enable the 'appearance' of the political actor in the second order of political community. On that, Arendt says: the 'non-time space in the very heart of time, unlike the world and the culture into which we are born, cannot be inherited and handed down by tradition' (LM I: 210). In a sense, she is right – the event of natality is 'given' by others only insofar as it requires disclosure (witness) and welcome by others; it cannot depend on being given by a tradition that, to remain in place, would memorialise and thus erase it. Levinas makes a similar point: the alterity that interrupts presence and so temporalises time is '*immemorial* time', which, while signified in the face of the other, is not given by anyone and cannot be temporalised, known or erased. But granting that the disjunctive temporality characteristic of the event of natality is not given by anyone still leaves in place the issue of inequalities among agents in the giving of lived time required for the disclosure and welcome of natality. The connection between the way time is lived by bodies and the performance and welcome of natality is demonstrated by the connection between giving lived time and giving birth. That is, there is a mutual dependence of expressions of natality (and the attendant disruption of the continuity between past and future) and the *embodied living of historical time*. It is precisely in this relation that the giving of lived time is distributed inequitably through the body politic and the labour force, with the consequence that some people are expected to give time for others without acknowledgement and without the 'appearance' and welcome of their uniqueness.

Lisa Guenther, in *The Gift of the Other* (2006), goes some way toward spelling out the connection between giving birth and giving time in her diagnosis of the politics of reproduction, with particular reference to Levinas and some reference to Arendt. By highlighting the way gestation postpones the arrival of the future–present, Guenther demonstrates how the expectant mother gives time to allow the child to whom she gives birth to be an expression of natality. For the expectant mother, the future newborn signifies natality in the sense of both the unknown future and the stranger – 'a future that does not belong [to her], but for which [she is] nevertheless responsible' and which she welcomes into the home (Guenther 2006: 102). Guenther also implies a connection between the rupture of im-memorial time (the event of natality) and the embodied living of historical time in remarking that 'the pregnant woman already inhabits a world [. . . and it is] into this time of representation and consciousness [that] the anarchy of birth erupts' (Guenther 2006: 100). To put that point another way, rather than a 'discrete absence' or a passive provider of hospitality, the maternal body is the bearer of historical time, a lived temporality and a mode of belonging to a world that is disrupted and transformed through gestation and birth. If it was not for this maternal body giving lived time for the welcome of the new beginning, the birth of a child would not signify the event of natality to anyone, and nor therefore would this first-order birth make a difference to the common world. Further, even though the mother's gift of birth and gift of time are not 'chosen', in the sense that 'the giving of time *to* the other is made possible [not by the self but] *by* the other' (Guenther 2006: 102), nevertheless, Guenther argues, neither giving time nor giving birth should be forced (a point we have discussed in detail in Chapter 3). Extending Arendt's politics and Levinas's ethics to mothers, the 'equality of all persons' (or equality of unique distinctness, as Arendt would put it) *and* 'reproductive choice for women', Guenther argues, are necessary to hold 'open the space in which an ethical response [of hospitality] might arise' (Guenther 2006: 148–50). To this we would add that without reproductive choice for women, the welcome of natality upon which the expression of uniqueness depends would be meaningless. Moreover, *both giving birth or deciding not to should be recognised as equally valid actions that signal a new beginning*, that signal the actor (the mother) is an agent contributing to the potentiality of being together that grounds inter-relationality and democratic plurality. She is therefore as worthy of hospitality as any labouring body and as those to whom she extends the welcome.

The patriarchal basis of our 'laws' of hospitality come to the fore if, through the combination of biopolitical synchronising of the home and the nation and the deregulation of labour time, there is an increased expectation that women, in giving birth, will give lived time to others in the home and the workplace in the service of transforming, for others, any immediate relation to 'life' (pure 'enjoyment' or cyclic time of 'biological life' or anything resembling 'life process') into historical patterns of embodied existence that are then opened to an unforeseeable future in political community. Those who are expected to give lived time in this way, without being given hospitality and, therefore, time by others may well be reduced to if not 'bare life' then something like the timeless present. Like the women of Derrida's analysis of hospitality, *these bodies may be cut to pieces*. And the more that those deprived of hospitality are thereby deprived of time for thinking, language and action, hence the time to contest the norms that govern us, the more that the preconditions of democratic plurality are undermined.

While in *The Human Condition* Arendt explains this tendency toward biopolitics with totalitarian elements in terms of the 'rise of the social', where public life takes on the principles of government of the household, the suggestion here is that there is something of the reverse in operation. The tendency toward totalising biopolitics in a micro-managed democracy can be equally well explained by an undermining of the welfare state by the rise of economic rationalism and neo-liberal notions of freedom from politics, combined with dominance of discourses of national security. Under these conditions, the task of reining in the unpredictable (that is, the event of natality, in Arendt's terms) is siphoned off from public life into the home. At such times, democratic politics would eliminate felt instability, not only through micro-management of labour and public life, by war, border closures, censorship and racism, but also through appeal to 'family values' and the security that women are assumed to provide by giving time to others in the home. But then, the 'home' too falls prey to totalising micro-management, through an intensification of biopolitics.

III. Natality and Responsibility: Acting Against Biopolitics

A key question raised by the analysis so far is this: if biopolitics, including policies attending to national security as well as labour, can not only be unethical (that is, discriminatory on the basis of sex, race, sexuality, religion and other categories of difference) but also impact on bodies to suppress natality and inter-relationality, then how can this be reversed? This is partly a question of who is responsible for any unethical or negative impact of government policy (particular citizens or the state, the Prime Minister, or the government? Eichmann, or the Nazi regime he served?), a question that is difficult to answer given that democratic government is supposedly the voice of the people. But it is also a question about how to reverse the normalisation or 'coordination' of the population that may have been conditioned through those policies; that is, if citizens – because they have been conditioned to accept the discriminatory treatment of some groups as the norm, or, as suggested in section II, because the dispersal of labour time has left them discombobulated and disconcerted without time for politics – go along with government policies that seem unethical to some, how can that conditioning be undone so that citizens are reawakened to the event of natality and to ensuring equality of unique distinctness? Arendt tries to answer these questions in her reflections on responsibility and judgement. In the process she redefines responsibility so it is less about blame and account-ability for past deeds and more about reawakening *conscience* (judgement of what is right and wrong), which amounts to reawakening inter-relationality and political action based on the disclosure and welcome of natality. In examining her analyses of responsibility, our aim in this section is to build an account of responsibility that best addresses the discriminatory biopolitics and nationalism characteristic of our times.

In her reflections on responsibility Arendt is less concerned with responsibility of the state (political or collective respon-sibility) than she is with the personal responsibility of those, including her friends, who fell in line with the Nazi regime and failed to act against it. She defines political responsibility as the collective responsibility that every government and nation assumes for the 'deeds and misdeeds of the past' and for setting 'the time aright', whereas personal responsibility is individual and refers to deeds and misdeeds for which the doer alone is accountable (RJ: 27–8). But restricting personal responsibility to *accountability* is inadequate for Arendt's purposes of explaining how even her friends, while not guilty of immoral acts them-selves or culpable for the acts of a criminal government, could have so easily accepted a reversal of standards in the treatment of 'others' that was apparent in the early stages of Nazi Germany.

To Arendt, this compliance with immoral or at least dubious government policy indicated that prior to (but a likely condition of) mass internments and 'exterminations', there was an 'almost universal breakdown, not of personal responsibility [in the sense of legal accountability], but of personal *judgment*', that is, a breakdown of *conscience*, the judgement of what is right or wrong, a general 'moral disintegration' (RJ: 24).

Here, Arendt is implicitly criticising the conventional *juridical* concept of *self-responsibility*, which emphasises accountability, duty and blame in terms of criteria provided by the prevailing legal and/or moral code. The concept is inadequate insofar as it assumes an individual self with the *capacity* to act autonomously, to 'own' that act, and to know its significance and value in terms of some juridico-moral code. It also assumes that the self is already temporalised, can remember past acts, anticipate (or promise) future acts, and lives an unbroken continuity from past to future. Insofar as it is assumed that such capacities are given, the philosophical debate about responsibility has centred on whether conscience (understood as conscious awareness of the difference between right and wrong) and hence agency are driven and *determined* by the juridico-moral code we inherit or arise from our *freedom* to oppose or affirm that code. However, if we are to explain the moral disintegration of public life in which Arendt is interested and the apparent indifference of her friends, then conscience cannot be determined by either the moral norms or the particular laws of the society into which we are born. Some alternative explanation is required.

The inadequacy of the juridical concept of self-responsibility and the enduring relevance of Arendt's alternative analysis are demonstrated by the impact of policies of contemporary liberal democratic governments that single out groups of people for special treatment that would not be tolerated by the wider community. We have mentioned some examples above, such as government policies that allow asylum seekers to be held in detention camps but that many citizens consider to be immoral and illegal; anti-terrorism legislation that some argue puts in jeopardy fundamental rights and freedoms of a nation's own citizens (provisions allowing preventive detention without charge, anti-sedition provisions that criminalise activities that urge disaffection against the government); or, in Australia, the Northern Territory Intervention of 2007, where the government suspended the Racial Discrimination Act 1975 in order to assume control over Indigenous communities.

Even if we grant that the intent behind these initiatives is not immoral (since they are justified in terms of improving the health, welfare and security of the nation's population), they can precipitate a crisis of conscience in that wider community when there is a felt conflict between the laws and programmes of government and the *normative basis* of people's moral sensibility. In such situations, conscience seems to vanish. Instead of considering the moral status of those government initiatives, we hold the target groups responsible for their own suffering or for any felt insecurity in a populace, and/or we follow the government's example in our conduct toward these target groups, or we do nothing. In any case, volatile emotions or passive compliance or confusion about what is right and wrong infect our conduct toward others. What is at issue under such conditions is not only whether individuals should be held accountable for acts committed in accordance with the standards for the treatment of others implied in those government measures. The question is also: what happens to the capacity for responsibility, and to the normative basis of conscience, judgement and conduct, when the laws and moral norms that supposedly guide our conduct without thinking are apparently undermined by a government that remains, nonetheless, anonymous and not responsible?

This was Arendt's concern (RJ: 26–7, 29). The government she had in mind was totalitarian in the sense discussed in Chapter 2: not a dictatorship but a totalising biopolitical government that reaches beyond public affairs into all 'spheres of life' and that 'coordinates' human existence toward some uniform national end (RJ: 33–4) or, in other ways discussed in section II of this chapter, discombobulates citizens sufficiently to reduce their capacity for politics. Even though Arendt may not adequately explain *how* conscience can be awakened or dampened and why personal responsibility can fail under such government (given that she neglects the role of the body in the inter-relational disclosure and welcome of natality), she does pinpoint what is at stake in such a failure: the uniqueness, equal worth and 'dignity' ('humanness') of each person. She also therefore indicates why conscience must be restored if the world of potentiality and plurality that we share is to endure or at least remain a regulative principle. The following is a summary of the main points Arendt makes about personal responsibility.

First, crucial for a revision of the juridical sense of responsibility is Arendt's argument, in partial accord with both Nietzsche and Kant, that conscience is not determined by the laws and the moral norms we inherit. As Arne Vetlesen shows, Arendt actually points to two kinds of conscience (Vetlesen 2001: 12, 25). There is that ever-present conscience that operates habitually and is influenced by prevailing norms and laws (RJ: 186; LM II: 200) embedded in the common world that conditions us. But there is also that conscience that is a 'by-product of thinking' (LM I: 193). In *The Life of the Mind*, thinking is presented, following

Kant, as *critical* of tradition: as an internal dialogue with oneself (Socrates' 'two-in-one') (for example, LM I: Chapter 18) and, diagrammatically, as the experience of a battle between the past tradition the person inherits and an open future that contradicts the past (LM I: 208). Arendt aligns conscience with this kind of thinking: conscience is the 'experience' of the thinking ego doing battle with itself (for example, LM I: 191). Judgement of right and wrong is not exactly the same as thinking because judgement is directed externally, to particulars in the world. Nevertheless, through the 'experience' of judgement of 'particulars' without reference to a universal, conscience makes thinking 'manifest in the world' (RJ: 188–9; LM I: 193). The thinking that conscience makes manifest is not knowledge of the good, norms or laws, but 'negative' critical thinking – the *challenging of all established criteria*, values and 'accepted rules of conduct' (RJ: 188). This second kind of conscience is what matters to Arendt: this is the experience of the capacity to judge what is right or wrong *for oneself* and is, presumably, what can still be experienced by those living in a world being coordinated by a morally dubious biopolitical government.

Second, in linking conscience to reflective critical thinking, Arendt posits a connection between the experience of conscience and the event of natality and, hence, the undeterminable and futural character of the self. That is, reflective thinking and judgement of right and wrong (experienced as conscience), along with our finitude, temporalise the self in a way necessary for both moral responsibility and the contestation of tradition that is a hallmark of democracy. Again recalling *The Life of the Mind*, Arendt's account of the historicity of the self explicitly borrows from Nietzsche's and Kafka's concepts of time to formulate the idea that the 'path paved by thinking' 'produces a rupture' between the thinker's past and future (LM I: 205). Arendt argues that reflective thought clears away established universals so as to judge particulars anew and this judgement (thinking made manifest and experienced as conscience) opens the gap between past and future. Reflective thinking and judgement therefore disrupt any kind of time continuum, including everyday activities that are 'spatially determined and conditioned' (LM I: 205), as well as the 'timeless present' (LM I: 207). While, as finite beings, we inherit a tradition of laws and moral norms that would determine the path we take, the act of thinking manifest as judgement of particular cases of right and wrong opens an undetermined future or begins the world anew (LM I: 210). This event of natality is foreclosed in a dampening of conscience and failure of personal responsibility. So, the crisis of conscience that Arendt explores is not precipitated by a conflict between two sets of moral norms (that which is inherited and its converse, instituted through some forms of biopolitical government) but, we suggest, by discriminatory biopolitics and attendant publicity that, by attempting to 'coordinate' the population, *quashes the self's futurity and with this the expression through judgement of natality generated within oneself.*

Hence, third, in undermining the futural aspect of human existence, government that fosters the kind of severely conditional hospitality outlined in section I not only reverses accepted norms of conduct toward others but also jeopardises the welcome of the other's unique distinctness and thereby destroys human plurality in general.[14] This implies that judgement (and therefore conscience) actualises what Arendt had referred to in *The Human Condition* as the 'who' as opposed to the 'what' of the person (HC: 179). Indeed, she says explicitly in her 1965 lecture 'Some questions of moral responsibility' (RJ: 49–146) that '[m]orality concerns the individual in his singularity' (RJ: 97). However, her model of conscience in these later reflections on moral responsibility is explicitly Kantian and Socratic and bypasses any implied connection between conscience and *political* community, which had been the prerequisite for the disclosure of natality in *The Human Condition*. (Indeed, thinking is an internal self-relation and along with moral judgement should ordinarily remain separate from politics – for example, LM II: 200.) In her accounts of responsibility Arendt describes conscience as the experience of judging particulars (as right or wrong) autonomously and rationally (after Kant) *and* as a self-relation, that is, as self-awareness and an internal dialogue with oneself (after Socrates) (for example, RJ: 76; see also LM I: 179–93). As an internal dialogue between the habitual (conditioned) self and the self's other internal witness, judgement expresses the person's *autonomous* capacity to disrupt tradition and embark on a new path, which is experienced as an internal 'difference in identity' (RJ: 183–4). Conscience (the experience of judgement) thereby actualises the person in their uniqueness: it is an experience and expression of natality. The process of thinking, actualised autonomous moral judgement, does require others but only as witness to its manifestation in action. It is apparently a mode of expressing natality by and for oneself: thinking so understood is the 'human way of [. . .] taking one's place in the world into which we all arrive as strangers' (RJ: 100) and implies that humans 'exist in the plural' (RJ: 96).

This capacity to discourse with oneself (including the judgement of what is right and wrong) is, for the later Arendt, the basis of normativity in two senses: it is the capacity through which we arrive at our *own* norms of conduct; and as a capacity in others, it expresses the uniqueness and moral worth or 'dignity' to other persons ('this root-striking process of thinking' is what distinguishes a 'person' from a 'nobody' – RJ: 100). Acting according to conscience, being responsible in a non-juridical sense, rather than being coordinated by a totalising biopolitics, is, she says, how one can regain what those in 'former times', including Kant, 'called the dignity or the honor of man: not perhaps of mankind but of the status of being human' (RJ: 48).

Finally, with this idea of conscience in place, Arendt is left with the crucial question: *what provides the normative criterion of judgement*, if not the moral norms we inherit or those government policies that may have reversed the norms of conduct of public life? Arendt falls short of providing an answer that would explain how to reverse unethical trends in democratic government and the apparent compliance with those trends on the part of the majority of a population. On the basis of the idea that judgement is experienced as a reflective self-relation in the form of a dialogue with oneself, Arendt argues that the criterion that limits what one permits oneself to do is set by what would allow one to live at 'peace with oneself' (RJ: 108). Following Socrates, conscience, she argues, is guided by the desire to avoid self-contradiction or, following Kant, the desire to avoid self-contempt.[15] Put simply, 'it is better to suffer wrong than do wrong' (a dictum she claims, while originating with Socrates, underlies all moral philosophy) because you could not, logically and with dignity, live with that other part of yourself that you would kill or make suffer.

Without rejecting Arendt's account of thinking and moral judgement, there is a problem with the way it confines the explanation of what *animates* judgement and action to an internal self-relation. This does not explain what prompts this internal self-contradiction in the first place. What is it about *witnessing* the unjust or immoral treatment of others by government policy, or by individuals, that reawakens conscience sufficiently to animate political action? The following is Arendt's explanation, in a 1964 interview with Günther Gaus, of what pricked her conscience and prompted her turn from philosophical thinking to political action in pre-war Nazi Germany:

> I would say February 27, 1933, the burning of the Reichstag, and the illegal arrests that followed during the same night. The so-called protective custody. As you know, people were taken to Gestapo cellars or to concentration camps. What happened then was monstrous, but it has now been overshadowed by things that happened later. This was *an immediate shock* for me, and from that moment on *I felt responsible*. That is, I was no longer of the opinion that one can simply be a bystander. I tried to help in many ways. (EU: 4–5, emphasis added)

This suggests that, for Arendt, responsibility involves a *responsive conscience* that propels the person to action without having to pass through any internal deliberation. This conscience somehow resists or overcomes 'coordination' by a totalising and morally dubious, if not bankrupt, regime, a conscience sufficiently responsive to mobilise the self into political action *prior to* the 'abyss' and horror of totalitarianism and a holocaust toward which compliance may otherwise lead (RJ: 55). If that is the case, then the criteria for conscience must be built into the experience of witnessing the disclosure of natality by others. As we will see, other aspects of Arendt's account of the disclosure and witnessing of natality within the web of human inter-relations can help explain how external events can prick a person's conscience in these terms. Meanwhile, her accounts in *Responsibility and Judgment* and *The Life of the Mind* of the self-relation behind conscience do not explain the 'immediate shock' Arendt felt in the wake of the illegal internments, nor why *her* conscience was thereby pricked enough to mobilise action but not that of her friends (although they may have been more disturbed and less compliant than they appeared to Arendt).

The difficulty here is that Arendt explicitly excludes affect and feeling from judgement and conscience.[16] Just as Kant opposes reason to inclination, Arendt at other times distances conscience, and therefore the uniqueness or 'singularity' of a person, from 'a way of feeling beyond reason and argument [or] of knowing through sentiment what is right and wrong' (RJ: 107). This is because she assumes that basing conscience on sensibility appeals to undisciplined affects and biological processes that threaten to drive the self to act from necessity, thus destroying the capacity for (political) action and hence the 'in-between' fabric of the common world that joins but also separates people (for example, OR: 59/76; HC: 50–1). Or, if based on feeling, conscience is simply reactive to these undisciplined affects and biological processes. Either way, Arendt says, 'feelings indicate conformity and non-conformity [between old habits and new commands], they don't indicate morality', that is, independent judgement of right and wrong (RJ: 107). This stance is behind Arendt's criticism of Nietzsche's focus on feeling and the body in his schema for the revaluation of value: the only criterion of conscience or standard of moral judgement he came up with, Arendt claims, was 'Life itself' (RJ: 51). Levinas is also critical of Nietzsche on this score: while admiring Nietzsche's account of human existence as embodied and open to a world, Levinas claims Nietzsche's materialism, based as it is on 'will to power', contributes to a philosophy of material expansion that becomes the 'philosophy of Hitlerism' (Levinas 1990: 69–71), a reading of Nietzsche refuted by the analysis below. Arendt's criticisms, however, as we go on to argue, overlook the complex role the body and affect play in responsive conscience, responsibility and political action. This matters for explaining how conscience can be confronted by witnessing events in the world that strip others of the capacity to begin something new in the world. Such a consideration also assists in explaining *how* conscience can be dampened and personal responsibility might fail under totalising or discriminatory biopolitical government. For this, we turn temporarily to Nietzsche's critique of the juridical notion of self-responsibility to which Arendt's account of conscience is partly indebted.[17]

Like Levinas, Nietzsche holds that affectivity is taken up into the conditioned subject in such a way that passion or feeling is inseparable from thinking and judgement. And, consistent with Foucault, this occurs through discipline of the body according to prevailing codes of conduct. Hence, in his approach to responsibility Nietzsche locates the condition of conscience, normativity and responsibility not first of all in reflective thinking or judgement, but in *responsiveness* based on what we will call *somatic reflexivity*. For him, what opens that gap between past and future is the constitution of a corporeal and affective self-relation that manifests as a futural ability to respond to circumstances with conscience and in excess of existing law and custom. As with Arendt, this moves the debate about responsibility beyond the impasse between freedom and determinism by proposing that the relation between the self and moral custom and law is constitutive (and therefore habitual), but can also be excessive, critical of, and potentially transformative of norms, values and all established criteria of judgement. Nietzsche's idea that this constitutive and transformative relation involves feeling, or the channelling of affect into action and thought, is crucial for explaining how a democratically elected government could, by aiming at coordinating nation and home, have such a rapid and potentially destructive impact on a population.

It is in the first three sections of the second essay of *On the Genealogy of Morals* (1967a) that Nietzsche provides his most systematic account of how independent judgement or conscience arises, and hence the capacity for 'genuine' responsibility. Rather than being given, the capacity for the usual (and compliant) juridical *self*-responsibility (where the person can be held accountable for their acts) is *made* through training, through a process of discipline and punishment that Foucault elaborates in his account of the production of the docile body or compliant subject (discussed in Chapter 2). For Nietzsche, this training historicises the self such that the person has the ability to anticipate a future and, through a selective memory, to recoup in the future a past that is now present. Thus we can make promises and participate in social relations. This is not the kind of promising that Arendt puts at the heart of coalition-building to curtail the 'boundless' consequences of action. It is a kind of promising that forms a compliant self and rigid society that Nietzsche and Arendt reject. At the same time, the person's memory gets imbued with prevailing moral norms (and meaning in general). For Nietzsche, it is the social codification of experience through discipline, rather than reflective thinking or judgement, that temporalises the self. This is also Nietzsche's explanation for how we are conditioned: culture is inaugurated, '*not* in the "soul"' or 'through a mere disciplining of thoughts [. . .]: one first has to convince the body' (Nietzsche 1968: 47).

While this social disciplining of the body is how we come to embody a juridico-moral code and are 'coordinated' and normalised by it, crucial for Nietzsche's idea of *conscience* is that, through the same disciplinary process, we also embody an affective, self-reflexive and self-critical *relation* to that code (for example, Nietzsche 1973: 19). In its reflexivity, the body attempts to enhance pleasure and move beyond pain, but as pleasure and pain, along with 'everything of which we become conscious', are already codified, 'interpreted through and through' (Nietzsche 1967b: 477), somatic reflexivity involves contestation and transformation in the meaning of experience, of affects and their relations. Independent judgement experienced as conscience, for Nietzsche, does not originate as a thinking self in dialogue with itself but rather as the body doubled: accompanying habitual evaluative action, normalised according to convention, are both affects *and* the futural force of re-evaluation beyond mere affect (or 'life process'). This is sensibility and 'will to power' described as the force of critical re-evaluation whereby 'whatever exists, having somehow come into being, is again and again reinterpreted to new ends' (Nietzsche 1967a: 77) and where 'the whole thing called reflection' is 'mastery over the affects' (Nietzsche 1967a: 62; see also Nietzsche 1973: 48–9). 'Genuine' self-responsibility, then, for Nietzsche, involves promising, acting and owning those acts on the basis of one's conscience, composed of one's *own* evaluations and judgements, that thwart and transform the work of a normalising biopolitics and its imposition of a few 'demands of social existence as *present realities* upon these slaves of momentary affect' (Nietzsche 1967a: 60–2). That agency and reflective thinking are grounded in somatic reflexivity is also what makes the self unique (singular) and opaque to itself and to the judgements of others. This is a responsive conscience, an embodied expression of natality, that opens the gap (the gateway called the moment) between the past and a future that contradicts the past

(Nietzsche 1978: 155–60), which Arendt takes up in *The Life of the Mind* (LM I: 202–13).[18]

In a way, Nietzsche ends up in a similar place to Arendt, when, for her, the reflective thinking normally conducted away from politics must, in the form of judgement expressed as conscience, become a 'kind of action' in challenging totalitarian and bio-political government (RJ: 188). The difference is that Nietzsche does not assume that reflective thinking and judgement come before or are ever divorced from the body's affective relation to a world or from the speech and action that, for Arendt, make up the fabric of the political. Hence his account can explain the *immediate* impact of the burning of the Reichstag on Arendt, how this precipitated a crisis of conscience and a 'feeling' of responsibility. Nietzsche's account of conscience also explains how critical thinking (revaluation of value) and action survive the coordination of the population by biopolitics and also why the kind of biopolitical government discussed in this chapter can generate such division, conflict and heightened passions among citizens. But there is also a lot Nietzsche's account of responsibility cannot do.

Nietzsche's philosophy of the body is not without its problems. Arendt is right to be suspicious of his idea of responsibility, but for another reason besides its corporeal and affective basis. The salient problem is that there is no internal *limit* to the creative forces that seem to necessarily accompany conscience, with the consequence that imperialism haunts Nietzsche's picture of genuine self-responsibility, as Arendt also notes (RJ: 134–5). The problem lies in Nietzsche's individualism (which is also a problem with classical liberalism's notion of free will that Nietzsche criticises) and that he posits no criteria of conscience beyond expansion of the self's critical and creative powers. He also fails to distinguish between the creative power of revaluation and will to power as a *force*, the expression of which is both inevitable and usually aggressive.[19] So, the only criterion the conscience of the genuinely responsible individual for judging what would be the right or wrong thing to do is *not* 'life itself', as Arendt suggests, but maintaining one's *own* reflexivity, one's *own* uniqueness. Nietzsche would preserve this for the self by proliferation of indifference to the suffering in others. Arendt, on the other hand, does limit the creative powers inherent in action and other expressions of natality. This limit lies with others. As discussed in Chapter 1, Arendt redefines the field of freedom as the experience of natality through action within the *togetherness* of human affairs (that is, freedom is the 'potentiality of being together'). Hence limiting the unpredictable consequences of action is the same as limiting the consequences of freedom as pure potentiality. But instead of limiting freedom by imposing laws to restrict individual action (which is where classical liberalism takes us), for Arendt, limiting freedom must involve actions with the same *collective* character integral to freedom as she understands it, if the status of all natal beings as beginners of the new is to be equally preserved. It is here that we can find another criterion of conscience more suited to Arendt's political philosophy, that is, in the preservation of the uniqueness of others within human interactions at all levels.

IV. Ethics Meets Politics: Personal Responsibility and Political Responsibility

In her political philosophy Arendt provides a way to address this question of the role that witnessing the plight of others plays in pricking one's conscience and hence the extent to which personal responsibility entails responsibility for others. This requires linking the experience of natality through conscience, and hence the indeterminate and futural dimension of self-responsibility, with responsibility for preserving the uniqueness and futurity of others. It is within this link that morality meets politics. In briefly making this connection we will retain some idea of the corporeal reflexivity and affectivity that Nietzsche (and also Levinas and Nancy) assumes as a basis of responsibility. This requires bypassing some of the Kantian elements in Arendt's discussions of moral responsibility – the model of judgement (as a manifestation of reflective thinking set apart from feeling) and her criteria for judgement (the desire to avoid self-contempt or, following Socrates, self-contradiction)

In her earlier accounts of the political, Arendt implies an alternative criterion of judgement that would limit what we can do in good conscience, alternative to those discussed in her accounts of responsibility and moral judgement. But this is not simply a question of making politics more morally good: Arendt, as with most political philosophers, is keen to keep the usual notions of morality out of politics. In *Responsibility and Judgment* she clearly distinguishes the two but in a way that implicitly maintains her unique idea of politics: 'The difference between ethics and politics is this: The political concern is not whether the act of striking somebody unjustly or being struck is more disgraceful. The concern is exclusively with having a world in which such acts do not occur' (RJ: 93). Ordinarily, moral judgement is individual and should stay out of politics, whereas politics concerns *collective* dialogue and action and the maintenance of law, regarded as 'essential to the integrity of our common humanity' (RJ: 22).[20] This is why Arendt describes the moral crisis with which we began in terms of 'border-line phenomena' (RJ: 104–5): moral judgement is relevant to politics, Arendt claims, only in times of crisis, when customary moral standards, which would ordinarily guide action without thinking, have been suspended or reversed in the public realm. It is also why Arendt needs to posit judgement, experienced as conscience, as the bridge and arbiter between thinking and morality, on the one hand, and politics and law, on the other. Morality and law usually intersect, Arendt says, only insofar as they 'deal with persons' rather than institutions and systems (RJ: 57) and only insofar as they presuppose the same 'power of judgment' of what is right and wrong (RJ: 22). But there is a way to show an ongoing mutual dependence of individual conscience and both inter-relationality and political community, an ongoing mutual dependence of personal responsibility and political responsibility, and, hence, of ethics and politics. This relationship is implied by two aspects of Arendt's political philosophy, outlined below.

First, Arendt ties the preservation of the uniqueness of the self's reflexivity (the uniqueness of autonomous judgement) to that of others and to the preservation of plurality in the world in general. While in her reflections on the failure of personal moral responsibility she claims that thinking and judgement arise from a self-relation isolated from others (being-with-others is the domain of politics, of speech and action, not judgement and thinking), she does acknowledge that this internal dialogue with oneself carries the 'trace of company' and, hence, a trace of the plurality that being-with-others implies (RJ: 106). What she means by 'trace of company' there is that the division within the self from which the internal dialogue of judgement arises is a division left over as a 'memory' of engagement with other selves. As we discuss further in Chapter 5, aside from suggesting that the internal dialogue we have with ourselves is simply a replica of dialogues we have with others, this imagined engagement with other selves points to the communicability of reflective thinking and judgement and how we can take into consideration the perspectives of others with whom we share the world. However, Arendt applies only *aesthetic* judgement (and its 'enlarged mentality') directly to collective political thinking (for example, BPF: 220–1). In any case, there is another way to link the more immediate experience of conscience or the judgement of right and wrong with political community and inter-relationality that does not require passing through internal deliberations. The 'trace of others' in moral judgement could refer to that witness and welcome of the uniqueness of others that make up the fabric of the world and it could be this unique distinctness of others itself that inspires thinking and judgement in the first place. In other words, the very *fact* of the (other) person's uniqueness and self-responsibility (which is acting autonomously according to conscience rather than through duty or by law) is disclosed and welcomed in the 'togetherness' of political community. Moreover, recall that this inter-relational disclosure of uniqueness can be understood as the principle of democratic plurality. Is not this disclosure and welcome of unique distinctness also a moral principle or, rather, the primary *criterion of conscience*? Presumably, then, conscience and personal responsibility (the internal dialogue that discloses uniqueness) are dependent upon the assumption of political responsibility, where 'setting the time aright' consists in maintaining a world that fosters the capacity for responsibility and hence the unique distinctness of everyone.

This connection between personal (moral) and political (collective) responsibility is reinforced by a second aspect of Arendt's notion of the political outlined in *The Human Condition* (which is also her second departure from Nietzsche). As discussed in Chapter 1, there she distinguishes power (or what Nietzsche would call 'will to power') from force. Power, for Arendt, is not Nietzsche's notion of an excess of creative force arising from self-responsibility that tends to appropriate others in affirming oneself. Recall that, for Arendt, power is the 'potentiality in being together' in political community; power is the disclosure of uniqueness where multiple potentialities are 'actualized but never fully materialized' through 'speech and action' (HC: 200–1; also HC: 50–3). The condition of this power, and therefore of political community, is not the same as the criteria of moral judgement that Arendt formulates in her later work (the desire to avoid self-contradiction and self-contempt). Rather, its condition is that the 'space of appearance', the space of disclosure of the uniqueness of others, is preserved as potentiality rather than transformed into a space of permanence, of things in relation (HC: 204). Crucially for the argument here, the 'only limitation' of this power of potentiality 'is the existence of other people [. . .] because human power is the condition of plurality' (HC: 201). Force, on the other hand, through 'violence can destroy power' (HC: 207) in various ways already discussed, including a coordinating biopolitical nationalist government with severely conditional laws of political hospitality. For Arendt, this loss of relationality signals an affront to the human condition and a failure of political responsibility. To be without the welcome of political hospitality is to be deprived of relationality engendered in the welcome. Without this web of the 'in-between' of the sharing of singularity is 'to be isolated, is to be deprived of the capacity to act' (HC: 188). To shut out strangers from political community is to condemn them to 'utter loneliness, where no communication, let alone association and community, is possible'; this is a 'dead' life (HC: 215) and 'it has ceased to be a human life' in the sense of being considered of *equal value* as initiators or beginners (HC: 176).

This is what Arendt witnessed with the events surrounding the burning of the Reichstag and it is what we are witnessing in Australia, the US and Europe regarding the treatment of refugees: in a complex web of biopolitical racism that has a patriarchal basis, we bear witness to strangers being denied political community, strangers being barred from the world of the disclosure of natality to and by others. Witnessing the foreclosure for others of the 'capacity' and 'appearance' of natality within community would prick our conscience if the disclosure and welcome of natality is as much a moral principle as it is a principle of democratic plurality. And we would *feel immediately responsible* and compelled to act if, indeed, bodily comportment toward a world and others is already part of belonging to a world as it is to oneself.

So, if we combine Arendt's two insights from her political philosophy with insights from some account of the corporeal and affective basis of conscience and responsibility such as Nietzsche's (or Nancy's account of bodily 'inclination' toward the singularity of others, or Levinas's account of how the labouring body temporalises dwelling in and belonging to a world), we can make two claims. First, both personal responsibility and political responsibility would share the same *normative basis* in a secular liberal democracy: preserving the capacity for responsibility of all persons. The normative link between the ethical and the political is provided by the body (acting, speaking or doing whatever) that, in its futurity, is the expression of uniqueness and of another origin of a world – the affective, responsive body that embodies the norms we inherit and through which we dwell, but also that is sufficiently reflexive to inaugurate 'conscience', that is, the contestation and transformation of those norms. But, bodies are so enabled only through the disclosure of their uniqueness in the collectivity of a world of plurality. Nancy's ultimate interest in theorising the operation the 'exposure' of uniqueness (the disclosure of natality) between humans is, like Arendt's, political: he is concerned with the political erasure of this sharing of singularity in its contemporary forms – genocide, mass deportations, incarceration and abandonment of refugees and other deleterious forms of what we refer to as biopolitics. Nancy, like Arendt, focuses on the preconditions of this erasure but he also sees it as an ethical as well as a political problem. In 'Corpus' (Nancy 1993: 189–207) Nancy describes two ways that a body will be deprived of exposure to the other or 'exposition' (as the unique site of the taking place of meaning, or as the site of the event of natality as Arendt might say): through rejection by others on the basis of perceived difference or foreignness (the consequence of which is akin to Arendt's notion of 'utter loneliness' – HC: 215), or, conversely, through incorporation by others on the basis of perceived sameness, an appropriation that would also dissolve the limit between agents (for Arendt, the assumption of shared commonness characteristic of the rule of no-body would have this effect) (Nancy 1993: 206).

The second claim that can be made is that the *power of potentiality* that sustains the plurality of the human world is corporeal and affective. Hence, biopolitical moves that convert power to force or to deprive strangers of community at all would impact on, and be felt by, bodies, including bodies that are not the explicit target of those political policies and their publicity but are nevertheless part of the collective that is 'coordinated' by them. This feeling would be manifest as a crisis of conscience in the modes outlined earlier. What would temper that feeling, and the violence or passivity that can emerge from it, would be a critical politics that preserves the independence of the self's reflexive and therefore critical powers by assuming responsibility for the preservation of the independence and unique value of the responsiveness of all.

We are suggesting, with and beyond Arendt, that morality is a borderline political issue in the sense that when initiatives of government precipitate a conflict and then a dulling of conscience within a citizenry, what becomes evident is that these initiatives have not simply undermined customary moral standards. What is also undermined at a more fundamental level is the very basis of *normativity* that underlies the capacity to contest and transform norms and simultaneously express the uniqueness of a human being. Contestation of norms and the expression of uniqueness underpin both liberal democratic politics *and* morality, irrespective of the particular values in question. The basis of normativity, or the criterion of conscience, in both politics and morality, in a secular democracy is not so much that contained in Arendt's account of moral judgement (at least not the version she gleans from Kant and Socrates). Taking into account the corporeal and affective basis of conscience, the more fundamental basis of normativity and the condition of judgement is maintaining the *collective exposure to each other of the uniqueness of the futurity of bodies*. Government that puts this in jeopardy, by abandoning political responsibility for maintaining the conditions for this (at all levels: nation, workplace and home), has separated itself from the collectivity of the populace that it would then coordinate. If citizens fall in line with this, through fear or indifference, then we join with our ruling governments and put in jeopardy the very fabric of the world we share as well as the democratic plurality we espouse.

These considerations enhance rather than lead to the abandonment of a political ontology of hospitality without which these bodies would be nothing. By adapting Arendt's political ontology to accommodate this philosophy of the body, we can say that, for the sake of preserving the world for the welcome and disclosure of the natality and uniqueness of *these bodies*, the hospitality of democratic politics is inspired toward justice. And a democratic polity could not survive without remaining open to and giving time for the uniqueness that these futural bodies are. Conversely, justice and democracy are compromised if, within the partitioning of time, particular groups of people are expected to give time more than others to allow others to be expressions of 'natality' and thereby also to have time for agency, judgement and the contestation of tradition. Further, the more that there is an abdication of political responsibility for preserving the world for the disclosure of the uniqueness of bodies, the more these bodies will collapse into the timeless present. With this goes the capacity to contest traditional laws of hospitality, which is the hallmark of democracy.

Notes

1   As discussed in Chapter 1, Nancy puts this principle, most succinctly, as follows: what opens us to ourselves, to each other and to 'potentiality' is the 'sharing' of the 'incalculable' uniqueness of each and all together or the 'affirmation' of the 'uniqueness' of all of us in all our relations (Nancy 2010: 24).

2   Arendt is clear that a 'common world' or 'reality' is not guaranteed by shared ideas or similar identities but rather the contrary – by human plurality, 'differences of position' or the disclosure of natality between speakers and

actors (HC: 57). This can be lost through totalitarianism, as we have seen in Chapter 2, but equally the common world can be destroyed by 'mass society or mass hysteria' (HC: 58) or, to update Arendt's terminology, by mass consumerism, celebrity idolatry and 'popularism'.

3 Arendt at times seems to formulate 'subjectivity' or agency in these terms, as *responding to* and openness to the other's uniqueness, for example when she discusses the disclosure of natality as the 'in-between' that keeps human existence open to potentiality. And crucially, she also formulates this 'in-between' as the common world or 'reality', which 'relates and separates men at the same time' (HC: 52). But at other times, especially in her engagements with Kant and her discussions of responsibility and judgement (and her account of 'representative thinking'), Arendt emphasises an internal self-relation as *prior* relations with, and the witness of, others rather than as always already a *response* to the other's unique distinctness. Even though such judgement and thinking are 'communicative' and so engage others (at the level of imagination), they are initiated from within the self and so are not exactly what Derrida (or Levinas) means by subjectivity, nor what Nancy means by being-singular-plural. The analysis in this section ignores this possible difference between Arendt's and Derrida's, Nancy's and Levinas's accounts of 'subjectivity'. Where Arendt's emphasis on the self's internal self-relation becomes a potential (although resolvable) problem for the analysis in this chapter is in section III, on responsibility and the faith she places in moral judgement (as she formulates it via Kant and Socrates) as a motivator of political action.

4 On this point Derrida is arguably at odds with Levinas, who seems to argue for the priority and the one-way directionality of the unconditional welcome of the other. As that debate is not directly relevant to our analysis, we leave aside Levinas's position regarding the conditionality of human inter-relations. See Bettina Bergo (2011) for an insightful and sympathetic critique of Levinas on this issue for perhaps neglecting embodied, affective and 'the lived fact of intersubjectivity', which, from the perspective of the analysis in this chapter, is precisely where the patriarchal and racist dimensions of hospitality play out (Bergo 2011: 18).

5 Perhaps surprisingly, since the mid-1990s Australia has been a key destination for a steady flow of refugees escaping conflicts in the Middle East, Afghanistan and South East Asia, many of whom – between 200 and 20,000 per annum – have attempted to enter the country, unofficially, by fishing boat from Indonesia. However, since August 2001, except for a brief period in 2009–12, the Australian government has blocked entry to

any such 'unprocessed' arrivals and held these people in offshore detention camps, a practice rightly condemned by the United Nations and Amnesty International. The ramification of this practice far exceeds the immediate devastating impact on the thousands held in these camps.

6 There has been much discussion and debate about the significance of Levinas's acknowledgement of the 'feminine welcome', which is beyond the scope of the analysis here. Derrida ties Levinas's account of the 'feminine welcome' specifically to political hospitality (Derrida 1999: 70–101). Also see Chanter (2001: 241–62) and Guenther (2006: 58–73) for critical accounts more sensitive to a feminist philosophical perspective.

7 See the news report 'Polish lawmakers push on with near-total ban on abortion', *The Guardian*, 23 September 2016 <https://www.theguardian. com/world/2016/sep/23/polish-lawmakers-anti-abortion-bill> (accessed 12 October 2016). The ruling party backed down in the face of a wave of mass protests by women in Poland, demonstrating again how crucial reproductive choice is to the maintenance of the mutual disclosure of natality upon which agency, democratic plurality and freedom depend.

8 The policy began by, and still involves, the Australian Navy escorting these boats away from the coast of Australia to detention camps on islands offshore. To justify the policy and to secure popular support, the Minister for Immigration announced, in a televised press conference in October 2001, that, according to a report from the Navy, people on one such boat were throwing their children overboard, presumably to thwart the Navy's mission. The announcement was accompanied by comments suggesting that people with such values would not be welcome in Australia. By the time it was revealed, several months later, that the report was false, it had served the government's purpose of demonising the refugees. After several official enquires, no one has been held accountable for what has been put down to a miscommunication. For a full analysis of the refugee policy and its relation to the 'war on terror' that began shortly after, see David Marr and Marian Wilkinson (2003).

9 This campaign was centred on the slogans 'Let's look out for Australia' and 'Be alert, but not alarmed'. It involved television advertisements and a pamphlet (with fridge magnet) distributed to every Australian household advising members of the public to report anything 'unusual or suspicious in their neighbourhood or workplace'. The campaign illustrates how comprehensive the Howard government's conviction was that national borders can be secured and conditional hospitality controlled through the 'home'.

10 For discussions of these changes to the workforces in Australia and the UK

that have enhanced job insecurity and job status insecurity, see De Ruyter and Burgess (2003) and Gallie et al. (2017).

11 The argument here is not that democracy, and the contestation of tradition at its heart, requires 'slow' time rather than the 'speed' characteristic of modern life. Rather, the point is that, aside from the issue of speed, lived time is dispersed for some more than for others and the giving of lived time in support of hospitality is distributed inequitably. See also William Connolly's thought-provoking discussion of 'Democracy and time' (Connolly 2002: 140–75).

12 Derrida's formulation of 'democracy to come', as an always futural event not unlike Arendt's notion of 'potentiality', arises in the context of his expansive deconstructive critique of the concept of sovereignty as understood by Bodin, Hobbes, Rousseau and Schmitt in his book *Rogues: Two Essays on Reason* (Derrida 2005).

13 This has been reconfirmed by economists and sociologists in studies conducted in Australia since the mid-1990s. See, for example, Pocock (2006).

14 Vasti Roodt (2001) provides a comprehensive analysis of this point through a comparison of Arendt and Nietzsche, but with reference to politics and their shared notions of the historicity of the self rather than conscience and responsibility.

15 Arendt discusses this point at length in several places, for example, RJ: 44–5, 86, 97, 181–8; and LM I: 184–93.

16 Bat-Ami Bar On (2002) also finds Arendt's neglect of affect and feeling a problem in her interesting and otherwise admiring account of Arendt's thoughts on restoring critical thinking and political action in societies ruined by political violence.

17 For a more comprehensive analysis of Nietzsche's notions of conscience and responsibility in relation to Arendt, see Diprose (2008).

18 In this gap, the past, including the juridico-moral code one has inherited or that is in the process of being reversed, is neither forgotten nor entirely recuperated: it is revised and either affirmed or contested through transforming the 'it was' into 'thus I willed it', as Nietzsche puts it in 'On redemption' (Nietzsche 1978: 137–42). In this way one keeps the future open, sacrifices oneself or 'goes under' in the process, while taking responsibility for one's own 'destiny' – see 'Zarathustra's prologue' (Nietzsche 1978: 9–25).

19 This is apparent in descriptions of will to power as 'appropriation, injury, overpowering what is strange and weaker, [. . .] imposition of one's

own forms' (Nietzsche 1973: 259; see also Nietzsche 1967a: 12) and in Nietzsche's concept of 'great politics' that follows from revaluation of value become flesh: 'politics merged entirely with a war of spirits' and the explosion of 'all power structures of the old society' (Nietzsche 1967a: 'Why I am destiny' 1).

20 This opposition between the solitary activity of thinking and collective action is not just in Arendt's explicit discussions of moral responsibility but runs throughout her work (for example, HC: 324–5; BPF: 259–60).

5

Natality and Narrative

In Chapters 3 and 4 we extended Arendt's notion of acting against the (patriarchal, racist, theological and heteronormative) biopolitical suppression of natality by addressing biopolitical issues, modes of embodiment and types of action that Arendt may not have counted as political. In Chapter 4 this exercise entailed, in part, re-examining the animating affections of action in terms of the criteria of conscience (that prompt us to act as well as guide us to do the right thing). In short, we proposed that if inter-relational disclosure and welcome of natality and uniqueness can be understood as the principle of democratic plurality, then it is also a kind of moral principle or, rather, the most fundamental criterion of conscience. The analysis revealed how Arendt's philosophy of natality and politics of action points toward an important connection between ethics and politics: conscience, personal responsibility and hence action are dependent upon the assumption of political responsibility, which consists in all of us, including lawmakers and members of government, not only acting *against* 'conditions under which people no longer wish to live' (OT: 442) but also acting *for* a world that fosters the capacity for responsibility and hence the unique distinctness of everyone – a world that would welcome the refugee and a world of public, domestic and work conditions under which anyone could live freely, in Arendt's sense of the word.

In this chapter we develop Arendt's notion of political action in a different direction by examining the relation between natality and narrative at stake in Arendt's famous claim, unusual in the context of both biopolitics and narrative studies, that political action '"produces" stories' the way other activities, such as work, produce objects (HC: 184). Because of this explicit connection with action, storytelling is intertwined with the event of natality, which constitutes for Arendt the ontological condition of action: because 'action has the closest connection with the human condition of natality [. . .] natality, and not mortality, may be the central category of political, as distinguished from metaphysical, thought' (HC: 9). Can we claim that natality, by implication, may also be 'the central category' of a narrative produced by action?[1] Yet, what kind of story is created by action, in Arendt's sense of the word, and what kind of a narrative is capable of manifesting, and perhaps sheltering, the condition of natality with its three inter-related meanings – the enactment of a new beginning in history, human plurality, and the disclosure of uniqueness through words and deeds? As we witness again and again, all these inter-related meanings of natality – the new beginning, uniqueness and the affirmation of human plurality – are the target of racist biopolitics and neo-liberalism as more new groups of people are 'insulted', 'injured' and expelled from the common world (MDT: 16). However, the mutual co-implication between action and narrative also expands the possibilities of countering these disastrous effects of biopolitics.

This explicit relation between action and stories seems to limit our reflection on narrative to a genre of life stories, which respond to political events; however, we hope to show that the implications of Arendt's claim are relevant to all narratives and perhaps to artworks in general. Although Arendt herself does not give us a coherent and well developed theory of narrative, following the implication of her philosophy of natality, we will have to assume that any narrative created by action is also an act in its own right, which enables a new beginning. This new beginning can be understood in multiple ways: as a new interpretation of actions, as a new interpretation of historical events, or as the very capacity to create a new beginning through language. Second, such narrative discloses the uniqueness of actors. And finally, stories produced by action retrospectively reveal its meaning, and this implies a crucial role of memory, with its specific temporality, characterised by an awareness of 'what is no longer'. Since the effects of action transpire in the course of the event without leaving durable tangible 'products', action relies for its preservation on stories, which constitute what Kristeva calls a politics of memory. By forming and contesting the politics of commemoration, narratives preserve and renew the effects of action into the future; they sustain the temporality of what is not yet. Thus, the peculiar temporality of narrative crosses over the gap between what is no longer and what is not yet. Consequently, a narrative capable of manifesting the condition of natality negotiates between seemingly incompatible tasks: it at once participates in the politics of commemoration and constitutes a new event; it negotiates between the singularity and plurality of actors; and it bridges the gap between no longer and not yet. In so doing, storytelling contests biopolitical normalisation, historical causality and the erasure of events from the past. A narrative in this sense departs from the politics of representation, legitimations of the dominant history, or the aesthetic ideologies of realism, and foregrounds instead a discontinuous temporality between past and future. At the same time, Arendt's notion of narrative provides a crucial alternative to information technologies, dominant in the age of biopolitics and neo-liberalism: statistical analysis, big data and the predictive modelling of the future.

In order to develop an Arendtian approach to narrative outlined above, this chapter examines the following problems: the implications of the event of natality for aesthetics, presupposed by the link between action and narration; the negotiation between uniqueness and human plurality in the narrative form; the role of memory, tradition and temporality; language and metaphor; and the worldly character of narrative. Taking all these elements of the narrative into account, we develop what Kristeva and Cavarero have called in different ways an ontological dimension of storytelling, namely, the status of human life as a narratable bios. Ultimately, we will argue that the concept of bios based on narratable lives further complicates the *bios–zoe* distinction and separates this distinction from the logic of sovereignty.

I. Narrative Between the Politics and Aesthetics of Natality

Arendt's claim that it is political action, rather than individual authors (HC: 184), that produces politically relevant stories situates the event of natality on the border between aesthetics and politics.[2] The mutual relation between action and stories (HC: 184) contests Adorno's political pessimism and expands the possibilities of transformative political action as the only weapon we have against totalitarianism, racist biopolitics and the destruction of the planet. For Arendt, both political acts and narrative acts have transformative potential, even though they occur in the midst of historical domination. That is why Adriana

Cavarero and Shari Stone-Mediatore deploy Arendt's concept of narrative for a feminist analysis of storytelling as a means of the political expression of marginalised subjectivities. Furthermore, in Arendt's work both political and aesthetic acts are mutually related: transformative political practice produces stories while narrative supplements action by making it memorable (Kristeva 2001), pertinent to political life, and by retrospectively shaping its meaning. This intersection between action and narrative allows us to situate the event of natality on the border between aesthetics and politics.

Although Arendt's own reflections on artistic practice are limited, several of her critics have debated the aesthetic elements of Arendt's theory of political action (Bernstein 2000: 277–92; Curtis 1999; Dietz 2000; Kateb 1983: 30–5; Sjöholm 2015). Curtis even goes so far as to argue that Arendt's philosophy as a whole takes 'an aesthetic turn' (Curtis 1999: 10–13). As Sjöholm argues, for Arendt, artworks, like political actors, are characterised by the capacity of sensible appearance in the public space. These aesthetic elements of the political are irreducible to what Benjamin calls an aesthetic unity of politics because Arendt rejects any notion of action and narrative based on the model of fabrication, understood as the realisation of a pre-existing model. Instead, she argues that politics requires a plurality of participants, conflicting perspectives and the acknowledgement of unpredictability. What her critics identify as 'aesthetic' elements of politics are, therefore, not the aesthetic unity of the people, but, on the contrary, the multiplicity and particularity of the sensible appearances of actors and artworks in the public space (Sjöholm 2015: 1–30), the expression of the uniqueness of political agents (Curtis 1999: 23–66) and the creation of a new beginning in political life (Ziarek 2012: 10–26). In the context of feminist and philosophical debates about aesthetics and politics, the main intervention that Arendt allows us to make is that political action, like art and thinking, is irreducible to a means–ends rationality and standardised behaviour produced by biopolitical normalisation. This claim subverts the usual opposition between a narrow view of politics driven by pragmatic interests and the creative artistic practice that exceeds such instrumentalism. As we have discussed in Chapters 1 and 3, for Arendt, not only artistic practice but also political action has to be considered in non-instrumental terms.

By rejecting the instrumentality and the substitution of action by standardised behaviour, Arendt also contests any ideological uses of narrative in particular to suggest a fictitious unity of the people or unified history, both of which are evident for example in Trump's slogan 'Make America great again'. On the contrary, if we can speak of the aesthetic dimensions of political action in Arendt's work, these would include: first, the negotiation between the plurality and uniqueness of political actors; and second, the creation of a new beginning, which creates ruptures in history and unpredictable events in public lives. To suppress these characteristics of the politics of natality – plurality, uniqueness and a new beginning – one indeed has to replace the political by biopolitics, fascist populism, or the neo-liberal model of the government as business. By contrast, the aesthetic element of action in Arendt's work consists in the disclosure of the uniqueness of political agents in the context of human plurality.

Why is this relation between human plurality and uniqueness an aesthetic as well as a political problem? The new beginning in public lives and the singularity of actors – natality – can be called the aesthetic dimensions of the political because their particularities exceed the available general political, philosophical and linguistic meanings and norms. Evocative of the modernist artistic slogan 'Make it new', the new beginning created by action, whether it occurs on a miniscule local or a revolutionary collective scale, initiates something unexpected, 'infinitely improbable' (HC: 178): it interrupts historical continuity and the re-production of the relations of power/knowledge in which it is situated. Action can initiate a new beginning precisely because, as we have shown, it creates inter-relational agency and new forms of political power in the context of the already constituted relations of power/knowledge. Although this unpredictable novelty is what action shares with experimental artistic practice, at the same time it contests the traditional aesthetic notion of the originality of the isolated artist or genius. And since the new beginning in politics is intertwined with a transformation of both inter-human relations and human relations to the world, such transformation is fundamentally different from the production and consumption of the ever-same 'novelty' of commodities. Consequently, narrative produced by such action does not imply a politically engaged literature, based on the representation of major political events, or on collective or individual identities, or on the persuasion of people to engage in specific initiatives;[3] rather, such narrative, like action that it retrospectively completes, is situated at the crossroads of politics and aesthetics of natality.

II. Narrative Disclosure of Uniqueness and Human Plurality

What is most directly linked to the politics and aesthetics of natality is the narrative disclosure of singularity and uniqueness in the web of relations, including relations of gender, class and race. As we have argued in Chapter 1, since uniqueness exceeds not only any political category of classification and normalisation but also general attributes of identity, it cannot be defined but merely implied in the form of an address to another: 'who are you?' Any answer to such a question in the form of self-definition – for example, I am a white feminist immigrant – is necessarily general, shared by other white feminist immigrants, and therefore slides into a general attribute of identity, which Arendt calls 'whatness'. As Arendt underscores, 'The moment we want to say *who* somebody is, our very vocabulary leads us astray into saying *what* he is' (HC: 181). This fundamental linguistic problem of uniqueness pushes the communicable generality of meaning to the limits of expression: 'The manifestation of who the speaker and doer unexchangeably is [. . .] retains a curious intangibility that confounds all efforts toward unequivocal verbal expression' (HC: 181). This challenge of the 'intangible' uniqueness posed to political, ordinary and philosophical languages is precisely what calls for narrative in the first place. That is why Arendt claims that uniqueness manifesting itself in acting with others 'eventually emerges as the unique life story of the newcomer, affecting uniquely the life stories of all those with whom he comes into contact' (HC: 184).

We are left, however, with a question about how uniqueness can be expressed as a unique life story. This question about the narrative disclosure of uniqueness is most debated among feminist theorists responding directly or indirectly to Arendt (Butler 2005; Cavarero 2000; Kristeva 2001). In her *Relating Narratives*, Cavarero, for example, argues that our desire for narrative is intertwined with a desire for our own uniqueness, narrated by others. From this point of view, she re-reads the foundational Western narratives in light of the conflict between universality and singularity and argues that this conflict has been historically gendered – and we should add racialised as well. Cavarero returns to the drama of Oedipus and interprets it as a paradigmatic Western masculine tragedy of a narrative universality suppressing singularity and sexual difference (Cavarero 2000: 52–3). This suppression is expressed in an exemplary way in Oedipus's answer – 'Man' – to the Sphinx's riddle.[4] In her response to Cavarero's interpretation of Arendt, Butler concedes (Butler 2005: 30–40) that uniqueness in narrative emerging from the address to the other provides an alternative to Nietzsche's punitive account of morality and to Hegel's reciprocity of recognition. However, according to Butler (2005: 36), any narrative account of singularity is interrupted by the indifference and generality of discursive norms, which make us not only recognisable to others but also 'substitutable' (Butler 2005: 37–9). Second, giving a narrative account of my life fails to account for those relations to others that precede my memory. Ultimately, norms, relations to others and the disconnection of narrative from lived bodily experience reveal uniqueness at the price of my 'opacity to myself' (Butler 2005: 37–9).

However, in the context of Arendt's work, these tensions between exposure and opacity, between singularity and the generality of norms, or 'who' and 'what', do not undermine irreplaceable singularity but precisely characterise its specific politico-aesthetic mode of disclosure in language, action and narrative form.[5] Indeed, as Kristeva points out, such revelation is characterised by the uncanny interplay between disalienation and estrangement (Kristeva 2001: 83, 86). Or, as Arendt argues, the manifestation of uniqueness to others is paradoxically interconnected with the obscurity of agents to themselves: the manifestation of the "'who", which appears so clearly and un-mistakably to others, remains hidden from the person himself' (HC: 179). Consequently, the narrative disclosure of uniqueness is likewise intertwined with darkness and obscurity, which can never be expressed or represented but, on the contrary, consti-tutes a limit of any expression, representation or appearance. However, the paradoxical implication of Arendt's work is that this irreducible enigma of uniqueness manifesting itself in action presents not an obstacle but, on the contrary, the very possibil-ity of narrative, which has to shelter this enigma: because such opacity is intertwined with our appearance to others prior to our relation to ourselves, it also positions those others – whether they are actors or spectators – as potential storytellers. These potential storytellers are situated in the multiplicity of inter-human relations and, therefore, their narrative point of view, invariably gendered, racialised and culturally specific, can never aspire to the position of the objective or omniscient narrator, because it always represents a partial, contingent perspective in relation to other perspectives. Nonetheless, these partial narrative perspectives are not isolated because they anticipate and are addressed to other possible and equally partial points of view.

Since life is narratable, thanks to others in their role as potential storytellers, the crucial implication of this indebted-ness of narration to others lies not in my dispossession from my own story, as Butler argues but, more fundamentally, in the reframing of any autobiography as always already a biography: '*Who* somebody [. . .] was we can know only by knowing [. . .] his biography' (HC: 186). The reason why the primary genre of any life story is biography rather than autobiography is that every auto/biography takes place in the context of stories told or withheld by others, who complete and disseminate their meaning. It is especially the case with the worldly events of the appearance and disappearance of subjects – birth and death – which, if narratable at all, are always told by others. Likewise, because action depends on human plurality, the very possibility of a life story, in Arendt's sense of the word, including auto-biography, emerges from the multiplicity of potential witnesses and storytellers, and this debt has to be reflected in the narrative form. It is because of such dependence of stories on others as potential storytellers that Arendt emphatically rejects of any idea of self-authorship, or 'self-fashioning', before such a rejection became a hallmark of postmodernism. As she puts it, 'nobody is the author or producer of his own life story' (HC: 184). This inseparable relation between uniqueness and plurality is another crucial reason why narrative is linked to the condition of natality.

The relation between uniqueness and human plurality allows us to reinterpret the role of the storyteller and expose its difference from the conventional individual author. According to Arendt, any storyteller concerned with the narrative expression of the actor's uniqueness has to take into account other multiple, often conflicting points of view of the narrated events. Reflected in narrative structure as the narrative point of view, the predicament of the storyteller can be theorised in the context of Arendt's analysis of the spectator in *The Life of the Mind* (LM I: 92–8) and in her political reinterpretation of Kant's *Critique of Judgment*. In her posthumously published *Lectures on Kant's Political Philosophy* (LKPP: 62–5) Arendt develops an analogy between the political judgement of historians, or spectators of action reflecting on a specific political event, and the aesthetic judgement of taste reflecting on a beautiful object. We can expand this analogy even further and suggest a similitude between spectators and storytellers, because any spectator is a potential storyteller. What is at stake in this analogy between the historian, the spectator, the storyteller and the audience of art is the judgement of the particular without a general concept – this event, this object, this agent, this work of art, rather than a judgement about history, nature, humanity or art in general. For Arendt, Kant's greatest political discovery in his theory of reflective judgement is the communicability of the particular to others without general concepts or norms. These rules are either unknown or should not be imposed because they fail to express uniqueness. Nor should these rules and their application be exempt from judgement, since, as Arendt repeats after Kant, there is no rule for the application of the general law or concept. Just as whatness – the series of attributes of identity, which can be communicated to others – cannot account for human unique-ness, so too aesthetic norms of beauty cannot explain why this art or landscape is beautiful, nor can democratic political ideals of freedom and equality tell us how we should act or judge in this particular case. Arendt's recovery of Kant's reflective judgement in the context of her philosophy of natality not only is crucial for the narrative expression of uniqueness but is even more urgent in the context of the convergence of biopolitics and neo-liberalism in Western democracies. Because of this con-vergence, we see an ongoing devalorisation of judgement and its replacement by metrics, statistical analysis and big data in the service of biopolitical normalisation and racial profiling.

For Arendt, the generality of reflective judgements does not depend on concepts or norms but on their communicability to others. She never ceases to marvel that the seemingly most private aesthetic judgement based on senses and affect – the pleasure in the particular for Kant, but for Arendt also the outrage, joy, laughter or anger[6] – is at the same time the most other-directed judgement (LKPP: 67–8). As Arendt suggests, the communicability of the particular is Kant's most important contribution to politics, aesthetics and, we should add, storytelling (LKPP: 43, 63). Like judgements of taste, stories concerned with particular events and the singularity of actors have to be communicable to others. Reinterpreting Kant in the context of her philosophy of natality, Arendt argues that what makes these judgements communicable is the so-called enlarged mentality, that is, taking other points of view into account when we judge something singular. Judging from others' points of view – one of the most contentious aspects of Arendt's political theory[7] – presupposes human plurality in the world, which in the context of Arendt's own work links aesthetic judgement with the politics and aesthetics of natality. In Arendt's interpretation of Kant, what enables taking others' viewpoints into account is neither empirical data nor statistical analysis of the population, but the 'force of imagination' (LKPP: 43). Throughout her work, Arendt defines imagination as the capacity to represent what is absent in the form of the 'invisible' mental image and sees it as a precondition not only of memory but also of perception. As the capacity to represent what is absent, imagination enables us to put ourselves in the position of potential others and to reflect on my judgement from their standpoints: 'the force of imagination [. . .] makes the others present and thus moves in a space that is potentially public. [. . .] To think with an enlarged mentality means that one trains one's imagination to go visiting' (LKPP: 43). Taking possible points of view of others into account – enlarged mentality – does not amount to an objective standpoint transcending human plurality but, on the contrary, to an inter-relational *sensus communis* (LKPP: 70–2). That is why, for Arendt, this enlarged mentality is not a condition of objectivity but of 'realness', which both normalising and totalitarian tendencies of biopolitics destroy.

Crucial for the spectator, the storyteller and even the thinker (LKPP: 43), an enlarged mentality can be achieved thanks to what Arendt reinterprets as the two operations of reflection in reflective judgement. The first step is negative and critical. By considering my own judgement from the perspective of potential or actual others, I might distance myself from my own dogmatism, conditioned norms, habitual behaviours or un-reflective opinions, and thus achieve some relative impartiality, or what Kant calls 'disinterestedness' (LKPP: 73). The positive achievement of enlarged mentality lies in sociability, in being and acting with others, which does not depend merely upon the satisfaction of our '*needs* and *wants*' (LKPP: 74). In other words, as Rodolphe Gasché suggests, for Arendt (differing from Kant) the reflection of the reflective judgement consists in taking into consideration others with whom we share the world in common, and whose potential or real viewpoints are represented by imagination (Gasché 2013–14: 112–14). For Gasché, reflection in Arendt's notion of reflective judgement is a kind of internal deliberation with others, and therefore it is communicable from the start (Gasché 2013–14: 112–14).[8]

By drawing on Arendt's analogy between spectators and storytellers, we have argued that storytellers concerned with com-municability of the particular have to take into account multiple possible points of view thanks to their reflective judgement and enlarged mentality. Stories and narratives, whether fictional or biographical, can convey this critical concern with communi-cability of singularity of agents and events on the level of narrative form by rejecting the objective point of view of the omniscient narrator, and exploring instead other narrative possibilities. And conversely, Arendt's reflections on singularity and plurality in the narrative allow us to draw out the philosophical and political implications of narrative form and to reinterpret the stakes of the aesthetic experimentation with the narrative point of view (or focalisation). For example, when a story is told from a limited third- or first-person narrative point of view, this narrative form calls for taking into account other narrative perspectives in the process of reading. Other narrative possibilities might consist in multiple and conflicting narrative points of view, which, through this multiplicity, enact the enlarged mentality in narrative form. This is the case, for example, in Virginia Woolf's *To the Lighthouse* or Akira Kurosawa's film *Rashomon*. Adopting an unreliable or ironic point of view, as for example in Nella Larsen's *Passing*, a story can make us question the narrator's fears and prejudices, and by extension compel a reflection on the limitations of our own point of view.

Another mode of the expression of uniqueness in a narrative form is suggested by Arendt's reinterpretation of Kant's exemplary validity. As Arendt points out, any time we communicate a particular as an example without knowing a general law or norm, which it might illuminate, we nonetheless imply that this particular is valid for more than one case. Because we do not know the general concept which a particular might illustrate, when we judge that a particular – this particular story, this particular event or this particular character – has exemplary validity we are with dealing with a reflective judgement (which itself has only exemplary validity, as if it were an example of *sensus communis*). An example is therefore a particular which is chosen to express something more than itself, some communicable generality, even if this generality cannot be defined. As

Arendt writes, '"example" comes from *eximere*, to "single out some particular" [. . .]. This exemplar is and remains a particular that in its very particularity reveals the generality that otherwise could not be defined' (LKPP: 77). What is critical for Arendt is that an example can express this exemplarity without comparison with another example or illustrating a general concept or a norm. By reflecting on this action, this story or the uniqueness of this person revealed through action, we offer these particulars as examples of what acting, narrative and uniqueness can be.[9] A story can be read as an example of human plurality of acting in concert or of human uniqueness without referring to a general definition or normative standard of what action, plurality or uniqueness are. Although examples are always culturally and historically specific, they provide nonetheless an alternative not only to concepts but, more importantly, to statistical analysis, big data and predictive analytics. This cultivation of reflective judgement and exemplary validity through narrative is all the more crucial in the age of ever more advanced information technologies, which drive biopolitical normalisation, management and predictions of political 'behaviour' in the future.

Nonetheless, when we critically choose exemplary events, persons or situations conveying uniqueness, this choice has to be intertwined with a further reflective judgement about why this story, or this event, and not others should be chosen as exemplary. As Arendt puts it, 'the judgment has exemplary validity to the extent that the example is rightly chosen' (LKPP: 84). Such reflection on the choice of exemplary events should be guided not by uncritical acceptance of socio-political norms or narrative conventions, but by reflective judgement, which might allow us to distance ourselves from these norms by imagining other points of view and other possibilities. Exemplarity is therefore antithetical to the biopolitics of normalisation, outcomes, metrics and so forth. Indeed, as Arendt concludes her reflections on Kant, even historical and political concepts are not objective but have only exemplary rather than scientific validity: these concepts 'have their origin in some particular historical incident, and we then proceed to make it "exemplary" – to see in the particular what is valid for more than one case' (LKPP: 85). Here we see a spectacular reversal in Arendt's thinking on judgement: this forgotten mere exemplary validity of historical and political concepts submits these concepts to reflective judgement, rather than using them as a basis of determinant judgements or statistical modelling of politics.

By responding to feminist debates about narrative (Butler, Curtis, Cavarero, Stone-Mediatore) we have discussed so far three aspects of narrative that enable the narrative disclosure of uniqueness and the affirmation of plurality in Arendt's notion of storytelling. First, we argued that uniqueness, which appears to others in the form of a question – 'Who are you?' – positions those others in the role of potential storytellers. Second, the communicability of singularity in narrative form calls for a partial, contingent viewpoint of the storyteller, which nonetheless has to be communicable to others. Such communication occurs thanks to reflective judgement, which calls for imagination and a critical refection on the narrator's and storyteller's points of view from the perspectives of others. By reflecting on the others' perspectives thanks to imagination, reflective judgement intertwined with the limited narrative point of view performs enlarged mentality rather than an objective or a subjective representation of reality. And finally, we pointed out that the narrative disclosure of uniqueness has a status of exemplary validity.

However, there is another reason why action enables stories: because the events it enacts constitute the possibility of a plot. Arendt briefly refers to the Aristotelian notion of plot or *mythos*, imitating, or more precisely, re-enacting, action (Aristotle 1989: 13–14). Based on the theatrical (rather than pictorial) Aristotelian notion of mimesis,[10] narrative, by re-enacting action, becomes a new performative act in its own right. For both Arendt and Aristotle, plot, which establishes a temporal sequence among the selected events, cannot be explained by the psychological or moral makeup (that is, by their whatness) of the characters, just as, for Arendt, action cannot be explained by the identity or the intention of actors. Despite these similarities, Arendt's and Aristotle's understandings of the plot, or *mythos*, differ. In contrast to the Aristotelian definition of *mythos*, the Arendtian notions of action and plot neither have a clear sense of an ending nor are based on the causal, linear relations between a beginning, a middle and a well defined ending. This is the case because Arendt focuses primarily on the way action creates a new beginning, which in turn calls for a new story. Without a new beginning, there is neither need nor desire for a new story. Paradoxically, it is this open-endedness of action, its lack of a predictable *telos*, that generates storytelling, which reveals the meaning of action retrospectively through the act of narrative recollection. Furthermore, such a retrospective disclosure of the meaning of action through the narrative act is itself incomplete and antithetical to predictive analytics; it engenders further, often conflicting, plots and the interpretations of these narratives. A non-chronological, non-linear plot can dramatise such a retrospective significance of action and point to a crucial role of memory in storytelling.

III. Narrating the Past: On Memory, Imagination and Metaphor in Storytelling

As Kristeva argues, any story inspired by action, any biography, is implicated in the politics of remembrance (Kristeva 2001: 75–6). Thanks to commemoration, stories preserve and renew the effects of action into the future. Political action recalled in narrative can belong to the most recent past, almost contemporaneous with the act of telling, or it can belong to a distant forgotten history. Consequently, the temporal gap between the event and the narrative act can be minimal or almost insurmountable, but no matter how distant or near the past, memory at stake in storytelling has to bridge this temporal hiatus. Only then can it enable the survival of the disclosed uniqueness and the new beginning enacted in the past. We can say in reference to Arendt's analysis of remedies of action that narrative itself is one of the cures for the fragility of action, which emerges from action itself rather than from other activities. Narratives complete action, preserve its occurrence across generations and enable the questioning of its meaning: 'without this thinking completion after the act, without the articulation accomplished by remembrance, there simply was no story left that could be told' (BPF: 6).

Arendt is aware of the fragility and influence of commemoration – action can fail to create its narrative accounts. Bereft of a narrative, action is in danger of disappearing from history or having a lesser influence in political and historical life. Hence Arendt's concern with the survival of actions and their articulations as stories. For instance, the role of historical and political narrative is crucial in Arendt's comparison of the influence of the American and French Revolutions. As she argues, the

French Revolution, even though it failed, played a much greater role in political thinking than the American Revolution, which, according to Arendt, succeeded, precisely because of the different narratives these events inspired. And, as Kathryn Gines points out, it is a failure of remembrance, indicative of a larger political failure in the West, that Arendt does not discuss the Haitian Revolution in this context (Gines 2014: 12–13, 74–6). Conversely, excluded or subjugated groups can mobilise story-telling for the expression of their resistance in order to keep a possibility of freedom alive. For Arendt, an exemplary case of such narratives of emancipation is a 'hidden tradition' of Jewish artists and writers, writing as self-conscious pariahs, who, by rejecting enforced assimilation, 'achieved liberty [. . .] by the sheer forces of imagination' ('The Jew as pariah', RLC: 70).

To explore this relation between narrative and remembrance of the past, in this section we examine Arendt's theory of memory and its links with imagination and metaphor (discussed most extensively in *The Life of the Mind, Volume I*).[11] In particular, we focus our analysis on two effects of memory in narrative form: first, on the temporal dislocation of the storyteller dwelling on the past; and second, on the imaginative and metaphorical re-construction of the past, creating a narrative reappearance in the world of what can no longer appear. Both of these aspects of memory in narrative contest any metaphysics of presence. Not only do narrative acts of recollection *not* make past events present, but, on the contrary, they dramatise the storyteller's withdrawal from here and now. In order to remember the past, we have to leave the immediacy of our sense experience and our world behind. This dislocation from one's own present moment reveals the complexity of the temporal predicament of the storyteller; storytellers have to absent themselves from their current preoccupations in order to recall the events and actors who are no longer here, and who perhaps have never been present in either storyteller's own or even collective memory. Such temporal withdrawal of the storyteller from the present is a precondition of the narrative recollection of the uniqueness of agents and events from the past.

Because the storyteller is preoccupied with what is no longer, narrative can bridge the temporal gap between the event and the act of telling, but at the price of creating another temporal abyss in the situation of the storyteller: by dwelling on the past, the story-teller is also no longer here and now. The temporal withdrawal for the sake of the past is followed by the spatial withdrawal from the space of appearance. In the context of thinking, this with-drawal leads to solitude, characterised by mental dialogue with oneself. However, in the context of narrative, the storyteller's provisional disappearance from the current world of appearances is more complex because it occurs for the sake of the survival of those who can no longer appear in our world. Just as the actor is always already exposed to other participants of action prior to being for oneself, so, too, the storyteller is exposed to – or haunted by, as Derrida or Toni Morrison would say – by past lives and events. Following Arendt, we can call this double – temporal and spatial – displacement of the storyteller a double reversal of space and time: the present becomes absent in order to allow the disappearing past to reappear; the distant becomes near and near becomes distant. As Arendt writes, this dislocating activity of memory is profoundly '"out of order"' (LM I: 78, 85) insofar as 'it inverts all ordinary relationships: what is near and appears directly to our senses is now far away and what is distant is actually present. While thinking I am not where I actually am; I am surrounded not by sense-objects but by images that are invisible to everybody else' (LM I: 85). Although Arendt does not refer in her analysis of memory to psychoanalysis, the very expression 'While thinking I am not where I actually am' resonates in an uncanny way with Lacan's description of the split subject of the unconscious: 'I think where I am not, therefore I am where I do not think' (Lacan 1977: 166). Since memory and recollection are basic experiences of both thinking and storytelling, these spatio-temporal dislocations, gaps and disorder (LM I: 88) also characterise in explicit or implicit ways the retrospective character of narrative form.

By recalling the past, stories also transform it. Because re-membrance 'has to do with things that are absent, that have disappeared from my senses' (LM I: 85), it entails first of all a transformation of 'what was' into 'what is no longer'. Arendt calls this transformation 'desensing' (LM I: 87). 'Desensing' does not mean the purging of memory from all sensibility but rather calls our attention to the interplay between the disappearance of the past from sense experience and its reappearance as an invisible memory image created by imagination. In other words, recollection does not bring past events and actions fully into the presence of the storyteller or the reader, but calls our attention to the paradoxical status of past appearances, which 'are' 'no longer'. 'Being no longer' evokes neither presence nor absence, neither appearance nor its loss, neither representation nor unrepresentability. Arendt refers briefly to the vanishing of Eurydice in the Orphic myth to convey this disappearance of the past from sense perception as a condition of its reappearance in narrative, but, as Julia Kristeva suggests, Arendt plays the role of both Eurydice and Orpheus (Kristeva 2001: 98–9). Moreover, by tracing Arendt's references to various Greek myths, we could just as well say that she reflects on Eurydice from the point of view of Penelope's weaving and unweaving, which, for Arendt, exemplifies constructive and destructive aspects of thinking, memory and, by extension, narrative itself (LM I: 88).

The transformation of 'what was' into an invisible memory image, which bears witness to what is no longer, occurs, according to Arendt, thanks to imagination. Referring to diverse philosophical sources, from Aristotle and Augustine (LM I: 77) to Kant, Arendt consistently defines imagination as 'the condition for memory' (LKPP: 80). As she explains in her 1970 lecture on Kant's *Critique of Judgment*, entitled 'Imagination', in philosophical tradition, 'to give the name "imagination" to this faculty of having present what is absent is natural enough. If I represent what is absent, I have an *image* in my mind – an image of something I have seen and now somehow reproduce' (LKPP: 79). However, as Arendt argues by referring to Kant's schematism in the *First Critique*, imagination can transform the past into an invisible memory 'image' only because it already participates in sense perception. By creating a certain kind of schematic general shape, something like an invisible image, imagination allows us to synthesise the multiplicity of sensations into a recognisable and communicable particular. For example, by providing a general shape (or schema) of a house that all houses somehow share, imagination enables us to recognise this particular object as a specific house and communicate it to others. Such an invisible image is created by the synthetic power of imagination 'inherent in all sense perceptions' (LKPP: 83–4).

Thus, when Arendt writes in *The Life of the Mind* that imagination 'transforms a visible object into an invisible image' and in so doing provides 'the mind with suitable thought-objects' (LM I: 77), she stresses the active role of imagination in both sense perception and memory. The 'gift' (LM I: 76) of imagination allows us to recall from the vast reservoir of memory the most suitable images for creating a narrative account of the past. Arendt calls these recalled invisible images of the past 'thought–objects' (LM I: 77) or 'thought–event[s]' (BPF: 10). As we can see, for Arendt imagination is not limited to art alone because it is also essential to memory and recollection. And perhaps narrative acts of recollection combine both the creative imagination characteristic of the work of art and the so–called reproductive imagination in the service of memory (LM I: 86). In fact, we might want to question the very distinction between productive and reproductive imagination since both of them, for Arendt, are transformative. If, nonetheless, Arendt seems to privilege imagination's role in remembrance it is because such a role foregrounds more strongly the temporal aspect of 'what is no longer', which forms an awareness of the past: 'Only because of the mind's capacity for making present what is absent can we say "no more" and constitute a past for ourselves' (LM I: 76). Even the future temporality of 'not yet' depends on this experience of 'no more'. By stressing the active role of imagination in sense perception, memory and the work of art, Arendt foregrounds both the temporal and representational status (as invisible image) of appearances, which have 'disappeared from [. . .] our field of perception', and which reappear in narratives (LM I: 86).

This reappearance of memories of past actions and lives in narrative form depends on its linguistic, metaphoric articulation. Language is fundamental not only for Arendt's theory of action and narratives but also for her account of memory (LM I: 98). Through a meaningful articulation, narrative enables invisible memory images of the past to reappear in the world – to disclose to others 'what otherwise would not be a part of the appearing world at all' (LM I: 98). Specifically, it is the task of metaphor to re-inscribe memory images formed by imagination into the sensible web of appearances in the world. Metaphor can perform this task because of its two outstanding characteristics: first, metaphors themselves are relational – they disclose similarity among heterogeneous relations in the world; and second, metaphors enable the formation of intelligible concepts – such as 'actuality' or 'category' – out of common experiences or activities in the world.[12] Thanks to their metaphoric construction, concepts are marked by memory traces of such worldly belonging. Like Nietzsche, Arendt emphasises the metaphorical genealogy of conceptual language. However, as Derrida cautions us in 'White mythology', reclaiming metaphorical origins of concepts may not necessarily be subversive, because such derivation seems to reproduce the classical philosophical oppositions between the sensible and the intelligible, the original and the derivative, proper and improper, forgetting and remembrance, among others. From Plato, Aristotle and Hegel, to Nietzsche, Freud and Jacobson, philosophical excavations of the metaphorical roots of concepts, writes Derrida, often amount to a search for a forgotten proper origin of meaning, which seems to be independent from all means of linguistic 'transport' (Derrida 1982: 229). Consequently, the 'epistemological ambivalence' (Derrida 1982: 261) of metaphor in philosophy is limited by the privilege of proper meaning, historical continuity, similarity and, ultimately, the return to the self-presence of the subject (268–9). By contrast, Derrida's deconstruction of the opposition between concept and metaphor stresses instead the unpredictable polysemy, which undermines similarity, and the self-presence of the subject. And, perhaps not surprisingly, Derrida ultimately associates this loss of the proper meaning and the eclipse of self-presence with death, as if he were forgetting that natality is another marker of finitude: 'metaphor, then, always carries its death within itself. And this death, surely, is also the death *of* philosophy' (Derrida 1982: 271).

Although, for Arendt, metaphor reconnects even the most abstract thoughts and concepts with sensibility, her account of figurative language is no longer bound to the values of proper meaning or the isolated subject. Nor does she rely on the affinity between metaphor and death to undermine these values. On the contrary, metaphor inscribes invisible memory images within the plural world of appearances because it is characterised by a fundamental transferability. As a bridge over the abyss separating the visible and the invisible, past and present, the particular and the general, the sensible and the conceptual, metaphor performs 'the transition from one existential state, that of thinking, to another, that of being an appearance among appearances' (LM I: 103). In narrative accounts of past lives and actions, metaphor performs such transferability on several different levels: first, it transmits memories over the temporal gap between a past event and its retrospective disclosure in a story; second, it mediates between singularity that escapes concepts and the generality of meaning that can be shared with others; and finally, it enables the desensing memory of the storyteller to appear in a sensible form to multiple readers.

What is unique in Arendt's theory of metaphor and narrative is once again the primacy of human plurality and being in the world with others: 'in bridging the gulf between the realm of the invisible and the world of appearances' (LM I: 108), metaphor 'indicates in its own manner the absolute primacy of the world of appearances' (LM I: 109). In so doing, metaphor contests the delusion of the two-worlds theory based on the opposi-tion between being and appearance: metaphoric relationality is 'a kind of "proof" that mind and body, thinking and sense experience, the invisible and the visible, belong together' (LM I: 109). As she concludes, 'there are not two worlds because metaphor unites them' (LM I: 110), even though unification is like a bridge over the abyss.

This threefold metaphoric transferability between the deed and the word, past and future, the sensible and the abstract, the singular and the shared, disappearance and reappearance reveals another connection between narratives and natality (LM I: 121). By referring to Aristotle, Arendt argues that metaphor not only discloses thinking, memories and judgements to others, but, unlike the philosophical associations of writing with death (from Plato to Derrida, Foucault and Barth), it associates mental activity with 'the sensation of being alive' (LM I: 123). Ultimately, for Arendt, it is a forgetting of metaphor in the history of philosophy that explains the persistent association of memory and thinking with death. As she points out, our temporal withdrawal from being with others for the sake of past actions and lives is turned into an exaggerated metaphor of death – into our final exit from the world: 'in a metaphorical sense, we have *dis*appeared from this world, and this can be understood [. . .] as the anticipation of our final departure, that is, our death' (LM I: 83). By forgetting this metaphorical anticipation of death, philosophy and narrative theory have been exclusively preoccupied with dying[13] rather than with natality or survival of the past (LM I: 84). 'The metaphor of death, or, rather, the metaphorical reversal of life and death [. . .] is not arbitrary, although one can see it a bit less dramatically [. . .] everything present is absent because something actually absent is present to his mind' (LM I: 84). It is perhaps this exaggerated and melodramatic forgetting of the metaphorical status of death that provokes feminine laughter in response to the tragi-comedy of philosophy (and we should add, narrative theory) (LM I: 83). As Arendt reminds us in her essay on Lessing, such laughter is a sign of reconciliation with the world. As this laughter suggests, the temporary disappearance of the storyteller from here and now, so often associated with death, has to be supplemented by the reappearance, or rebirth, of past events in a narrative form. In other words, the condition of mortality (the disappearance of the past) and natality (the reappearance of the past actions and lives thanks to their commemoration in stories) are intimately intertwined in narrative structure.

By stressing the dislocating effects of memory, a transformative role of imagination and metaphoric language in both historical and fictional stories, Arendt's work fits neither constructivist nor realist paradigms of narrativity and history. The constructivist approach in cultural studies, feminism, critical race studies, as well as in historiography studies, emphasises the fact that all experience, gender and race identities, subjectivity and history are produced by discourse, social conventions, technologies of representation and power. Associated in historiography with Hayden White (1981), Roland Barthes (1989) or Joan Scott (1992), constructivism in its various forms emphasises the fact that, as Stone-Mediatore puts it, rhetorical constructions 'of the narrative text generate a content that exceeds factual determination' (Stone-Mediatore 2003: 19).[14] By contrast, the aesthetics of realism is characterised by the objective point of view and the mirror-like representation of objective reality. As Frederic Jameson puts it, realism 'conceives of representation as the reproduction, for subjectivity, of an objectivity that lies outside it – projects a mirror theory of knowledge and art, whose fundamental evaluative categories are those of adequacy, accuracy, and

Truth itself' (Jameson 1984: viii). By presenting story as a mirror of life, realism downplays literary, linguistic and social conventions that make representation possible, while constructivism stresses the opposite, the determining role of these constructions in the formation of subjectivity and reality. Consequently, both constructivism and realism in narrative studies are at odds with Arendt's imaginative, metaphorical and transformative role of memory as well as with her notion of realness, inseparable from human plurality. By stressing the centrality of experience for storytelling, she at the same time argues that 'no experience yields any meaning or even coherence without undergoing the operations of' memory, imagination and language (LM I: 87). For Arendt, what is real is what is shared by others, who interpret, modify and question (HC: 198–9) judgements and stories of the past. As Cecilia Sjöholm rightly points out, realness, emerging 'at the level of judgment' and *sensus communis* (Sjöholm 2015: 91), is sustained by 'interaction at the level of stories' (Sjöholm 2015: 92, 90–6). And the defence of such inter-subjective realness acquires renewed urgency in the age 'fake news'.

IV. In the Wake of Tradition, or Narrative Temporality Between Past and Future

Narrative remembrance of past struggles for freedom acquires a political significance when it is inscribed into a shared 'framework of reference', assured by tradition (BPF: 6). Without this shared tradition, as Arendt's example of the French resistance fighters against Nazi occupation suggests, struggles for freedom can lose their public significance – they leave no testament in their aftermath.[15] Composed, as Cecelia Sjöholm (Sjöholm 2015:

317

90–6) points out, of multiple and often conflicting narratives and augmented by new stories, this shared and contested framework of tradition passes an inheritance of past actions and stories to future generations (BPF: 13). Arendt specifically refers to a Roman political model of tradition because it commemorates and transmits to future generations the legacy of a new beginning – the act of founding a new political realm. Within the framework of this political tradition, every new act of freedom renews and derives its legitimacy from the initial founding of the body politic ('What is authority?', BPF: 121–4). Arendt argues, however, that the Roman tradition commemorating a new foundation has been eroded in Western modernity, despite the revolutionary attempts to restore the experience of creating a new political order ('What is authority?', BPF: 140). To indicate this loss of a revolutionary tradition, she quotes René Char's aphorism: 'our inheritance was left to us by no testament' (BPF: 3).

Although Arendt underscores the importance of shared frameworks of tradition for remembrance and storytelling, this does not mean that, for her, traditions are devoid of destructive effects. As her work on anti-Semitism, imperialism, the Holocaust and totalitarianism (discussed in Chapter 2) shows, Western tradition has not been immune to racist ideologies, which legitimate domination, imperialism, violence, anti-Semitism and genocide. That is why Arendt contests the foundational narratives of Western humanism, in particular the narrative of human progress, which she consistently rejects as a shared political framework for remembrance and historical judgement. Arendt's criticism of progress resonates, on the one hand, with Walter Benjamin's indictment of historical catastrophes and, on the other, anticipates Jean- François Lyotard's diagnosis of the demise of the Western master narratives.[16]

Because of the ambiguous function of tradition, Arendt neither bemoans nor celebrates its loss. Nor does she situate her thinking in the philosophical scepticism and rebellions against traditional values, which she identifies with the work of Nietzsche, Marx and Kierkegaard (BPF: 17–40). Rather, she argues that the breakdown of tradition legitimating new beginnings has a threefold effect. First, it 'liberates' new narratives of action from hegemonic narrative examples, or what Lyotard calls master narratives. For Arendt an exemplary case of such new narratives of emancipation are often 'hidden traditions' of the struggles for freedom of the oppressed people, such as Jewish self-conscious pariahs ('The Jew as pariah', RLC: 69–90). Indeed, Arendt herself writes such a counter-narrative, a biography of Rahel Varnhagen, who, at the end of her life, becomes a female self-conscious Jewish pariah, and because of that 'find[s] a place in the history of European humanity' (RH: 227). Second, the disappearance of hegemonic traditions reveals a new temporal framework for public narratives, contestations and historical judgements. These political acts of remembrance, narratives and judgement occur in the temporal gap between past and future, which a political tradition used to bridge: 'this gap was bridged over by what, since the Romans, we have called tradition [. . .]. When the thread of tradition finally broke, the gap between past and future ceased to be a condition peculiar only to the activity of thought [. . .]. It became a tangible reality and perplexity for all; that is, it became a fact of political relevance' (BPF: 13–14). And finally, in addition to the conflict between narratives, the breakdown of the dominant tradition reveals the antagonistic temporality of storytelling.

Underlying every tradition, the temporal gap between past and future, as we discussed in Chapter 1, is not a modern invention because its status is ontological, coextensive with the condition of natality. As such, this gap 'cannot be inherited' but merely discovered 'anew' by each generation. However, such a temporal abyss used to be traversed by tradition, which legitimated new temporal disruptions created by every political act of freedom and provided a framework for narrative accounts of such actions. In other words, tradition provided a meaningful framework for the transmission of stories about past events to future generations. With the disappearance of tradition in modernity, the perplexing temporal hiatus between past and future acquires public awareness and, therefore, political significance. No longer bridged by a tradition, the antagonistic temporal break itself has become a new shared framework for storytelling and remembrance.

What are the implications of the absence of tradition for the public transmission of narratives? In an essay 'Between past and future', Arendt argues that the political consequences of the gap between past and future are disclosed in an exemplary manner in a short Kafka parable, 'He'. In other words, it is narrative, dependent on imagination and metaphor, that reveals such discontinuous temporality (LM I: 205). Consequently, narrative does not only recount political events but also provides an insight into the temporal conditions of storytelling. In Kafka's text, to which Arendt returns again in *The Life of the Mind* in order to discuss the temporality of thinking, an unnameable male protagonist is caught in the struggle between the forces of the past and the forces of the future. As this struggle with the past suggests, the most significant consequence of the breakdown of tradition is not the oblivion of the past but, on the contrary, the intensification of its force. Not merely an archive or a historical conditioning of the present, the past is an active antagonistic force confronting the future. Arendt once again refers to a modern writer, Faulkner this time, to underscore this active, dynamic understanding of the past: "'the past is never dead, it is not even past'" (BPF: 10). Likewise, Toni Morrison's novels, like the celebrated *Beloved*, dramatise the fact that the traumatic past of slavery and racial oppression continues to haunt present and future generations.

In her reading of Kafka, Arendt also reverses the usual understanding of the future – the future is not merely a utopian orientation of action, anticipation, political plans or a target of predictive analytics, but also an antagonistic force oriented toward the past. We can only speculate what is at stake in this struggle between past and future, since no details are given in Kafka's enigmatic parable. Does the past threaten to swallow the future through its conditioning or determining force? Does it fight against the oblivion of past actions, or perhaps struggle for the transmission of alternative possibilities of the political, which have never been realised? And what is a meaning of this counter-intuitive, non-linear, backward-oriented image of the future confronting the past? Does the future struggle to erase the past, or, on the contrary, to disclose its retrospective meaning, or perhaps to rescue new possibilities of acting and being in common repressed by dominant ideological narratives? What this means is that the multiple, contradictory legacies of past actions – for example, the legacy of feminist and anti-racist struggles – fight with the future for their survival. In its confrontation with the past, the future either belatedly discloses their meanings or actively erases them. Such a discontinuous and antagonistic relation between past and future also changes the understanding of present, which ceases to be associated with the self-presence of the subject, but acquires instead a strange meaning of the temporal abyss, which we have already discussed in Arendt's conception of memory. As Arendt puts it, present time is merely a 'gap', 'an in-between' (LM I: 205), a non-time in time.

Given the loss of tradition, public remembrance of past actions and their transmission as narratives occur in the ever-changing, antagonistic and historically limited interval between 'no longer' and 'not yet'. The agonistic interval between past and future is precisely where the collective significance of historical events – such as struggles against police brutality against black people in the US, or the gender war against women in Eastern Europe – is continually contested, judged, obliterated or recovered through conflicting narratives. Consequently, the temporal gap between past and future is a domain of political struggles, public remembrance, judgements and narratives about what has happened, what might have happened, or what could have happened otherwise. Narratives both disclose this antagonistic temporality and are implicated in it. One of the consequences of this temporal predicament of narratives is that the meaning of the past is never stable. For example, the meaning of an event that failed in the past can change dramatically when it is taken up by narratives as an inspiration for future generations. And conversely, an event that succeeded in the past can be forgotten, at least until it is recovered and judged again by subsequent generations of storytellers, actors and historians.

In the absence of tradition, public remembrance of past actions in the interval between 'no longer' and 'not yet' creates the superimposition of two battlegrounds. The first battleground described above – the struggle between the forces of the past and the forces of the future – is associated with the ontology of natality and mortality. The antagonistic interval in time appears thanks to the insertion of a finite embodied subjectivity into time which occurs for the first time with the event of birth (BPF: 10), that is, thanks to the condition of natality. And, vice versa, Arendt claims that these antagonistic forces of time act on the body (BPF: 11). This insertion in time situates an embodied being between birth and death, and in turn splits the temporal continuum into antagonistic forces and tenses (LM I: 203, 210). Occurring at the site of the temporal antagonism, the second battleground begins with the force of human acting, narrative and judgement, all of which require human plurality. Indeed, as Arendt writes, Kafka's parable 'begins when the course of action has run its course and when the story which was its outcome waits to be completed' (BPF: 7–8). If the first battleground between past and future is created by the ontology of natality, the second battleground is initiated by the politics of natality, because the activities of acting, remembrance and storytelling add a third force to the struggle between past and future.

Although Arendt has been criticised by Lyotard and Mouffe, among others, for not considering antagonism in her appeal to Kant's enlarged mentality (that is, judging by taking others' points of view into account) and to *sensus communis*, these criticisms ignore her view of antagonistic temporality, or the temporal dimension of antagonism. In her elucidation of the double battleground between past and future, Arendt argues that we do not know the starting points of the forces of past or future, but we know their terminus, which is the moment when they clash. By contrast, the third force of embodied, human activities – action, judgement, narrative – begins at the site of the temporal antagonism, but we do not know its telos. This deflection of the antagonism between past and future differs both from the bridging function of tradition and even more so from transcendence of historicity – a transcendence Kafka's character wants to achieve in order to judge history. Rather, this third deflecting force of human activity generates a temporal distance 'sufficiently removed from past and future to offer [. . .] a position from which to judge the forces fighting with each other with an impartial eye' (BPF: 12).

Although Arendt calls Kafka's parable a breath-taking 'thought-event' (BPF: 10), she also criticises the limitations of his text. What is ripe for a feminist theory of narrative and natality is not only Arendt's non-linear notion of time but also her critique of the male protagonist in Kafka's story. First of all, Arendt reinterprets the pronoun 'he' neither as a (always implicitly masculine) transcendental subject nor as an individual empirical subject, but rather in the sense of a historical generation, that is, in the context of human plurality, which is one of the most important features of the politics of natality. Consequently, she objects that Kafka's male protagonist, in the manner of a universal, isolated, philosophical subject, desires to transcend the struggle and temporality in order to reach the transcendent position of an objective judge of history – a desire characteristic of the old dream of the Western metaphysics of 'a timeless, spaceless, suprasensuous realm as the proper region of thought' (BPF: 11). In *The Life of the Mind*, Arendt claims that the 'demise' of metaphysical transcendence, 'permit[s] us to look on the past with new eyes, unburdened [. . .] by any traditions [. . .] without being bound by any prescriptions' (LM I: 12). Kafka's character is not aware that, with the breakdown of tradition, the conflicting gap between past and future is the only shared framework of judgement, memory and storytelling. By contrast, the Arendtian plurality – which might be more appropriately indicated by the plural pronoun of 'they', referring to those who live, act and think with others in the interval between past and future – knows that there is no transcendence of this antagonist gap. It is precisely this inter-ruption of historical time that opens a possibility of a new beginning and a new story, both of which are intertwined with the condition of natality.

Arendt suggests that the deflecting third temporal force originating in the antagonistic interval between past and future is 'the perfect metaphor' for the experimental activity of thinking based on memory (BPF: 12). Disclosed through Kafka's parable, this is perhaps an even more striking metaphor of the temporal predicament of narrative, which also contains 'an element of experiment in the critical interpretation of the past' (BPF: 14). In making this suggestion, we follow arguments, advanced by such diverse thinkers as Lukács, Ricoeur and Anderson, about the constitutive relationship between temporality and narrativity. For Ricoeur, for example, narrative's main referent is temporality itself and, vice versa, the temporal structure of existence is expressed in language as narrative (Ricoeur 1981: 165; Ricoeur 1984: 3–4). In their work, both Arendt and Ricoeur critique the illusion of chronology and historical continuity usually reflected in the linear structure of the plot. Following Ricoeur's suggestion that narratives express temporalisation of existence, we could say that, for Arendt (though not for Ricoeur), narrative inscribes what can no longer appear – the struggles of the past generations – in the antagonistic interval between past and future. As we have argued in the previous section, the storyteller withdraws from the shared space of appearances in order to create a narrative reconstruction of 'what is no longer' for future generations. This narrative inscription of what can no longer appear in the web of inter-human relations is possible thanks to the metaphoric language of narrative – and not just its content.

The paradoxical temporal situatedness of narrative also confronts storytellers and interpreters of narratives with a new task. This task of storytellers and interpreters, and we would add anti-racist feminist thinkers, is not only to critically recount the past but also to preserve this agonistic interval in time and its paradoxical negative determination 'by things that are no longer and by things that are not yet' (BPF: 9). As Arendt's puts it, the task of any thought experiment, which we claim narrative also performs, is not 'to retie the broken thread of tradition or to invent some newfangled surrogates with which to fill the gap between past and future' but rather to discover 'how to move in this gap' (BPF: 14). By contrast, domination, discipline, normalisation and different forms of biopower, not to mention new forms of instant communication technologies and predictive analytics, aim to close this interval in order to restore historical continuity and institute a softer or stronger version of historical determination. As we have seen in Chapter 2, ultimately it is the logic of totalitarianism armed with terror which aims to eliminate the temporal discontinuities and antagonisms from history, by destroying the human condition of natality. By contrast, the task of narrative is to keep the spatio-temporal gap of enquiry open as the possibility of freedom.

We have argued in this section that the spatio-temporal agonistic gap in time created through the insertion of the embodied relational natal being becomes a public temporal predicament of storytelling. The political significance of this temporal predicament has been disclosed by the loss of unified tradition, which used to bridge (but not eliminate or hide) the hiatus between past and future. In her concluding remarks on the temporal predicament of the disintegrated tradition, Arendt calls for experimental thinking, which 'can be won, like all experience in doing something, only through practice, through exercises' (BPF: 13). The task of such intersubjective experiment is to 'gain experience in *how* to think' rather than offer 'prescriptions on what to think' (BPF: 14). This experimental activity is even more pertinent for narratives – historical, political and, of course, literary. The political role of storytelling is to recall and perform this agonistic interval again and again, whenever thinking, action or judgement seems to repeat habitual conclusions. In Arendt's words: 'this small non-time-space in the very heart of time, unlike the world and the culture into which we are born, can only be indicated, but cannot be inherited and handed down from the past; each new generation, indeed every new human being [. . .] must discover and ploddingly pave it anew' (BPF: 13). No matter which events and characters they commemorate, narratives also have the task to disclose 'this small non-time-space in the very heart of time' anew as a condition of freedom. And perhaps the Arendtian notion of polis as 'organized remembrance' (HC: 198) is implicated in this task as well.

V. The Worldly Character of Narrative: Art, Objects . . . and Passions

In sections III and IV we have discussed the temporal predicament of narratives, which have to articulate and transmit memories of 'what is no longer' across the antagonistic gap between past and future. Furthermore, in the aftermath of tradition, narratives have to guard this temporal interval whenever domination, biopower, historical causality and, especially, totalitarian 'logic' of historical development threaten to close it. By developing Arendt's remarks on art in the context of storytelling, we argue that narratives receive unexpected assistance in their task of transmission from objects in the world. Narratives have worldly existence not only because they enable the sharing of memories in the web of human appearances but also, as Sjöholm persuasively argues, because they appear as sensible objects in the world (Sjöholm 2015: 3, 37–58). In general, as part of the world, objects persist – they have a relative permanence, which actions and memories lack. Because of their durability, objects in the world form a material framework for human affairs and remembrance. This support of objects for memory and narrative modifies Arendt's claims about the distinction between poesis and praxis, work and action. Although action itself occurs without the intermediary and 'stabilising' effect of things (HC: 182), memories and narratives of such action cannot exist without the help of objects. And since action is completed through memory and its retrospective articulation in narrative, we could say that action itself requires the assistance of objects *ex post facto*. And the same retrospective dependence on objects pertains to the narrative disclosure of uniqueness, because the memory of the storyteller needs the support of objects in order to function at all. Consequently, we have to consider the role of narrative not only in relation to action and temporality, but also in relation to objects in the world.

What also calls for such an analysis of narratives' relation to the world is the ambiguous status of storytelling, which belongs both to politics and to fabrication. On the one hand, stories are produced by action itself and retrospectively reveal its meaning through the backward glance of the storyteller or the historian. Yet insofar as they are written, insofar as they exist as books, monuments, drawings, dramas, films or artworks, they are also produced by fabrication. Consequently, narrative is an act and an object, praxis and poesis. As Arendt emphatically argues, actions, ideas and events

> must first be seen, heard, and remembered and then trans-
> formed, reified as it were, into things – into sayings of poetry,
> the written page or the printed book, into paintings or
> sculpture, into all sorts of records, documents, and monuments.
> The whole factual world of human affairs depends for its reality
> and its continued existence, first, upon the presence of others
> who will have seen and heard and will remember, and, second,
> on the transformation of the intangible into the tangibility of
> things. (HC: 95)

It is as created things and 'fabricated' objects that narrative acts of recollection acquire durability, which action, which transpires in the performance itself, lacks. As Arendt puts it, the element of fabrication in narrative enables action and enacted stories to survive: 'acting and speaking men need the help of *homo faber* in his highest capacity, that is, the help of the artist, of poets and historiographers, of monument-builders or writers, because without them the only product of their activity, the story they enact and tell, would not survive at all' (HC: 173).

This survival of stories and memories of action thanks to fabricated objects manifests itself in an exemplary way in the work of art, whether or not art commemorates historical events. Why is this the case? What is the relation between political event, memory, storytelling and artworks? For Arendt, all art, including narrative arts, is the highest form of fabrication, one which surpasses its status as a fabricated object. What distinguishes artwork, including fictional narratives, from other produced objects, is its uselessness. What Arendt means here by the uselessness of art is not just art's autonomy but something more specific, namely, the fact that art is neither destroyed by consumption, as for example bread is by eating, nor worn out by use, as for example a pair of shoes is by walking. Precisely because artworks are not consumed or used up, they acquire both a relative permanence and a worldly character:

> Because of their outstanding permanence, works of art are the most intensely worldly of all tangible things; their durability is almost untouched by the corroding effect of natural processes, since they are not subject to the use of living creatures [. . .]. Thus, their durability is of a higher order than that which all things need in order to exist at all. (HC: 167)

Removed from human consumption and use, fictional narratives, like all art, manifest the permanence of the world, its relative independence from the needs and desires of its producers: 'Nowhere else does the sheer durability of the world of things appear in such purity and clarity' as in art (HC: 168). Instead, artworks reveal the world as the shared dwelling place, as 'the non-mortal home for mortal beings' (HC: 168). For Sjöholm, this worldly character of art objects in fact expands the ontology of plurality beyond human appearances, because it 'bears witness to the inherently plural character of being' (Sjöholm 2015: 3). Or, as D'Entrèves, among other Arendt scholars, writes, thanks to art, the world shared with others gives us 'a sense of belonging', 'a touchstone of reality' (D'Entrèves 1994: 37). As we have seen in Chapter 2, it is precisely this character of the world that refugees and migrants are deprived of. And because art shelters memories and the notion of a shared world, arts and artefacts, as Sjöholm (2015: 31–3) argues, are destroyed in the dark times of persecution and domination.

This endurance of the world beyond the satisfaction of human needs, desires and beyond the human life span provides a material support for memories and stories, which is all the more crucial in the wake of lost or destroyed traditions. Although the world and tradition are created by different human activities – fabrication in the case of the world, and culture/polis/arts in the case of tradition – what these artefacts share is their support for human memory and actions. As we have seen, tradition used to provide one of the frameworks for sharing collective memories. Arendt makes an even stronger claim about the relation between memory and the world: without the endurance of material things, and in particular the endurance of artworks, our capacity for recollection, and thus our capacity for thinking and story-telling, would perish. That is, 'remembrance and the gift of recollection [. . .] need tangible things to remind them, lest they perish themselves' (HC: 170). The durability of things and their 'relative independence' from their producers not only give the life of perpetual beginners some degree of stability but in fact they are essential for remembrance. Arendt points out that our memories and even our identities persist only by 'being related to the same chair and the same table' (HC: 137). As D'Entrèves argues, without a human world of material objects, 'our actions would not form coherent stories' (D'Entrèves 1994: 37).

This function of the world as a support for memory and storytelling is disclosed in the work of art. Whether artworks are fictional or not, whether they relate particular events or not, they enable recollection in a more essential way: whatever its 'content', art discloses first of all the fact that recollection cannot exist without the permanence of the world. And since recollection is the basis of both thinking and storytelling, art supports and reveals the worldly character of these activities as well. Consequently, all narratives, fictional or not, reveal a mutual dependence between memory, storytelling and objects. It is through its character as a non-utilitarian object, and not merely through representation, that art reveals the shared world, which in turn supports memory, thinking and the uniqueness and identities (who and what) of actors, who are perpetual beginners.

Art and narratives not only disclose the relative permanence of the world but also transform it into 'a place fit for action and speech' (HC: 173). In other words, the key relation between art and natality lies not only in the support for memory, but, more importantly, in the transformation of the world into a place for speech and action. In what sense is this transformation of the fabricated world into a place fit for action possible? Because they are created as non-instrumental objects, artworks have the capacity to reveal the non-instrumental character of the world to which they belong. Consequently, art objects, including narrative arts, change our relation to the world – the world becomes a shared dwelling place in which other non-instrumental activities, such as thinking, acting and speaking, can take place: 'In order to be what the world is always meant to be, a home for men during their life on earth', the world as human artifice must also be 'a place fit for action and speech' (HC: 173). Intertwined with the aesthetic and politics of natality, this transformation of the world into a place fit for action, and thus fit for human plurality, is incompatible with the Benjaminian worry that any aestheticisation of politics implies the organic wholeness of the people, without difference or dissent.[17] Likewise, the world transformed by art into a place of acting contests the Adornian thesis that all politics is dominated by instrumentality and that art is the only activity free of such instrumentality. By contrast, the work of art in Arendt's thought prepares the world for non-instrumental, transformative action, which depends on human plurality and engagement. Art supports the meaning of the world as a place of belonging and action, even though such a notion of the world is continually threatened by the processes of biopolitics, globalisation, imperialism, racism and neo-liberalism.

Artworks and narratives acquire their 'intensely' worldly character (HC: 167) thanks to the process of materialisation, or what Arendt calls reification. As we can see, reification for Arendt is a positive process, which has to be distinguished from the Marxist notion of commodity fetishism (HC: 210) and from Lukács's reification, developed in the 1920s in his *History and Class Consciousness*. As Etienne Balibar points out, the Lukácsian term 'reification' (*Verdinglichung*) is synonymous with the instrumental treatment of people as things in a capitalist system: 'in the world of commodity values, *subjects are themselves evaluated* and, as a result, *transformed into "things"'*, that is, into commodities (Balibar 1995: 69). By contrast, for Arendt, reification in art contests the instrumental, market-driven relations not only to persons but also to objects and the world.[18] She refers to the Greek older notion of reification as poesis, that is, to the fabrication of objects according to a certain purpose or a model. The reification in art and narratives, however, does not consist in the realisation of a pre-existing model, purpose or idea, characteristic of all other forms of fabrication. There is no pre-existing blueprint in art, just as there is no such model in thinking or acting. Because materialisation in art is no longer controlled by the violent imposition of a pre-existing model, it is less violent with respect to its materials than a utilitarian fabrication. To further describe this artistic process, we can refer here to what Adorno calls the process of composition from below (Adorno 1997a: 108). Such composition consists of the interaction between thinking, passion and materiality. In other words, although materials are transformed in the process of artistic composition, they themselves play an active role in this process. For Arendt, though not for Adorno, this non-violence in artistic composition also contributes to the transformation of the world into a place fit for action. It is precisely because reification in art and narrative does not actualise a pre-given model that artistic activity and storytelling can transform our relation to objects and the world into non-utilitarian, non-violent and non-instrumental terms.

According to Arendt, the reification in art and stories does not realise a pre-existing model for two reasons. In life stories 'produced' by action there is no such model because action itself lacks it. In this case, reification consists in the re-enactment of action in the process of writing, that is, in the Aristotelian theatrical imitation of acting itself in the construction of the plot (HC: 187). The most perfect example of such a re-enactment of action is drama and theatre, 'the political art par excellence' (HC: 188). In order to contest the pre-existing model of reification in the case of other arts, Arendt claims that artistic activity is inspired by the 'capacity' of thinking and passion (HC: 168–69). When inspired by experimental thinking (BPF: 14), art and narrative are non-utilitarian 'thought things' (HC: 169); when created by action, they are acts in their own right. To borrow from Adorno, who also stresses a double – dynamic and objective – quality of art, artworks are both things and 'force fields' (Adorno 1997a: 176). Arendt's turn to passionate thinking as an inspiration for art is probably dictated by the fact that thinking, for Arendt, is the only other human activity (in addition to action) that is non-utilitarian – that 'has neither an end nor an aim outside itself' (HC: 170). 'Permeating' the entirety of human existence (HC: 171), thought inspiring art is essentially different from practical cognition characteristic of the sciences, which pursue specific goals and produce measurable results (LM I: 62–5).

Although one might contest the separation between acting and thinking as two different sources of narrative, what is nonetheless interesting in Arendt's turn to thinking in the context of art is her emphasis on the interconnection between opposite forms of sensibility characteristic of the work of art: on the one hand, its sensible appearance as an object in the world, and, on the other, as the materialisation of passionate thoughts. Although, for Arendt, passion is mute apart from its bodily mode of expression through gestures, facial expressions and so forth, blushing for example (LM I: 30–7), thinking makes passions and affects articulable through art, written accounts and narratives: as a 'human capacity which by its very nature is world-open and communicative', thinking 'releases into the world a passionate intensity from its imprisonment within the self' (HC: 168) thanks to art and language. As Arendt puts it in a very suggestive claim, 'thought is related to feeling and transforms its mute and inarticulate despondency [. . .] until they all are fit to enter the world and to be transformed into things, to become reified' (HC: 168). Because Arendt links narratives with the expression of passionate intensity, she most frequently discusses passions and emotions, including political emotions such as anger, lament, indignation, laughter and gladness, in the context of her analysis of other artworks and artists, for example in her lecture on Lessing (MDT: 3–31). In the case of stories inspired by action, this passionate intensity might refer to the joy and 'delight' of acting and being together, which Arendt conveys in her epigram from Dante (HC: 175) preceding her discussion of action in *The Human Condition*. Her opening epigram to the 'Action' chapter is from Isaac Dinesen: '[a]ll sorrows can be borne if you put them into a story or tell a story about them' (HC: 175). As this epigram implies, stories can also convey grief and lament over the destruction of the world, communities and human beings.

Whether inspired by passionate thinking or action, art and narratives require artistic technique. To a certain degree, this technique can be taught, but it also emerges from the process of experimentation. Nonetheless, the excellence of the technique cannot account for a genuine metamorphosis of both passionate thought and art materials – such as language, stone, sound, paint, industrial refuse – that occurs in the process of artistic creation. Arendt, however, is ambivalent about the effects of the material metamorphosis of passionate thought. On the one hand, transcending the laws of nature, the artistic materialisation of thinking, like a phoenix, can turn ashes into flame: 'it is as though the course of nature which wills that all fire burn to ashes is reverted and even dust can burst into flames' (HC: 168). As this metaphor of rebirth suggests, the process of materialisation in art transforms the world itself into a place fit for action, memory and the disclosure of natality. Yet, on the other hand, insofar as passionate thinking is associated with interiority – a view Arendt herself modifies in *The Life of the Mind* and contests in her lectures on Kant – its transformation into an object in the world is certain 'deadness'. For Arendt, the metaphor of death, which is opposite to the metaphor of rebirth, indicates a rather traditional idea of a 'distance between thought's original home in the heart or head of man and its eventual destination in the world' (HC: 169). Yet, as this quote also suggests, although thought inspiring art has its 'original home' in interiority, its ultimate destination is the world shared by human plurality. Second, thinking transformed into an art object becomes communicable and acquires public appearance (HC: 168), and this exposure to human plurality is a crucial feature of the condition of natality. Finally, the unforeseeable

NATALITY AND NARRATIVE

metamorphosis that thinking undergoes in the artistic process, its novelty, is another manifestation of natality. Arendt's metaphoric descriptions of materialisation in art suggest that art engages both conditions of finitude: natality and mortality.

Insofar as they undergo materialisation, written narratives of actions have hybrid status: they are passionate thought objects, performative acts and worldly things. For Adorno – not to mention many contemporary artists – this heterogeneous status of art means that artworks are both objects and non-violent relations of forces. By materialising action, narrative in Arendt's account connects storytelling with passionate thinking, on the one hand, and with objects in the world, on the other. It allows action to endure by materialising memories, and, vice versa, transforms the world into a place fit for acting. Thanks to this materialisation, action becomes communicable not only in the context of the inter-human web of relations but also in the more than human context of objects in the world. Hence a chiasmatic relation between memories and the materiality of art, between subjects and objects in the world: the world assists memory, which is the source of art; the art object in turn reveals to us that we need the world in order to remember, think, act and tell stories. Indeed, as Sjöholm (2015) also observes, this existence of the artwork as a created object foregrounds, in addition to human plurality, the crucial role of material objects for thinking, acting and remembering.

VI. Narrative *Bios*

These multiple relations of narrative to action, singularity, judgement, memory, imagination, metaphoric language and the

337

material world constitute what Arendt calls a narrative *bios*. As Arendt writes:

> [t]he chief characteristic of this specifically human life, whose appearance and disappearance constitute worldly events, is that it is itself always full of events which ultimately can be told as a story, establish a biography; it is of this life, *bios* as distinguished from mere *zōē*, that Aristotle said that it 'somehow is a kind of praxis'. (HC: 97)

A life of speech and action 'will always be a story with enough coherence to be told' (HC: 97). The interpretation of political *bios* in terms of narratability is further suggested by Arendt's own claim that life deprived of action and speech is dead to the world, that is, it stops being *bios* and becomes superfluous, or, to use Agamben's term (1998), is reduced to bare life. Indeed, in her intellectual biography of Arendt, the first chapter of which is entitled 'Life as narrative' (Kristeva 2001: 3–99), Kristeva singles out the narrative formation of political forms of life, understood as *bios* rather than *zoe*, as one of Arendt's most important contributions to political theory. Yet, what are the implications of this formulation of *bios* as narrative?

The first implication is that narrative *bios* entails a new shift in narrative studies away from structuralist classifications of narrative elements or the debates about the epistemic function of narrative representation (its relation to truth and ideology). What is stressed instead are the ontological functions of narrative, namely, the way the narrative act changes the status of collective and singular lives. As we have suggested at the beginning of this chapter, in our approach we stress natality (although we do not exclude mortality) as the primary ontological dimension of narrative, because it is a condition of action, human plurality and uniqueness, but also of storytelling produced by action. In a different way the sociologist Margaret Somers links an onto-logical dimension of narrative to social being, social identity, in order to challenge social sciences' primary preoccupations with 'observable social behavior – measured variously by social interests, rational preferences, or social norms' (Somers 1994: 615).[19] As we have argued in Chapters 1 and 2, for Arendt the substitution of action by statistically measurable behaviour is one of the manifestations of the rise of the social, which we reinterpret in this book as the rise of the biopolitical. Conse-quently, the ontological dimension of narrative, its disclosure and the safeguarding of political *bios* through remembrance of actions, provides an alternative to biopolitical standardisation of behaviour and its classification according to social norms.

The second point is that Arendt's notion of narrative *bios* is in fact synonymous with the etymological meaning of biography, which for her is the primary genre of a life story, always told by others. As the *Online Etymology Dictionary* tells us, although the word 'biography' comes from the Greek *bios* and *graphia*, 'record, account', '*biographia* was not in classical Greek (*bios* alone was the word for it)'. It enters English and French in the 1680s, probably from modern 'Latin *biographia*'.[20] It might be a historical accident, or a significant historical genealogy, that the modern term 'biography', with its etymological reference to narrative *bios*, is thus almost contemporary with Hobbes's *Leviathan* (1651) and, therefore, with modern contractual con-ceptions of sovereignty, citizenship and politics. As we argued in Chapters 1 and 2, Arendt consistently criticises this liberal conception of sovereignty and contract, which isolates citizens from each other, deprives them of or limits their power, and disregards the constitutive effects of action. Moreover, this contractual notion of citizenship is implicated for Arendt with imperialism and colonialism; for contemporary critical race and feminist theorists, in particular for Charles Mills (1997) and Patricia Williams (1991:15–43), such citizenship is associated with a patriarchal racial contract of white supremacy. As an alternative to contract theory, Arendt proposes political coalitions created for the sake of action, which generate new power and disclose the uniqueness of the relational agents in the midst of human plurality. Emerging from acting with others, the narrative act can therefore be understood as Arendt's more capacious modern formulation of *bios* beyond contractual transactions of power, biopolitical normalisation of identities or juridical rights. As a necessary supplement to any democratic notion of citizenship, a narrative *bios* as we present it in this chapter can take into account both singularity and human plurality in the world; agency and judgement; memory and the antagonistic temporalisation of human existence; uniqueness and the historically constituted, shared attributes of identity – 'who' and 'what'. Furthermore, it is in the context of narrative, and especially in the context of her reading of literary texts, that Arendt foregrounds aspects of *bios* that are sometimes downplayed in her political theory of action. The most notable of these are the role of the body, political passions, imagination, as well as the role of material objects in the world. Consequently, narrative might give us a richer and more capacious formulation of *bios*.

The narrative formation of the political *bios* might also undermine the sovereign power to devalue the political significance of dominated groups – refugees, racial minorities or immigrants – by suspending or limiting their rights. Although the rights of citizens can be suspended by the sovereign power in a state of emergency (Agamben 1998), sovereignty alone cannot altogether destroy inter-human relations, language and narratives, all of which constitute the political, worldly meanings of *bios*. One could even claim that sovereign decision cannot silence storytelling, which continues to circulate, bear witness to the past and present atrocities, remember past struggles for freedom as an incitement to actions in the present and future, offer alternative interpretations of the polis, protest against justice and thus preserve the web of human relations, even if this protest and testimony emerge belatedly and retrospectively.

Another important point of narrative *bios* is the paradoxical ubiquity and fragility of life stories in public lives. Such stories can emerge everywhere, since everyone can be a potential storyteller, and they can also be forgotten or marginalised in public lives. The narratability of life, its status as a *bios*, does not guarantee that every life will have a narrated story, because the telling or writing of such a story depends not only on witnessing and willingness to narrate a story, but also on numerous, often invisible and diffused power relations determining whose lives are 'worthy' of narration and memorialisation in the public sphere and whose lives 'do not matter'. Consequently, as numerous feminist theorists point out – Gloria Anzaldúa, Patricia Williams, Shari Stone-Mediatore, Margaret Somers, Adriana Cavarero, among others – public dissemination of stories is implicated in racist, gendered, capitalist and imperialist institutions and networks of power. In the context of the ever-growing circles of superfluous humanity, the dispossession or destruction of narratives compounds the injury and is one of the instruments of domination. As Margaret Somers eloquently argues, lives deprived of narration are further damaged and dispossessed, denied political significance:

> Since social actors do not freely construct their own private
> or public narratives, we can also expect to find that confusion,
> powerlessness, despair, victimization, and even madness are
> some of the outcomes of an inability to accommodate certain
> happenings within a range of available cultural, public, and in-
> stitutional narratives. (Somers 1994: 630)

Cavarero concurs that 'what is intolerable' is not only the life of
poverty and exclusion but also the fact 'that the life-story that
results from it remains without narration' (Cavarero 2000: 56–7).

What emerges from this brief discussion of narrative political
possibilities and narrative dispossession is a difficult question
about the relation between narrative *bios* and what Agamben calls
biopolitics of bare life and what Weheliye rearticulates as *habeas
viscus* – the second aspect of biopolitics discussed in this book. As
we have argued in Chapter 2, Arendt's work on totalitarianism
and superfluous humanity articulates a notion of damaged life
that predates Agamben's bare life: in both cases, such damaged
life is stripped of its cultural and political significance, deprived
of rights, reduced to naked existence, and exposed to unlimited
violence and terror. The key difference between Arendt and
Agamben is that for Agamben bare life remains the target of
sovereign power and reveals the biopolitical dimension of sovereignty, whereas for Arendt these lethal biopolitical operations of
statelessness, criminalisation of collective identities, terror, settler
colonialism, racism and the monstrous biopolitical experiments
in the camps are irreducible to sovereignty alone.

The question we want to pose is not about the form of
power that produces bare life, but rather about a counter-power
of narrative: can a narrative formation of the political *bios*,
despite the fragility and the possibility of suppression of alternative storytelling in public lives, offer new means of resistance

against ongoing political devaluation and criminalisation of dominated groups that we see in liberal democracies – refugees, racial minorities, immigrants, Muslims, Native Americans, undocumented workers – unfortunately, this list grows rather than diminishes. Can the creation, remembrance and dissemination of counter-narratives protect or recreate the political meanings of *bios*? Can narrative formulation of the political significance of lives offer a kind of fragile shelter, or a sanctuary (to refer to the title of Nella Larsen's short story 'Sanctuary') for the new targets of violence? Despite the fragility and marginalisation of life stories by hegemonic narratives, diverse feminist thinkers, such as Anzaldúa, Williams, Somers, Stone-Mediatore and Cavarero, among others, answer these questions in the affirmative. Counter-narratives and counter-histories, which challenge both the politics of narration, as well as the dominant values, jurisprudence, gendered and racialised identities, 'cultural tyranny' (Anzaldúa 1999: 37–45) and boundaries of the political, become powerful political weapons of marginalised or dispossessed groups. As Anzaldúa famously writes in *Borderlands/La Frontera*, narrative border crossings and code switching enable her to overcome 'the tradition of silence' and the linguistic terrorism of hegemonic English (Anzaldúa 1999: 75–86); to interrogate critically 'all three cultures – white, Mexican, Indian' she inhabits; and to form a new 'mestiza' consciousness (Anzaldúa 1999: 44, 102) on singular and collective levels. Through the invention of such multilingual, multicultural narratives, as well as through political critique, Anzaldúa performs 'the freedom to carve and chisel my own face, to staunch the bleeding with ashes, to fashion my own gods out of my entrails' (Anzaldúa 1999: 44). Referring to Anzaldúa's hybrid theoretical and narrative practices among other feminist writers, Stone-Mediatore proposes to reinterpret Arendt's theory of narrative in feminist terms in order to account for the multiple ways 'marginal experience narratives can contribute to a feminist democratic politics' (Stone-Mediatore 2003: 11).[21]

The final point we want to make is that the narratability of life, its status as *bios*, not only contests multiple power relations through narrative acts but also has to confront critically the politics of narrative form. Although Arendt does not develop a political or aesthetic reflection on narrative form, it is clear that not every story performs a disclosure of uniqueness in the midst of human plurality, or safeguards a new beginning – that is, not every story discloses narrative *bios*. In fact, quite the opposite is the case. The politics of narration has both normalising and subversive functions, which manifest themselves on the level of narrative form, and we as readers and interpreters of culture and politics have to rely on reflective judgement to be able to distinguish stories that enhance natality and those that suppress it. A case in point is Arendt's own misuse of Conrad's *Heart of Darkness* in *The Origins of Totalitarianism*. On the one hand, Conrad's ambiguous novella helps Arendt to diagnose anti-black racism as a precursor to totalitarianism, but on the other, Conrad, like Arendt herself, disregards the political singularity and political plurality of Africans. Other familiar gender, class and race master plots in Western culture – the Oedipal plot, the racial and gender meanings of the dark continent, the terrorist plot, the alien invasion plots (ranging from science fiction to immigration and refugee policy) – all perform disciplinary, normalising or exclusionary functions. As Lyotard writes, narratives can produce a legitimation of culture 'without having recourse to argumentation and proof', that is, without recourse to judgement (Lyotard 1984: 27). Especially the traditional narratives, mobilised by contemporary populist political discourses in the US and in Europe, provide 'immediate legitimation' by illustrating through their choice of the hero and the hero's successes and failures 'the know-how', namely, what should be done, what is good and what constitutes competence or incompetence (Lyotard 1984: 21–3).[22] The relationship between narrative and power determines the choice of the protagonists (for example, white patriotic male citizens rather than workers, women or people of colour) and villains (criminalised immigrants, refugees, terrorists), or the selection of significant events (Anzaldúa 1999; Barthes 1989; White 1981; Williams 1991). These 'master plots' – which, according to Jameson (1984: xii), persist either overtly or as a political unconscious – selected from the vast repertoire of possible stories, become hegemonic for a given society, a political group or a state. Consequently, for a story to disclose uniqueness and to open a new beginning, for a story to constitute narrative *bios*, it has to contest recurrent normalisation (and its obverse side, criminalisation of identities) of hegemonic narratives and invent new ways of storytelling. And vice versa, the politics of storytelling has to be attentive to marks of erasure, silencing and invisibility in the politics of narration. By acknowledging these erasures, the politics and aesthetics of narrative form challenge the way storytelling is entangled in the network of gendered power/ knowledge, which makes some narrative forms more readily disseminated and others more easily silenced. That is why, as Kristeva suggests, the Arendtian narrative *bios* involves complex negotiations among individual and public memories, contestations of the available narrative norms, modes of storytelling, discourses (Kristeva 2001: 75–6), as well as a confrontation with a politics of memory and culture.

345

Despite Arendt's, Butler's and Cavarero's disregard of textuality, the consideration of the political and aesthetic aspects of the narrative act necessarily brings back the question of form, or the manner of storytelling. That is why in the reconstruction of Arendt's narrative theory we have consistently showed the implications of her theories of judgement, imagination, uniqueness and metaphor, not merely for narrative content but also for the elements of narrative form, such as narrative point of view, plot, narrative temporality, theatrical mimesis, or performativity of its figurative language. We can recall at this point Adorno's claim that formal aspects of literary works, and in fact of all artworks, are implicated in political antagonisms, which the artworks both reproduce and contest (Adorno 1997a: 6). What we call here briefly a political function of narrative form is an ongoing formal struggle against normalisation and exclusion in order to keep the possibility of a new beginning, plurality and political uniqueness viable within languages and cultures. This formal struggle of storytelling is a kind of transposition, or an extension of political struggles by other means. Except that such struggle can no longer be defined as an extension of war by other means.

We have argued in this chapter that the ontological character of narrative – understood as a disclosure of the event of natality and the formation of political *bios* through remembrance of actions – contests two dimensions of biopolitics discussed in this book. First, narratives of natality offer an alternative to the standardisation of behaviour, statistics and normalisation – as well as to an ongoing criminalisation – of collective identities. Second, by reclaiming agency through the creation of counter-narratives, dispossessed groups both witness and resist the continuing production of what Arendt calls superfluous humanity. At the same time, we suggest that Arendt's dispersed reflections on narrative foreground those aspects of political *bios* that are sometimes downplayed in her political theory of action. The most notable of these are embodiment, political passions, imagination, as well as the supportive role of material objects in the world for remembrance, revelation of uniqueness and human actions. Consequently, in Arendt's work, narrative might give us a richer and more capacious formulation of *bios* than her explicitly political thinking.

We have also claimed that not every narrative, not every storytelling is equal to the task of manifesting the ontological condition of natality. Instead of providing standards of judging narrative acts and storytelling, we conclude instead with an example of storytelling in public art, deeply committed to the expression of singularity and shared plurality of human existence in democratic public spaces. We turn to the work of Krzysztof Wodiczko, a Polish immigrant artist who is best known for his projections of the images and voices of the most vulnerable persons – immigrants, refugees, the homeless, un-employed or battered women – on prominent public buildings and monuments in the cities across the globe, from New York to Hiroshima. The main concern of his art is to intervene and create more welcoming public spaces, where those who are deprived of the ability to speak through either domina-tion or stereotypes can acquire a possibility of articulating the complexity and singularity of their experiences. Because 'no aliens, residents, non-residents, legal or illegal immigrants have voting rights, nor any sufficient voice or image of their own in official "'public'", 'they have no chance to convey the often unbearable complexity of their lives' (Wodiczko 1999: 104). For Wodiczko, the role for art is to collaborate with immigrants, who are treated as if they had no history of their own, to create

347

a possibility of 'cross-cultural communication' (Wodiczko 1999: 115). For example, when the images and stories of marginalised persons are projected on familiar public architecture, strangers re-appropriate its authority in order to speak through it and communicate their own experiences to the public. Assisted by artistic practice, immigrants, refugees and the homeless also interrupt the traditions that monuments and public buildings are supposed to commemorate and in so doing insert into imaginary historical continuity a temporal gap between 'no longer and not yet'. One of Wodiczko's collaborative public art projects is called *Alien Staff* (1992–6), which is a kind of tall walking stick equipped with a loudspeaker and a small video player, projecting the face of its user. This artistic communication device allows migrants to address indifferent crowds, interrupt their habitual movements and attract attention. As Wodiczko explains, 'the task of the *Alien Staff* is to inspire, provoke, and assist in the process of communication among and between immigrants and non-immigrants' (Wodiczko 1999: 115). The person speaking though the staff appears in public as a singular 'human being who happens to become an immigrant, rather than as one who conforms to any preconceived category of immigrant, population or community of immigrants, or any other kind or type' (Wodiczko 1999: 116). At the same time, this singular but shared public appearance of strangers and their stories supported by art expands the public sphere, calls for a renewed effort of imagination and reflective judgement in order to create a more capacious *sensus communis*. Wodiczko's public art both provokes and creates 'a new form of communication in a non-xenophobic community' (Wodiczko 1999: 9). According to Wodiczko, 'each time the experience of a stranger is shared', public life is itself renewed and gives 'a democratic hope for us all' (Wodiczko

1999: 9). Indeed, this hope resonates with Arendt's own democratic politics of natality and with her reflections on the role of storytelling in such politics.

Notes

1 If that is so, Arendt's theory of narrative is not limited to the human condition of mortality alone, unlike the claims of so many philosophers and critics, in works from Walter Benjamin's 'The storyteller' (Benjamin 1968) to Maurice Blanchot's 'Literature and the right to death' (Blanchot 1981).

2 For further analysis of the implications of Arendt's notion of narrative for feminist aesthetics, see Ziarek (2017: 474–84).

3 Neither narrative nor action in Arendt's sense of the word is irreducible to what Blanchot criticises as a narrative command to act (Blanchot 1981: 37).

4 Cavarero's work is foundational to any discussion of the implication of Arendt's work for narrative studies. Our only disagreement with Cavarero lies in her reinterpretation of the uniqueness of a who as the unity of identity, disclosed at birth to others. Consequently, desire for one's own story is not a desire for this unity of identity.

5 For a discussion of the significance of the what–who distinction for feminist theories of intersectionality, see Ziarek (2016).

6 For Arendt's most explicit discussion of political passions, such as joy, anger or outrage, see her essay on Lessing, 'On humanity in dark times' (MDT: 6–16).

7 For Kathryn Gines, judging from the others' points of view in the context of racial inequality is presumptuous at best or pre-empting these others from voicing their own opinions at worst. That is why the enlarged mentality for Gines is one of the methodological flaws that makes Arendt unaware of the racial biases in her own judgement of African American civil rights politics (Gines 2014: 123–30). For a different account of Arendt's appropriation of Kant's reflective judgement that can allow us to articulate distinctions between those stories that promote critical thinking as well as public debate, and those that reproduce communal prejudices, see Stone-Mediatore (2003: 67–94).

8 As Gasché, among other of Arendt's critics, points out, Arendt leaves out Kant's discussion of the subjective principle of judgement, namely purposiveness without the purpose, consisting in the harmonious play of imagination and understanding (Gasché 2013–14: 111). For a discussion of the limitations of Arendt's and Lyotard's political reworking of Kant's aesthetic judgement, see David Ingram (1992). Ingram focuses on aesthetic judgement's relation to non-teleological history in Arendt's work. For an excellent feminist discussion of the importance of Kant's reflective judgement for Arendt's 'debate-enhancing' storytelling, see Stone-Mediatore (2003: 10, 69–94).

9 For Arendt, examples are analogous to the schema in the *Critique of Pure Reason* (LKPP: 84). Referring to Ricoeur's argument (Ricoeur 1984: x–xi), Stone-Mediatore, like Ricoeur, claims that stories themselves perform a function similar to schematism (Stone-Mediatore 2003: 35–6).

10 For an excellent discussion of the difference between pictorial and theatrical notion of mimesis, see Lichtenstein and Decultot (2014: 659–61).

11 Although Arendt's analysis of memory occurs in the context of thinking, it is even more pertinent to her theory of narrative (LM I: 87). For Arendt, not only life stories but in fact all thinking and judgements, including reflective judgements analysed in the previous section, are retrospective and therefore derived from experience. That is why she claims that every thought is an 'afterthought'. In this context, it is important to recall, as Peg Birmingham underscores, that our primary event of natality is 'itself beyond memory', even though our gratitude for it is 'the source of all remembrance' (Birmingham 2006: 79).

12 For instance, Arendt points to the metaphorical origins of Aristotle's Greek term for 'actuality' (*energeia*), which derives from the common adjective *energos*, 'indicating someone active, at work, busy' (LM I: 105).

13 As an example of such melodramatic concern with death one can cite, among others, Blanchot's famous essay 'Literature and the right to death', which connects language, literature and freedom to the ontological condition of mortality alone. This connection is based on the common assertion that 'when I speak: death speaks in me' because it allows the words to be separated from their live referent (Blanchot 1981: 43). Death is thus a condition of meaning, linguistic expression and the negation of the existent. In Blanchot's words, language is a 'deferred assassination' (Blanchot 1981: 43). Hence, for Blanchot, there is an affinity between death, understood as the negation of the world, and revolutionary terror, where absolute freedom is equated with the absolute death and with the

absolute negation of all particularity (Blanchot 1981: 39). Rather than
the anticipation of the final end, death and the tomb are the beginning of
writing: 'literature [. . .] *begins* with the *end* [. . .]. When we speak, we are
leaning on a tomb' (Blanchot 1981: 55). What is striking in this analysis
is, first, the inability to think beginning otherwise than a relation to death
and, second, the inability to think freedom beyond negative liberation.
Hence Blanchot considers death not only as the end of existence, but
also as the beginning of existence. By contrast, narrative considered in
relation to natality stresses the unpredictable beginning, the possibility of
something new, being with others, and the disclosure of singularity rather
than its absolute negation.

14 For a useful analysis of Arendt's theory of narrative in the context of
constructivist and post-structuralist approaches to historical narration, in
particular that of Hayden White, see Stone-Mediatore (2003: 18–45).

15 As Arendt writes, despite their location in the underground, and thus
outside any institutionalised public space, French insurgents, by acting
together against the Nazi occupation, managed to create among themselves relations of freedom. However, since their action left no narratives,
even the actors themselves failed to remember and name this brief event of
intersubjective public freedom.

16 Lyotard himself does not recognise his affinity to Arendt and criticises her
for the failure to address antagonisms in the formation of *sensus communis*.
For an excellent account of Lyotard's criticism of Arendt's reading of Kant's
Critique of Judgement, see Zerilli (2005: 154–5). As Zerilli aptly puts in her
response to Lyotard's criticism, Arendt's account of the community and,
by extension, of the shared framework of stories is neither empirical nor
transcendental but political (Zerilli 2005: 156). She also shows the consequence of Arendt's theory of reflective judgement for feminist politics of
freedom.

17 See Benjamin 'The work of art in the age of mechanical reproduction'
(Benjamin 1968: 217–52). For an excellent account of Arendt's relation to
Benjamin and Adorno, see Sjöholm (2015: 1–5).

18 For a discussion of Arendt's reification and Marxist commodification, see
Sjöholm (2015: 37–49).

19 Although Somers does not refer either to biopolitics or to Arendt's
approach to narrative, her emphasis on social being, action and 'inter-
subjective webs of relationality' (Somers 1994: 618) resonate with certain
aspects of Arendt's ontology of natality. The two important differences are,
first, that for Somers behaviour and action are synonymous and, second,

social identity explains action and agency, while for Arendt it is action that discloses agency and uniqueness (Somers 1994: 612–15). Somers's argument about the importance of ontological narrative in sociology is a striking example of W. J. T. Mitchell's claim that stories provide useful methodological approaches 'for all the branches of human and natural science' (Mitchell 1981: ix), including history, anthropology and sociology, and today we should update this list by adding critical race studies, law, disability studies, queer and transgender studies, among others.

20 The *Online Etymology Dictionary* at <https://www.etymonline.com/index.php?term=biography> (last accessed 14 November 2016). For a full etymology of 'biography' see also the *Oxford English Dictionary*.

21 As an example of such an enabling politics of narration, Cavarero gives women's narratives forming alternative public spaces during feminist consciousness-raising practices in the 1960s (Cavarero 2000: 55–66).

22 Moreover, by defining the narrators as the prior listeners to the story, and listeners as the potential narrators, the transmission of narratives illustrates how to listen and how to tell a story and how transmit it to other listeners, as well as, as Lyotard puts it, 'what has the right to be said and done in the culture in question' (Lyotard 1984: 23).

References

Adorno, Theodor W. (1997a), *Aesthetic Theory*, ed. Gretel Adorno and Rolf Tiedemann, trans. Robert Hullot-Kentor, Minneapolis: University of Minnesota Press.

Adorno, Theodor W. (1997b), *Negative Dialectics*, trans. E. B. Ashton, New York: Continuum.

Agamben, Giorgio (1995), 'We refugees', *Symposium: A Quarterly Journal in Modern Literatures*, 49(2), 114–19.

Agamben, Giorgio (1998), *Homo Sacer: Sovereign Power and Bare Life*, trans. Daniel Heller-Roazen, Stanford: Stanford University Press.

Aharony, Michal (2017), *Hannah Arendt and the Limits of Total Domination: The Holocaust, Plurality, and Resistance*, Routledge Studies in Social and Political Thought Series, New York: Routledge.

Allen, Amy (2002), 'Power, subjectivity, and agency: between Arendt and Foucault', *International Journal of Philosophical Studies*, 10(2), 131–49.

Anzaldúa, Gloria (1999), *Borderlands/La Frontera: The New Metiza*, 2nd edn, San Francisco: Aunt Lute Books.

Arendt, Hannah (1994), 'We refugees', in Marc Robinson (ed.), *Altogether Elsewhere. Writers on Exile*, Boston: Faber and Faber, pp. 110–19.

Aristotle (1976), *Metaphysics*, trans. Julia Annas, Oxford: Clarendon Press.

Aristotle (1989), *On Poetry and Style*, trans. G. M. A. Grube, Indianapolis: Hackett.

Baird, Barbara (2006a), 'The future of abortion', in Elizabeth McMahon and Brigitta Olubas (eds), *Women Making Time: Contemporary Feminist Critique and Cultural Analysis*, Mount Crawley: University of Western Australia Press, pp. 116–51.

Baird, Barbara (2006b), 'Maternity, whiteness and national identity', *Australian Feminist Studies*, 21(50), 197–221.

Balibar, Etienne (1995), *The Philosophy of Marx*, trans. Gregory Elliot and Chris Turner, London: Verso.

Bar On, Bat-Ami (2002), 'Ruin, repair, and responsibility', *International Journal of Philosophical Studies*, 10(2), 195–207.

Barthes, Roland (1989), 'The discourse of history', in *The Rustle of Language*, trans. Richard Howard, Berkeley: University of California Press, pp. 127–40.

Benhabib, Seyla (1995), 'The pariah and her shadow: Hannah Arendt's biography of Rahel Verhagen', in Bonnie Honig (ed.), *Feminist Interpretations of Hannah Arendt*, University Park: Pennsylvania State University Press, pp. 83–103.

Benhabib, Seyla (1996), *The Reluctant Modernism of Hannah Arendt*, Thousand Oaks: Sage Publications.

Benhabib, Seyla (2000), 'Arendt's *Eichmann of Jerusalem*', in Dana Villa (ed.), *The Cambridge Companion to Hannah Arendt*, Cambridge: Cambridge University Press, pp. 65–84.

Benhabib, Seyla (2010), 'Hannah Arendt's political engagements', in Roger Berkowitz, Jeffrey Katz and Thomas Keenan (eds), *Thinking in Dark Times: Hannah Arendt on Ethics and Politics*, New York: Fordham University Press, pp. 55–62.

Benjamin, Walter (1968), *Illuminations: Essays and Reflections*, ed. Hannah Arendt, trans. Harry Zohn, New York: Schocken Books.

Bergo, Bettina (2011), 'The face in Levinas: toward a phenomenology of substitution', *Angelaki: Journal of the Theoretical Humanities*, 16(1), 17–39.

Berkowitz, Roger, Jeffrey Katz and Thomas Keenan (eds) (2010), *Thinking in Dark Times: Hannah Arendt on Ethics and Politics*, New York: Fordham University Press.

Bernstein, Richard J. (1996), *Hannah Arendt and the Jewish Question*, Cambridge, MA: MIT Press.

Bernstein, Richard J. (2000), 'Arendt on thinking', in Dana Villa (ed.), *The Cambridge Companion to Hannah Arendt*, Cambridge: Cambridge University Press, pp. 277–92.

Birmingham, Peg (2006), *Hannah Arendt and Human Rights: The Predicament of Common Responsibility*, Bloomington: Indiana University Press.

Birmingham, Peg (2013), 'Heidegger and Arendt: the lawful space of worldly appearance', in Francois Raffoul and Eric Nelson (eds), *The Continuum Companion to Martin Heidegger*, New York: Continuum Press.

Blanchot, Maurice (1981), 'Literature and the right to death', in *The Gaze of Orpheus*, trans. Lydia Davis, New York: Station Hill Press, pp. 21–62.

Blencowe, Claire (2012), *Biopolitical Experience: Foucault, Power and Positive Critique*, Basingstoke: Palgrave Macmillan.

Bordo, Susan (1987), *The Flight to Objectivity: Essays on Cartesianism and Culture*, Albany: SUNY Press.

Borren, Marieke (2013), '"A sense of the world": Hannah Arendt's hermeneutic phenomenology of common sense', *International Journal of Philosophical Studies*, 21(2), 225–55.

Bowen-Moore, Patricia (1989), *Hannah Arendt's Philosophy of Natality*, New York: St Martin's Press.

Butler, Judith (1992), 'Contingent foundations: feminism and the question of "postmodernism"', in Judith Butler and Joan W. Scott (eds), *Feminists Theorize the Political*, New York: Routledge, pp. 3–21.

Butler, Judith (2005), *Giving an Account of Oneself*, New York: Fordham University Press.

Butler, Judith (2015), *Notes Toward a Performative Theory of Assembly*, Cambridge, MA: Harvard University Press.

Canovan, Margaret (1992), *Hannah Arendt: A Reinterpretation of Her Political Thought*, Cambridge: Cambridge University Press.

Canovan, Margaret (2000), 'Arendt's theory of totalitarianism: a reassessment', in Dana Villa (ed.), *The Cambridge Companion to Hannah Arendt*, Cambridge: Cambridge University Press, pp. 25–43.

Cavarero, Adriana (2000), *Relating Narratives: Storytelling and Selfhood*, trans. Paul A. Kottman, London: Routledge.

Cavarero, Adriana (2014), '"A child has been born to us": Arendt on birth', trans. Silvia Guslandi and Cosette Bruhns, *PhiloSophia*, 4, 12–30.

Cerwonka, Allaine and Anna Loutfi (2011), 'Biopolitics and the female reproductive body as the new subject of law', *feminists@law*, 1(1): 1–5.

Chanter, Tina (2001), *Time, Death, and the Feminine: Levinas with Heidegger*, Stanford: Stanford University Press.

Connolly, William (2002), *Neuropolitics: Thinking, Culture, Speed*, Minneapolis: University of Minnesota Press.

Curtis, Kimberley (1999), *Our Sense of the Real: Aesthetic Experience and Arendtian Politics*, Ithaca: Cornell University Press.

Davis, Angela Y. (2016), *Freedom Is a Constant Struggle: Ferguson, Palestine, and the Foundations of a Movement*, Chicago: Haymarket Books.

D'Entrèves, Maurizio Passerin (1994), *The Political Philosophy of Hannah Arendt*, London: Routledge.

Derrida, Jacques (1982), 'White mythology', in *Margins of Philosophy*, trans. Alan Bass, Chicago: University of Chicago Press, pp. 207–71.

Derrida, Jacques (1999), *Adieu to Emmanuel Levinas*, trans. Pascale-Anne Brault and Michael Nass, Stanford: Stanford University Press.

Derrida, Jacques (2000), *Of Hospitality: Anne Dufourmantelle Invites Derrida to Respond*, trans. Rachel Bowlby, Stanford: Stanford University Press.

Derrida, Jacques (2002), 'The aforementioned so-called human genome', in *Negotiations: Interventions and Interviews 1971–2001,* ed., trans. and intro. Elizabeth Rottenberg, Stanford: Stanford University Press, pp. 199–214.

Derrida, Jacques (2005), *Rogues: Two Essays on Reason*, trans. Pascale-Anne Brault and Michael Nass, Stanford: Stanford University Press.

De Ruyter, Alex and John Burgess (2003), 'Growing labour insecurity in Australia and the UK in the midst of job growth: beware the Anglo-Saxon model', *European Journal of Industrial Relations*, 9(2), 223–43.

Deutscher, Max (2007), *Judgment After Arendt*, London: Routledge.

Deutscher, Penelope (2007), 'The inversion of exceptionality: Foucault, Agamben and "reproductive rights"', *South Atlantic Quarterly*, 107(1), 55–70.

Deutscher, Penelope (2017), *Foucault's Futures: A Critique of Reproductive Reason*, New York: Columbia University Press.

Dietz, Mary G. (1995), 'Feminist receptions of Hannah Arendt', in Bonnie Honig (ed.), *Feminist Interpretations of Hannah Arendt*, University Park: Pennsylvania State University Press, pp. 17–50.

Dietz, Mary G. (2000), 'Arendt and the Holocaust', in Dana Villa (ed.), *The Cambridge Companion to Hannah Arendt*, Cambridge: Cambridge University Press, pp. 86–109.

Dikeç, Mustafa (2015), *Space, Politics and Aesthetics*, Edinburgh: Edinburgh University Press.

Diprose, Rosalyn (2002), *Corporeal Generosity: On Giving with Nietzsche, Levinas, and Merleau-Ponty*, Albany: State University of New York Press.

Diprose, Rosalyn (2008), 'Arendt and Nietzsche on responsibility and futurity', *Philosophy and Social Criticism*, 34(6), 617–42.

Diprose, Rosalyn (2010), 'The political technology of RU486', in Bruce Braun and Sarah Whatmore (eds), *Political Matter: Technoscience, Democracy and Public Life*, Minneapolis: University of Minnesota Press, pp. 211–42.

Disch, Lisa J. (1993), 'More truth than fact: storytelling as critical understanding in the political writings of Hannah Arendt', *Political Theory*, 21(4), 665–94.

Disch, Lisa J. (2011), 'How could Hannah Arendt glorify the American Revolution and revile the French? Placing *On Revolution* in the historiography of the American and French revolutions', *European Journal of Political Thought*, 10(3), 350–71.

Duarte, André (2008), 'Hannah Arendt, biopolitics, and the problem of

violence: from animal laborans to homo sacer', in Richard H. King and
Dan Stone (eds), *Hannah Arendt and the Uses of History: Imperialism, Nation,
Race, and Genocide*, New York: Berghahn Books, pp. 191–204.

Esposito, Roberto (2008), *Bíos: Biopolitics and Philosophy*, trans. and intro.
Timothy Campbell, Minneapolis: University of Minnesota Press.

Esposito, Roberto (2013), *Terms of the Political: Community, Immunity, Biopolitics*, trans. Rhiannon Noel Welch, New York: Fordham University Press.

Fetscher, Iring (2001), 'Equality', in Tom Bottomore (ed.), *A Dictionary of
Marxist Thought*, 2nd edn, Oxford: Blackwell, pp. 177–8.

Foucault, Michel (1970), *The Order of Things: An Archaeology of the Human
Sciences*, unnamed translator, New York: Random House.

Foucault, Michel (1979), *Discipline and Punish: The Birth of the Prison*, trans.
Alan Sheridan, Harmondsworth: Penguin.

Foucault, Michel (1980a), *The History of Sexuality, Volume I: An Introduction*,
trans. Robert Hurley, New York: Vintage/Random House.

Foucault, Michel (1980b), 'Body/power', in *Power/Knowledge: Selected Interviews and Other Writings 1972–1977*, ed. and trans. C. Gordon, Brighton:
Harvester Press, pp. 55–62.

Foucault, Michel (2000a), *Essential Works of Michel Foucault 1954–1984, Volume
I: Ethics: Subjectivity and Truth*, ed. James D. Faubion, London: Penguin.

Foucault, Michel (2000b), *Essential Works of Michel Foucault 1954–1984,
Volume II: Aesthetics, Method, and Epistemology*, ed. James D. Faubion,
London: Penguin.

Foucault, Michel (2002), *Essential Works of Michel Foucault 1954–1984, Volume
III: Power*, ed. James D. Faubion, London: Penguin.

Foucault, Michel (2003), *Society Must Be Defended: Lectures at the Collége de
France 1975–76*, trans. D. Macey, ed. M. Bertani and A. Fontana, New
York: Picador.

Foucault, Michel (2007), *Security, Territory, Population: Lectures at the College de
France 1977–78*, ed. Michel Senellart, Basingstoke: Palgrave Macmillan.

Foucault, Michel (2008), *The Birth of Biopolitics: Lectures at the College de France
1978–79*, ed. Michel Senellart, trans. Graham Burchell, Basingstoke:
Palgrave Macmillan.

Frazer, Elizabeth (2009), 'Hannah Arendt: the risks of the public realm',
Critical Review of International Social and Political Philosophy, 12(2), 203–23.

Gallie, Duncan, Alan Felstead, Francis Green and Hande Inac (2017), 'The
hidden face of job insecurity', *Work, Employment and Society*, 31(1), 36–53.

Gasché, Rodolphe (2013–14), 'Is determinant judgment really a judgment?',
Washington University Jurisprudence Review, 6(1), 99–120.

Gines, Kathryn T. (2014), *Hannah Arendt and the Negro Question*, Bloomington: Indiana University Press.

Glowacka, Dorota (2006), 'Community and the work of death: thanato-ontology in Hannah Arendt and Jean-Luc Nancy', *Culture Machine*, 8, n.p.n. <https://www.culturemachine.net/index.php/cm/article/view/24/31> (last accessed on 28 March 2017).

Glowacka, Dorota (2013), 'Philosophy in the feminine and the holocaust witness: Hannah Arendt and Sarah Kofman', in Myrna Goldenberg and Amy H. Shapiro (eds), *Different Horrors/Same Hell: Gender and the Holocaust*, Seattle: University of Washington Press, pp. 38–58.

Gottlieb, Susannah Young-ha (2003), *Regions of Sorrow: Anxiety and Messianism in Hannah Arendt and W. H. Auden*, Stanford: Stanford University Press.

Grönlund, K., A. Bächtinger and M. Setälä (eds) (2014), *Deliberative Mini-Publics: Involving Citizens in the Democratic Process*, Colchester: ECPR Press.

Guenther, Lisa (2006), *The Gift of the Other: Levinas and the Politics of Reproduction*, Albany: State University of New York Press.

Guest, Ross (2007), 'The baby bonus: a dubious policy initiative', *Policy*, 23(1): 11–16.

Hamacher, Werner (2004), 'The right to have rights (four-and-a-half remarks)', *South Atlantic Quarterly*, 103(2/3), 343–56.

Hamill, Graham and Julia Reinhardt Lupton (2012), 'Introduction', in Graham Hamill and Julia Reinhardt Lupton (eds), *Political Theology and Early Modernity*, Chicago: University of Chicago Press, pp. 1–21.

Hay, Colin (2009), 'Political ontology', in Robert E. Goodin (ed.), *The Oxford Handbook of Political Science*, Oxford: Oxford University Press, pp. 460–78.

Heidegger, Martin (1962), *Being and Time*, trans. John Macquarrie and Edward Robinson, New York: Harper & Row.

Heinemann, Torsten (2015), 'Biological citizenship', in Henk ten Have (ed.), *Encyclopedia of Global Ethics*, Dordrecht: Springer Science+Business Media, pp. 1–7 <https://link.springer.com/referenceworkentry/10.1007/978-3-319-05544-2_453-1> (last accessed 28 April 2017).

Honderich, Ted (ed.) (1995), *Oxford Companion to Philosophy*, Oxford: Oxford University Press.

Honig, Bonnie (1988), 'Arendt, identity and difference', *Political Theory*, 16(1), 77–98.

Honig, Bonnie (1993), *Political Theory and the Displacement of Politics*, Ithaca: Cornell University Press, pp. 76–125.

Honig, Bonnie (1995), 'Towards an agonistic feminism: Hannah Arendt and the politics of identity', in Bonnie Honig (ed.), *Feminist Interpretations of Hannah Arendt*, University Park: Pennsylvania State University Press, pp. 135–66.

Ingram, David (1992), 'The postmodern Kantianism of Arendt and Lyotard', in Andrew Benjamin (ed.), *Judging Lyotard*, London: Routledge.

Jaimes, M. Annette (1992), 'Federal Indian identification policy: a usurpation of indigenous sovereignty in North America', in M. Annette Jaimes (ed.), *The State of Native America: Genocide, Colonization, and Resistance*, Boston: South End Press, pp. 123–38.

Jameson, Fredric (1984), 'Foreword', in Jean- François Lyotard, *The Postmodern Condition: A Report on Knowledge*, trans. Geoff Bennington and Brian Massumi, Minneapolis: University of Minnesota Press.

Kateb, George (1983), *Hannah Arendt: Politics, Conscience, Evil*, New Jersey: Rowman and Littlefield.

Kottoman, Paul (2012), 'Novus ordo saeclorum: Hannah Arendt on revolutionary spirit', in Graham Hamill and Julia Reinhard Lupton (eds), *Political Theology and Early Modernity*, Chicago: University of Chicago Press, pp. 143–58.

Kristeva, Julia (2001), *Hannah Arendt*, trans. Ross Guberman, New York: Columbia University Press.

Lacan, Jacques (1977), *Érits: A Selection*, trans. Alan Sheridan, New York: Norton.

Lacoue-Labarthe, Phillipe and Jean-Luc Nancy (1990), 'The Nazi myth', trans. Ryan Holmes, *Critical Inquiry*, 16, 291–312.

Laduke, Winona (2015), *All Our Relations: Native Struggles for Land and Life*, Chicago: Haymarket Books.

Lemke, Thomas (2011), *Biopolitics: An Advanced Introduction*, New York: New York University Press.

Lettow, Susanne (2015), 'Population, race and gender: on the genealogy of the modern politics of reproduction', *Distinktion: Scandinavian Journal of Social Theory*, 16(3), 267–82.

Levinas, Emmanuel (1969), *Totality and Infinity: An Essay on Exteriority*, trans. Alphonso Lingis, Pittsburgh: Duquesne University Press.

Levinas, Emmanuel (1987), 'Meaning and sense', in *Emmanuel Levinas: Collected Philosophical Papers*, trans. Alphonso Lingis, Dordrecht: Martinus Nijhoff Publishers, pp. 75–108.

Levinas, Emmanuel (1990), 'Reflections on the philosophy of Hitlerism', trans. S. Hand, *Critical Inquiry*, 17, 62–71.

Lichtenstein, Jacqueline and Elizabeth Decultot (2014), 'Mimêsis', in Barbara

Cassin (ed.), *Dictionary of Untranslatables: A Philosophical Lexicon*, Princeton: Princeton University Press, pp. 659–74.

Lyotard, Jean-François (1984), *The Postmodern Condition: A Report on Knowledge*, trans. Geoff Bennington and Brian Massumi, Minneapolis: University of Minnesota Press.

Marr, David and Marian Wilkinson (2003), *Dark Victory*, Sydney: Allen & Unwin.

McWhorter, Ladelle (2009), *Racism and Sexual Oppression in Anglo-America: A Genealogy*, Bloomington: Indiana University Press.

Millar, Erica (2015), '"Too many": anxious white nationalism and the biopolitics of abortion', *Australian Feminist Studies*, 30(83), 82–98.

Millar, Ruth (2007), *The Limits of Bodily Integrity: Abortion, Adultery, and Rape Legislation in Comparative Perspective*, Aldershot: Ashgate.

Mills, Catherine (2008), *The Philosophy of Agamben*, Stocksfield: Acumen and Montreal: McGill-Queen's University Press.

Mills, Catherine (2011), *Futures of Reproduction: Bioethics and Biopolitics*, Dordrecht: Springer.

Mills, Catherine (2018), *Biopolitics*, London: Routledge.

Mills, Charles (1997), *The Racial Contract*, Ithaca: Cornell University Press.

Mitchell, W. J. T. (ed.) (1981), *On Narrative*, Chicago: University of Chicago Press.

Nancy, Jean-Luc (1991), *The Inoperative Community*, trans. P. Connor et al., Minneapolis: University of Minnesota Press.

Nancy, Jean-Luc (1993), *The Birth to Presence*, trans. Brian Holmes et al., Stanford: Stanford University Press.

Nancy, Jean-Luc (2000), *Being Singular Plural*, trans. Robert D. Richardson and Anne E. O'Byrne, Stanford: Stanford University Press.

Nancy, Jean-Luc (2010), *The Truth of Democracy*, trans. Pascale-Anne Brault and Michael Naas, New York: Fordham University Press.

Negri, Antonio (1999), *Insurgencies: Constituent Power and the Modern State*, trans. Maurizia Boscagli, Minneapolis: University of Minnesota Press.

Nietzsche, Friedrich (1967a), *On the Genealogy of Morals and Ecce Homo*, trans. Walter Kaufmann and R. J. Hollingdale, New York: Random House.

Nietzsche, Friedrich (1967b), *The Will to Power*, ed. Walter Kaufmann, trans. Walter Kaufmann and R. J. Hollingdale, New York: Random House.

Nietzsche, Friedrich (1968), *Twilight of the Idols and the Anti-Christ*, trans. R. J. Hollingdale, Harmondsworth: Penguin.

Nietzsche, Friedrich (1973), *Beyond Good and Evil*, trans. R. J. Hollingdale, Harmondsworth: Penguin.

Nietzsche, Friedrich (1978), *Thus Spoke Zarathustra*, trans. Walter Kaufmann, Harmondsworth: Penguin.

Norris, Andrew (ed) (2005), *Politics, Metaphysics, and Death: Essays on Agamben's Homo Sacer*, Durham, NC: Duke University Press.

O'Byrne, Anne (2010), *Natality and Finitude*, Bloomington: Indiana University Press.

Petryna, Adriana (2002), *Biological Citizenship: Science and the Politics of Health After Chernobyl*, Princeton: Princeton University Press.

Phillips, James (2013), 'Between the tyranny of opinion and the despotism of rational truth: Arendt on facts and acting in concert', *New German Critique*, 40(2), 97–111.

Pitkin, Hanna (1995), 'Conformism, housekeeping, and the attack of the blog: the origin of Hannah Arendt's concept of the social', in Bonnie Honig (ed.), *Feminist Interpretations of Hannah Arendt*, University Park: Pennsylvania State University Press.

Pocock, Barbara (2006), *The Labour Market Ate My Babies: Work, Children and a Sustainable Future*, Adelaide: Federation Press.

Repo, Jemima (2016), *The Biopolitics of Gender*, Oxford: Oxford University Press.

Ricoeur, Paul (1981), 'Narrative time', in W. J. T. Mitchell (ed.), *On Narrative*, Chicago: University of Chicago Press, pp. 165–86.

Ricoeur, Paul (1984), *Time and Narrative: Volume I*, trans. Kathleen McLaughlin and David Pellauer, Chicago: University of Chicago Press.

Roodt, Vasti (2001), 'Amor fati, amor mundi: history, action and worldliness in Nietzsche and Arendt', *Tijdschrift voor Filosofie*, 63, 319–48.

Rose, Nikolas (2007), *The Politics of Life Itself: Biomedicine, Power, and Subjectivity in the Twenty-First Century*, Princeton: Princeton University Press.

Ross, Alison (ed.) (2008), *The Agamben Effect*, special issue of *South Atlantic Quarterly*, 107.

Ross, Loretta (2006) 'Understanding reproductive justice', on the Trust Black Women website <http://www.trustblackwomen.org/our-work/what-is-reproductive-justice/9-what-is-reproductive-justice> (last accessed 29 October 2016).

Schmitt, Carl (1985), *Political Theology: Four Chapters on the Concept of Sovereignty*, trans. George Schwab, Chicago: University of Chicago Press.

Schott, Robin May (2010), 'Natality and destruction: Arendtian perspectives on war rape', in Robin May Schott (ed.), *Birth, Death, and Femininity: Philosophies of Embodiment*, Bloomington: Indiana University Press, pp. 49–69.

Scott, Joan (1992), 'Experience', in Judith Butler and Joan Scott (eds), *Feminists Theorize the Political*, New York: Routledge, pp. 22–40.

Silliman, Jael (2002), 'Introduction', in Jael Silliman and Anannya Bhattacharjee (eds), *Policing the National Body: Sex, Race, and Criminalization*, Cambridge, MA: South End Press, pp. ix–xxix.

Silliman, Jael, Marlene Gerber Fried, Loretta Ross and Elena R. Gutiérrez (2016), *Undivided Rights: Women of Color Organize for Reproductive Justice*, Chicago: Haymarket Books.

Sjöholm, Cecilia (2015), *Doing Aesthetics with Arendt*, New York: Columbia University Press.

Somers, Margaret (1994), 'The narrative constitution of identity', *Theory and Society*, 23, 605–49.

Sorial, Sara (2006), 'Hannah Arendt's concept of the political', *Cadernos de Filosofia*, 19–20, 373–91.

Stone-Mediatore, Shari (2003), *Reading Across Borders: Storytelling and Knowledges of Resistance*, New York: Macmillan, pp. 17–96.

Stopler, Gila (2015), 'Biopolitics and reproductive justice: fertility policies between women's rights and state and community interests', *University of Pennsylvania Journal of Law and Social Change*, 18(2), 169–207.

Taylor, Dianna (2002), 'Hannah Arendt on judgement: thinking for politics', *International Journal of Philosophical Studies*, 10(2), 151–69.

Taylor, Keeanga-Yamahtta (2016), *From #BlackLivesMatter to Black Liberation*, Chicago: Haymarket Books.

Topolski, Anya (2015), *Arendt, Levinas and a Politics of Relationality* (Kindle edn), London: Rowman & Littlefield.

Vatter, Miguel (2006), 'Natality and biopolitics in Hannah Arendt', *Revista de Ciencia Politica*, 26, 137–59.

Vatter, Miguel (2014), *The Republic of the Living: Biopolitics and the Critique of Civil Society*, New York: Fordham University Press.

Vetlesen, A. J. (2001), 'Hannah Arendt on conscience and evil', *Philosophy and Social Criticism*, 27(5), 1–33.

Villa, Dana (1999), *Politics, Philosophy Terror: Essays on the Thought of Hannah Arendt*, Princeton: Princeton University Press.

Villa, Dana (2000), 'Introduction: the development of Arendt's political thought', in Dana Villa (ed.), *The Cambridge Companion to Hannah Arendt*, Cambridge: Cambridge University Press, pp. 1–21.

Waldby, Catherine and Melinda Cooper (2008), 'The biopolitics of reproduction', *Australian Feminist Studies*, 23(55), 57–73.

Weheliye, Alexander (2014), *Habeas Viscus: Racializing Assemblages, Biopolitics, and Black Feminist Theories of the Human*, Durham, NC: Duke University Press.

Weinbaum, Alys Eve (2004), *Wayward Reproductions: Genealogies of Race and Nation in Transatlantic Modern Thought*, Durham, NC: Duke University Press

White, Hayden (1981), 'The value of narrativity in the representation of reality', in W. J. T. Mitchell (ed.), *On Narrative*, Chicago: University of Chicago Press, pp. 1–23.

Williams, Patricia (1991), *The Alchemy of Race and Rights: Diary of a Law Professor*, Cambridge, MA: Harvard University Press.

Wodiczko, Krzysztof (1999), *Critical Vehicles: Writings, Projects, Interviews*, Cambridge, MA: MIT Press.

Wolin, Sheldon S. (1977), 'Hannah Arendt and the ordinance of time', *Social Research*, 44(1), 91–105.

Zerilli, Linda M. G. (1995), 'The Arendtian body', in Bonnie Honig (ed.), *Feminist Interpretations of Hannah Arendt*, University Park: Pennsylvania State University Press, pp. 167–94.

Zerilli, Linda M. G. (2005), *Feminism and the Abyss of Freedom*, Chicago: University of Chicago Press.

Ziarek, Ewa Plonowska (2008), 'Bare life on strike: notes of the biopolitics of race and gender', in Alison Ross (ed.), *The Agamben Effect*, special issue of *South Atlantic Quarterly*, 107, 89–105.

Ziarek, Ewa Plonowska (2012), *Feminist Aesthetics and the Politics of Modernism*, New York: Columbia University Press.

Ziarek, Ewa Plonowska (2016), 'Shall we gender? Who? Where? When?', *Genders' Future Tense*, special issue of *Genders*, 1(1), n.p.n.

Ziarek, Ewa Plonowska (2017), 'Aesthetics and the politics of gender', in Ann Garry, Serene J. Khader and Allison Stone (eds), *The Routledge Companion to Feminist Philosophy*, New York: Routledge, pp. 474–84.

Index

References to notes are indicated by n.